The Quadrangle

This volume is dedicated to T. OĞUZ ALPÖZEN, R. Dbg., who negotiated the purchase of Newton's 'Quadrangle', thereby securing for the Danish Expedition the option of re-excavating the site where the Maussolleion stood

THE MAUSSOLLEION AT HALIKARNASSOS

Reports of the Danish Archaeological Expedition to Bodrum

volume 4

THE QUADRANGLE

The Foundations of the Maussolleion and its Sepulchral Compartments

by Kristian Jeppesen

Jutland Archaeological Society Publications XV:4, 2000

In Commission at Aarhus University Press

THE MAUSSOLLEION AT HALIKARNASSOS
The Quadrangle

ISBN 87-88415-03-1
ISSN 0107-2854

Pre-press: Narayana Press

Cover: Kristian Jeppesen
Translation and justification: P.J. Crabb
Printed by: Narayana Press

Type: Baskerville 11/12
Paper: Arctic Silk, 130 g.

Published by
Jutland Archaeological Society
Moesgaard
DK-8270 Højbjerg

Distributed through
Aarhus University Press
Langelandsgade 177
DK-8200 Aarhus N

The publication of this book has been supported by
The Carlsberg Foundation

Contents

Preface

In vol. 3,1-2 (1991) of the publications of the Danish Halikarnassos Expedition, Poul Pedersen published all the architectural finds made in the trenches excavated along the periphery of the Maussolleion Terrace during the campaigns 1966-67 and 1970.

The pottery collected from these and other investigations inside the Maussolleion Terrace (in particular the excavation of the foundation cutting, or 'Quadrangle', as Newton named it) will be published in a separate volume on pottery under preparation by a team working under the supervision of John Lund, MA, of the Collection of Classical Antiquities at the National Museum of Copenhagen. The volume is scheduled to appear in 2002.

Poul Pedersen's publication did not include the excavation of the Quadrangle, which is the subject matter of the present volume. However, an impressive part of the finds made in this area, the sacrificial deposit discovered at the bottom of the western staircase, was published in vol. 1 of the series (1981) by Flemming Højlund and Kim Aaris Sørensen.

In the present volume, the architectural evidence and the remains of sepulchral furnishings of marble are described and commented on by the present writer while in chapters 23-24 have been taken into account preliminary contributions by B. Bundgaard Rasmussen and J. Zahle.

The expedition is indebted to Professor John Gifford for his valuable description and discussion of the geological aspects of the Maussolleion site (Appendix 1).

The excerpts from Newton's report of his diggings reproduced in Appendix 2 will give the reader an idea of the results he achieved and the basis on which the recent excavators started their investigations in 1966.

In Appendix 3 will be found an analysis of the Commander de la Tourette's account of the complete demolition of the Maussolleion in 1522 AD (reproduced in extenso from the original text in Claude Guichard's "Funerailles et diverses manières d'ensevelir etc.", Lyon 1581). Attempts will be made to clarify its meaning where it does not directly appear from the context and depends on the interpretation of terms not currently used in modern French or used in a different sense.

Since I began studying Newton's finds in the British Museum in 1953, the Department of Greek and Roman Antiquities has generously permitted me to publish any item from Newton's excavations as yet unpublished. Not a few of these, as also the present volume will demonstrate, have added considerably to our knowledge of the Maussolleion by supplementing, or by being supplemented by, the recent finds.

The Quadrangle was re-excavated and measured during the campaigns 1970, 1972-4, and 1976-7 with the cooperation of Bodil Bundgaard Rasmussen and Jan Zahle as archeologists, and Henrik Hoffmeyer, Ernst Kallesøe, and Kjeld Kjeldsen as architects, the present writer participating in both capacities, while Flemming Højlund and Poul Pedersen were in charge of the excavation of the sacrificial deposit already referred to. A summary of agenda and results accomplished in this period will be found in volume 1 (1981) of the present series.

Apart from the plan of the re-excavated Quadrangle and most of the sections on pls. E1-15, the photos taken by Bodil Bundgaard Rasmussen (pp. 131-140), those published by courtesy of the Trustees of the British Museum (figs. 3.2-3; 4.1-3; 10.5-6; 11.1; 12.1; pp. 79-80; 106), and illustrations reproduced from printed papers (figs. 1.56; 10.1; 17.5; 28.9), all photos and drawings have been made by the present writer.

In addition to the description of finds that can be measured in metres or millimetres, the technical examination and definition of the materials they are made of, the reconstruction of the contexts from which they came, and the clarification of issues bearing on their date –

topics traditionally expected to be thoroughly dealt with in any complete excavation report – the present study also has the more ambitious aim of providing as much new evidence as possible for an all-round reconstruction of one of the Seven Wonders of the Ancient World and its history until recent times.

Given the sad fact that so little of the monument remains in situ, double attention has had to be paid to every bit of evidence available, earth-bound or written, ancient as well as medieval; and no less heedfully to the observations made by Newton on the site, when it had just been discovered and was investigated for the first time after the Knights had left it for good at their hurried retreat more than 300 years before. In several cases the conclusions that can be suggested must be based on working hypotheses involving a combination of observations made in different fields of enquiry. Some of them may eventually have to be modified or abandoned in favour of alternative ways of attaining the truth, or in the light of evidence so far unknown.

The present volume will be followed by one specifying the complete evidence available for a reconstruction of the superstructure of the Maussolleion. Much of the archeological material has already been published and commented on in connection with a discussion of ancient written sources relevant to the theme in provisional reports to which references will be made pending the final publication.[1]

Kristian Jeppesen

Introductory Note on Illustrations

A plan of the re-excavated foundations of the Maussolleion at a scale of 1:100 is reproduced on the folded plate inserted separately in the back of the book.

After extensive weathering had proved it necessary to cover all rock-cut parts of the Quadrangle by means of protective walls, measures to that effect were carried out in 1996. Henceforth, therefore, many details can be studied only by reference to the photos and drawings reproduced in the present volume.

This is also true of the 'Short Gallery', the tomb-robbers' mine, and the angular cutting east of the tomb chamber, which are now completely filled up with the many thousands of marble fragments which it has not yet been possible to identify.

Elevations of cross-sections describing the principal features of the excavated area at a scale of 1:100 are reproduced on the plates E1-15 also appended at the back of the book, cf. the plan fig. 1.54.

The text illustrations are separately numbered for each chapter (fig. 5.17, for example, meaning fig. 17 in chapter 5).

Figs. 1.1-52 provide a selection of excavation photos illustrating various particulars of the site, as indicated by arrows on the plan fig. 1.53.

The principal levels L1-14 at which the bedrock was levelled to fit the successive courses of foundation slabs laid upon them are plotted on the plan fig. 1.55.

The squares 4 × 4 m into which the Quadrangle was subdivided during the excavations are indicated on the plan fig. 1.57. Each findspot is specified by reference to two figures, the first referring to the series 1-16 counting from west towards east, the second to the series 1-12 counting from south towards north.

1. 'The Quadrangle'

The periphery of the quadrangular cutting in the bedrock, roughly 32.5 × 38.5 m in width and length, inside which the foundations of the Maussolleion were laid – termed by Newton 'the Quadrangle'- is not perfectly rectilinear, but somewhat irregularly cut. Where the vertical surface indicating its circumference is intact, traces remain of a pointed tool, probably a pick-axe,[2] and in some places (particularly clear at the SW and NE corners) it does not coincide precisely with the outline of the foundations, but deviates by a maximum of about 40 cm.

All along the Quadrangle, the bedrock is disfigured by cuttings testifying to previous quarrying activities. Since the rock is soft and easy to cut and shape, it was tempting to use it as building material for unpretentious structures. Three rock-cut column drums found lying at the NW corner are probably discarded quarry pieces from the time before the Maussolleion was erected.[3]

However, rock-cut ashlars were also used to some extent in the building of the Maussolleion, i.e. for the foundations of the peribolos wall[4] and for accessory structures abutting on the foundations of the monument such as the walls of the western staircase (chapter 3) and a number of roughly built pillars along the circumference of the Quadrangle, in particular on its longer sides (chapters 4-6).

The issue of what the site looked like before the monument was erected will be dealt with in a forthcoming volume by Jan Zahle and Kjeld Kjeldsen (cf. the provisional report in chapter 24). It seems evident, at any rate, that all preexisting structures were cleared away before the foundations were laid, that any cavity inside the Quadrangle, natural or man-made, was filled up with foundation slabs, and that eventually the whole area except the tomb chamber, its antechamber, and its corridor was completely covered with foundation slabs.

There are no remains suggesting that individual foundations were constructed to support external walls or partition walls inside the monument, and it may well be assumed that above the vault roofing the sepulchre and its entrance, and at least as high as the top of the podium on which the colonnaded structure rested, the inside of the building was entirely compact. The question whether there was a cella inside the circumference of the colonnade will be dealt with in the forthcoming volume on the reconstruction of the superstructure.[5]

Remains of walls dating after the complete demolition of the Maussolleion about 1522, and consisting of dry masonry of broken pieces of foundation slabs of tufa from the Maussolleion, survive in squares 12/7 and 13/6-7 (figs. 1.37,48). To the same period should probably be attributed a c. 20-40 cm wide, shallow groove cut in the surface of the platform of the levelled bedrock at level L9 in squares 6-11/11 and 11/9-11 (fig. 1.49 in the foreground), probably to carry off waste water into the cutting in the east wall of the tomb chamber whence it would have flowed into the Lower Gallery. Being c. 3 cm deep at its western extremity in square 6/11, it widens to a maximum depth of c. 23 cm between squares 8/11 and 7/11, then proceeds at a fairly even level (depth c. 9-11 cm) towards its end in square 11/9. It does not seem technically feasible that it could have been worked before the platform existed.

A similar groove, but of more irregular form, in squares 11/5-6, and 12/4, emptied into the Short Gallery or into the lower levels west of the groove. Several pry-cuttings cut in the same surface are so close to the groove as to render it unlikely that this could have existed before the foundations of the Maussolleion were laid.

Within the Quadrangle Newton found two wells, both almost correctly placed in his plan HD pl. iv (fig. 1.56) at the spots where they were re-

cently re-excavated: one at the NE corner of the tomb chamber belonging to 'Suliman' (square 10/10), the other situated on a higher platform in the eastern part of the Quadrangle (square 13/7) and belonging to 'Achmet'. Both were cut in the bedrock and are of the same circular type with footholds cut into the sides as in the three wells recently excavated along the east side of the Maussolleion Terrace, whose ancient date can be concluded from their undisturbed contents of datable pottery.[6]

On 1st October 1974 Achmet's well had been emptied to a depth of 4.45 m below the surface (i.e. to level c. 415), when groundwater prevented investigations at greater depths.

So far, the well had produced only marble fragments from the Maussolleion, and there seemed to be many more below.

It was therefore not possible to establish whether remains from earlier periods were to be found below the marbles and closer to the bottom of the well.[7]

When opened in the same year, Suliman's well also proved to be filled up with marble fragments from the Maussolleion, but technical problems prevented soundings below the depth of a couple of metres. However, the exceptional find of a fragment from an Acroterion base[8] demonstrated that it might prove worthwhile to resume investigations with better equipment, should this become available, which eventually happened in September 1996. Fragments from the Maussolleion were observed right to the bottom, and a dendrochronological examination of a well-preserved log of wood found just above the bottom will probably settle the terminus post quem, after which the fill was deposited, whether in Newton's day or earlier.[9]

The thickness of the individual foundation courses varies considerably, both as compared to other courses, and within one and the same course or foundation slab. Complete slabs and fragments of slabs of the standard type found scattered within the Quadrangle represent thicknesses varying between 23.9 and 34 cm, and side lengths varying between 86.6 and 96 cm. The slabs were made of greenish tufa probably extracted from quarries north of Myndos, which are still accessible.[10] The surfaces were flattened by means of a fine pointed chisel, while the claw chisel was only sparingly used. There is anathyrosis at all the vertical joints, and iron clamps fastened with molten lead across the middle of each joint connected the slab with the four neighbouring slabs adjoining it.

In some cases, pry-cuttings indicate the approximate position of the outline of a row of slabs in the superincumbent course, but there are no holes for the dowels that would have been required to secure the position of each course in relation to the courses below and above it. This omission may well have caused the marble revetment facing the exterior of the monument to loosen from the core of the masonry in consequence of earthquakes.

Inside the Quadrangle, the rock is flattened to fit courses of foundation slabs at various levels. Although the rock was easy to cut, the builders probably avoided cutting away more than strictly necessary to provide reasonably extensive platforms on which the courses of foundation slabs could be solidly laid.

The most spacious of these platforms is the one surrounding the tomb chamber on all sides (at level 678/679). In the eastern part of the Quadrangle, the bedrock rises steeply and reaches the maximum level 860 on the platform adjoining the NE corner. The difference in height between this level and the rock-cut bottom of the tomb chamber at level 478, 382 cm, corresponds with 13 courses of foundation slabs averaging c. 29.4 cm in height, cf. Fig. 1.55.

All the intermediate levels (L1-13) can be defined on the basis of rock-cut beds or foundation slabs in situ whose positions are indicated in brackets:

L1 478
(tomb chamber, rock-cut bottom, pls. E5-10)

L2 504/505
(tomb chamber, top of bottom course of pavement slabs of tufa, pls. E5-7, 9-10)

L3 531/532
(top of foundation slabs paving the platform in front of the entrance to the tomb corridor, pl. E4-6)

L4 560
(top of the lower foundation slab in situ south of the entrance to the tomb chamber, pl. E4, 6, 12)

L5 589
(top of foundation slab in situ above the last mentioned slab, pl. E4, 6, 12)

L6 613
(top of course of foundation slabs above the drain east of the tomb chamber, pls. E5, 10)

L7 643
(top of course of foundation slabs above the last-mentioned slab, ibid., pl. E5, 10)

L8 678/679
(rock-cut platform around the tomb chamber, pls. E1-2, 4-5, 7-8, 9-10)

L9 706/707
(rock-cut platform south of the tomb chamber, pls. E3-4)

L10 736/737
(top of course of foundation slabs in situ on the rock-cut platform south of the tomb chamber, pl. E4)

L11 767/768
(rock-cut platform at the SE corner of the Quadrangle, pls. E2, 11)

L12 798
(rock-cut rebate for the following course, ibid. pls. E2, 11)

L13 826/827
(rebates cut in the NE platform, pl. E2)

L14 860
(level of the NE platform, pl. E2)

L15 890
(top of course of foundation slabs surviving in situ on the NE platform, pl. E2)

Judging from individual foundation slabs in situ, the courses had in some places the following thicknesses (Cl, for example, meaning the course between Ll and L2):

C1 c. 27 cm
C2 27
C3 28
C4 29
C5 24
C6 30
C7 36
C8 28
C9 30
C10 30
C11 31
C12 29
C13 33
C14 30

That the thickness varied within one and the same course is also apparent, where the general level of the topmost platform (L14) was lowered a couple of centimetres to make room for a few slabs (square 13/10) that did not fit the neighbouring slabs in height: it was easier to cut the bedrock than to reduce the hard lava used for the foundation slabs.

A somewhat different procedure was followed in the area adjoining the south staircase. While the slabs of the lowest courses were laid parallel to the axis of the obliquely situated staircase, the irregular cavities remaining were not widened to fit a rectangular pattern, but filled up with slabs of a more or less irregular shape individually adjusted to serve that purpose. Similarly the foundation slabs filling up the large angular cutting in the bedrock extending across the area east of the tomb chamber were laid parallel to the sides of that cutting.

C8 laid around the tomb chamber (fig. 1.55, L8) was the first course comprising an extensive part of the Quadrangle (c. 23 × 20 m). The following courses widened gradually until C14 filled up the Quadrangle completely. The heights of the courses with which the cavities existing before the Maussolleion were filled up varied individually and were not adapted to match the general levels of the foundation courses until they reached L8.

Thus below C9 the courses filling up the part of the south staircase covered by the Maussolleion have the following heights:

C8 c. 26 cm
C7 25
C6 25
C5 26
C4 26
C3 22

while the heights of the courses filling up the cavity in the bedrock at the SW corner (fig. 1.59) are different:

C8 c. 23 cm
C7 26
C6 28
C5 32

Since the slabs of the bottom course in the angular cutting that abutted on the east wall of the tomb chamber were not bonded with this and not connected with it by means of clamps, it seems likely that the cutting was not filled up until the east wall (and probably the other walls of the tomb chamber as well) had been built.

The drain coming from the tomb chamber followed the bottom of the cutting before joining the eastern branch of the draining system that was intended to keep the Quadrangle dry, and the peculiar angular shape of the cutting suggests that there existed underneath it some kind of natural crevice before the Maussolleion was built. A series of steps cut to accommodate courses of foundation slabs in the side facing NE does in fact suggest that originally this side was not vertical, but inclined. The crevice appears to have been prolonged by means of the regular part of the cutting extending c. 5.6 m eastwards from the tomb chamber and centered exactly on its axis, in consequence of which disposition it misses its continuation in the crevice by half its width.

Pry-cuttings cut in the levelled surfaces of the bedrock and on top of the courses of foundation slabs remaining in situ (fig. 1.58, pl. E13) indicate that the courses covering the platforms were laid out in a grid arrangement and that care was taken to preclude, if possible, vertical congruence of the joints between any two consecutive courses. The foundation slabs on top of the courses in situ at the SW and NE corners, for example, were staggered half a slab-width in both directions.

Probably in consequence of this arrangement, the rows along the outline of the foundations at the SW corner (fig. 1.41) were composed of slabs one and a half times longer than those of the standard size, i.e. c. 135 cm, and similar slabs seem to have been used in the course on top of the group of slabs in situ at the NE corner (C14).[11]

Undoubtedly the trench cut in the bedrock near the south side of the Quadrangle and approximately parallel to it – termed by Newton 'Short Gallery' – was filled up with foundation slabs in exactly the same way as the area around the southern staircase, but these stones were removed by the Knights. As the width of the trench varies between c. 85 and c. 100 cm, a single row of foundation slabs of standard size would have sufficed to fill up this cavity.

Fig. 1.1. Quarry area S of the W staircase, looking SW (1972).

Fig. 1.2. N wall of the W staircase, looking E (1972). Cf. fig. 1.3. At the cutting of the bedrock part of the adjoining pillar, a previously abandoned blind alley of the Lower Gallery was struck at the corner.

Fig. 1.3. Lower landing of the W staircase and entrance to the tomb chamber, looking SE (1972).

Fig. 1.4. The lowest courses of the S wall of the W staircase, looking S (1972).

Fig. 1.5. The covered branch of the Lower Gallery crossing the lower landing of the W staircase, looking N (1972). Note the plug-block blocking the upper part of the gallery where it continues behind the N wall.

Fig. 1.6. View of the W staircase, looking N (1972). In the foreground the lowest courses of the S wall, behind this the stone pile later excavated that covered the bone deposit.

Fig. 1.7-8. Quarry cuttings at the NW angle of the Quadrangle, behind the pillar P18, looking NW (1972). Cf. fig. 1.9.

Fig. 1.9. In the foreground pillar P18, in the background the W staircase, looking SW (1972). Cf. figs. 1.8 and 1.10.

Fig. 1.10. In the foreground the pillars P1, P2, and P18, in the background the W staircase, looking SW (1972).

Fig. 1.11. The N side of the Quadrangle with pillars P1-3 and P18, looking W (1972).

Fig. 1.12. The N side of the Quadrangle with pillars P2-3, looking E (1972).

Fig. 1.13. The N side of the Quadrangle with pillars P2-3, behind which are seen the foundations for the N enclosure wall (1972).

Fig. 1.14. At the bottom of the photo pillar P4 resting on an eminence of the bedrock traversed by quarry cuttings, looking W (1972).

Fig. 1.15. The N side of the Quadrangle comprising pillars P18 and P1-7, looking E (1972).

Fig. 1.16. NE angle of the Quadrangle, looking NE (1972). In the foreground foundation slabs from course C14 in situ.

Fig. 1.17. NE angle of the Quadrangle, looking NW (1972), cf. fig. 1.16. In the foreground foundation slabs from course C14 in situ.

Fig. 1.18. Tomb chamber, looking S (1972). Excavation of the rock-cut cavity in the bottom of the tomb chamber under way (cf. chapters 22-23 and figs. 1.19/20/21/24/25).

Fig. 1.19. Tomb chamber, looking NE (1972). In the foreground the rock-cut cavity in the bottom of the tomb chamber (cf. fig. 1.18 etc.), in the background branch of the Lower Gallery continuing towards the E.

Fig. 1.20. Tomb chamber, looking NW (1972). In the foreground the rock-cut cavity in the bottom of the tomb chamber, in the background foundations in situ for the anteroom.

Fig. 1.21. Tomb chamber, looking E (1972).

Fig. 1.22. Tomb chamber, NW angle, looking NW (1972).

Fig. 1.23. Tomb chamber, NE angle, looking N (1972).

Fig. 1.24. Tomb chamber, NE angle, looking NE (1972).

Fig. 1.25. S side of tomb chamber, looking E (1972). On the right the tomb-robbers' mine.

Fig. 1.26. Entrance to the tomb chamber and plug-block tipped over as found, looking NE (1972). Cf. chapters 8, 10, and 13.

Fig. 1.27. Entrance to the tomb chamber, looking E (1972). Note pry-cuttings for the plug-block on the pavement in the foreground.

Fig. 1.28. Tomb chamber, looking W (1972). On the left the grave-robbers' mine.

Fig. 1.29. View of the W part of the Quadrangle with the tomb chamber in the foreground, looking SW (1972).

Fig. 1.30. The robbers' mine near the point where it stops, looking E (1972). On the right is seen the beginning of the supplementary mine driven southwards in the hope of eventually tracing the tomb chamber.

Fig. 1.31. The supplementary branch of the robbers' mine, cf. fig. 1.30 and elevation E11, looking N (1972).

Fig. 1.32. The last ramification of the tomb-robbers' mine, issuing from the supplementary branch fig. 1.31 and proceeding a few m westwards, looking W (1972). On the right foundation slab of course C8 in situ.

Fig. 1.33. The robbers' mine seen from the E, looking W (1972). Below on the left is the entrance to the supplementary mine, cf. fig. 1.30.

Fig. 1.34. The rock-cut platform dominating the E half of the Quadrangle and rising six foundation courses above the platform around the tomb chamber, looking SE (1972). In the background, the angular cutting indicating the eastward course of the drain coming from the tomb chamber.

Fig. 1.35. Easternmost part of the angular cutting seen on fig. 1.34, looking SE (1972).

Fig. 1.36. Easternmost part of the angular cutting, cf. fig. 1.35, looking NW (1972).

Fig. 1.37. Dry-rubble wall constructed of fragments of tufa blocks from the Maussolleion, square 12/7, looking S (1972).

Fig. 1.38. SW corner of the Quadrangle, foundation slabs in situ opposite pillar P15, looking S (1972).

Fig. 1.39. S side of the Quadrangle opposite cuttings for pillar P13, looking SE (1972).

Fig. 1.40. S side of the Quadrangle opposite pillars P10-11, looking SW (1972).

Fig. 1.41. SW angle of the Quadrangle, foundation slabs of course C9 in situ, looking S (1972).

Fig. 1.42. S staircase, looking W (1972).

Fig. 1.43. Covered passage built across the lower landing of the S staircase, looking W (1972).

Fig. 1.44. S staircase, lower landing, looking E (1972).

Fig. 1.45. E side of the Quadrangle, pillar P8, looking NE (1972).

Fig. 1.46. Overall view of the Quadrangle, looking E (1972). In the foreground the stone pile on the lower landing of the W staircase, in the middle the tomb chamber lined with protective rubble walls.

Fig. 1.47. Overall view of the Quadrangle, cf. fig. 1.46, looking E (1972).

Fig. 1.48. Overall view of the middle of the Quadrangle, looking S (1972).

Fig. 1.49. Overall view of the W part of the Quadrangle, looking SE (1972).

Fig. 1.50. Overall view of the W part of the Quadrangle, looking S (1972).

Fig. 1.51. Overall view of the middle of the Quadrangle, looking S (1972).

Fig. 1.52. N side of the Quadrangle with pillars P 3-7, looking NE (1972).

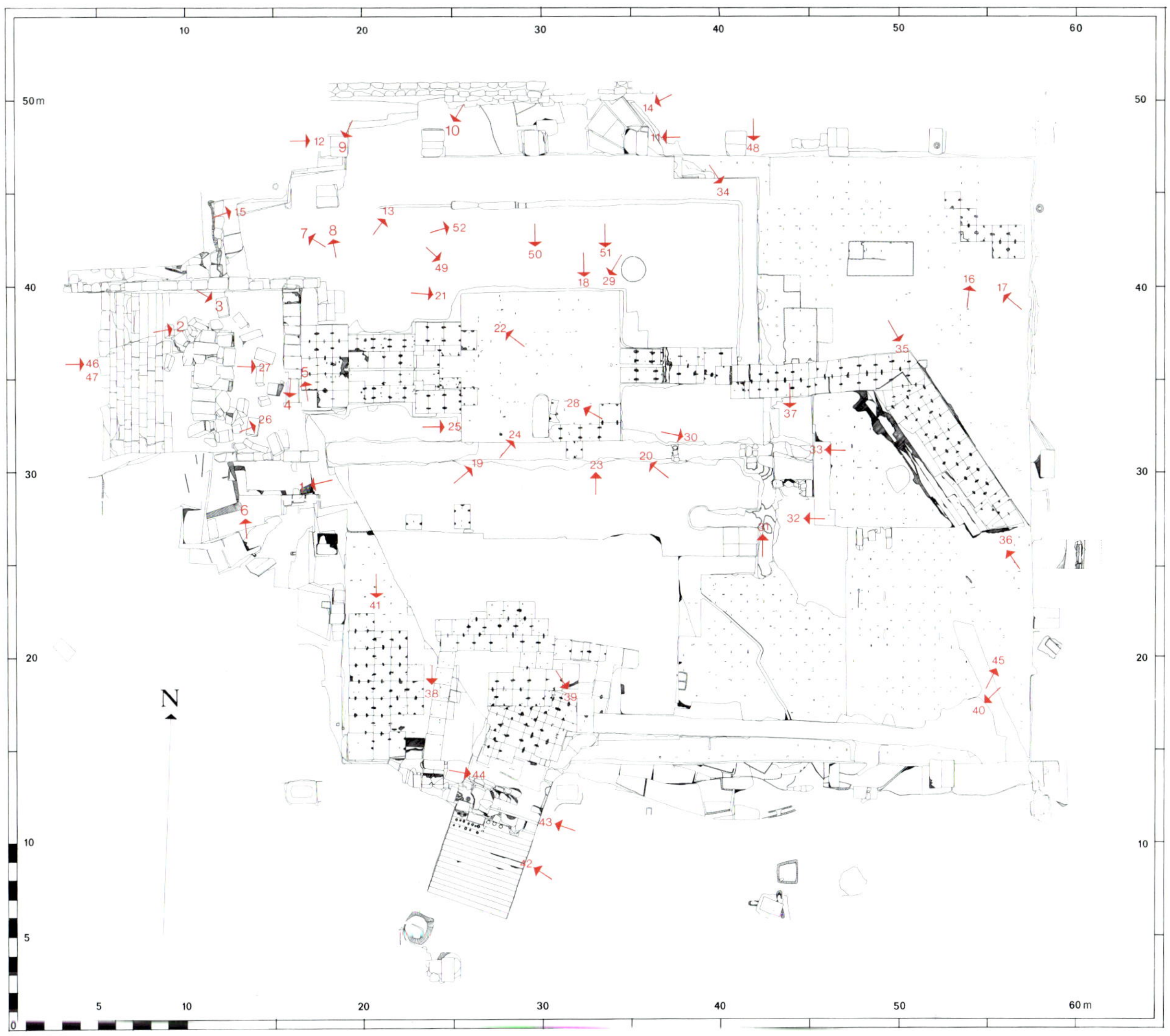

Fig. 1.53. Plan of the Quadrangle with superimposed arrows indicating the viewpoints from which the photos figs. 1.1-52 were taken.

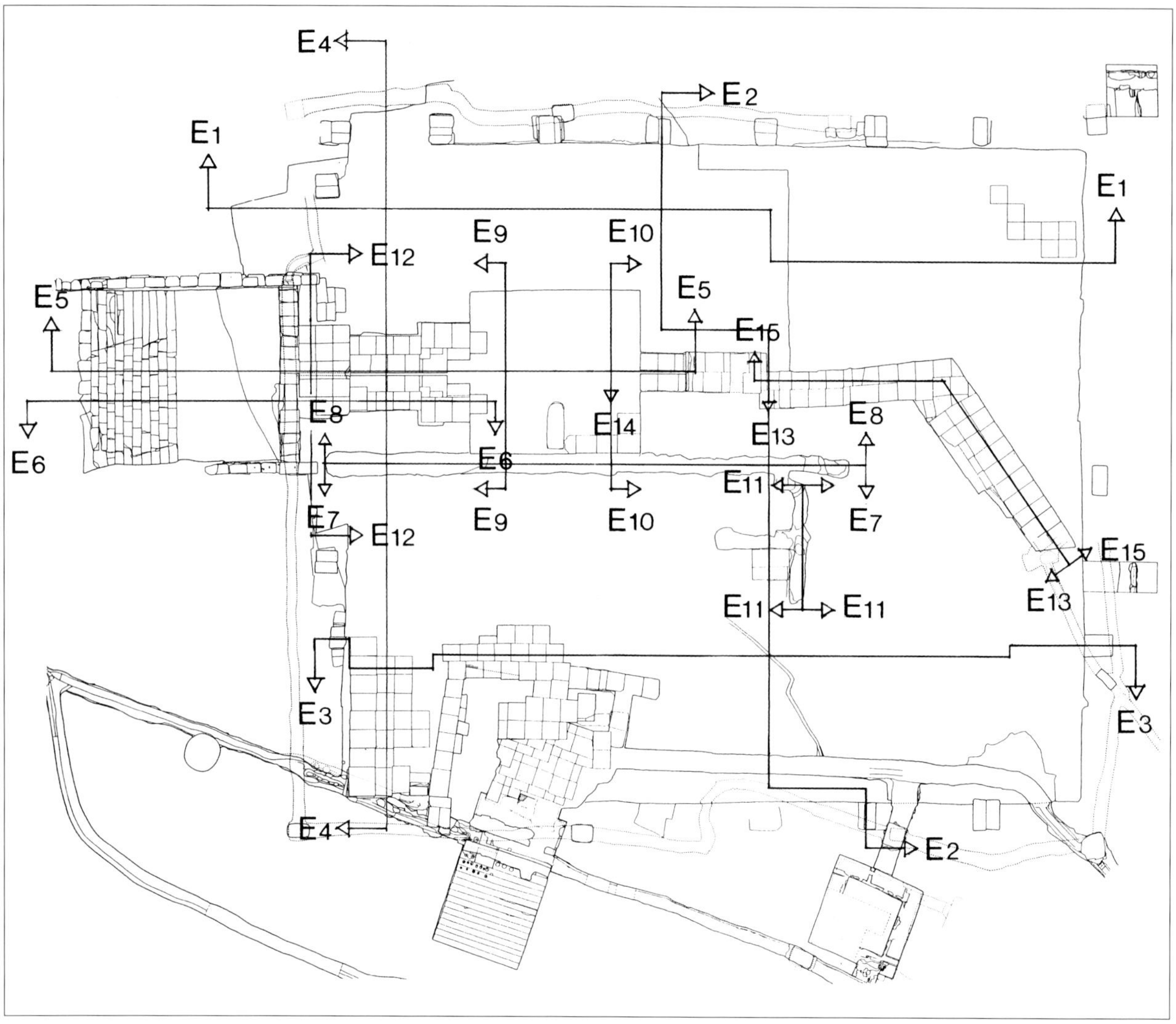

Fig. 1.54. Plan of the Quadrangle indicating the positions of the cross-sections E1-15 on the folded plates.

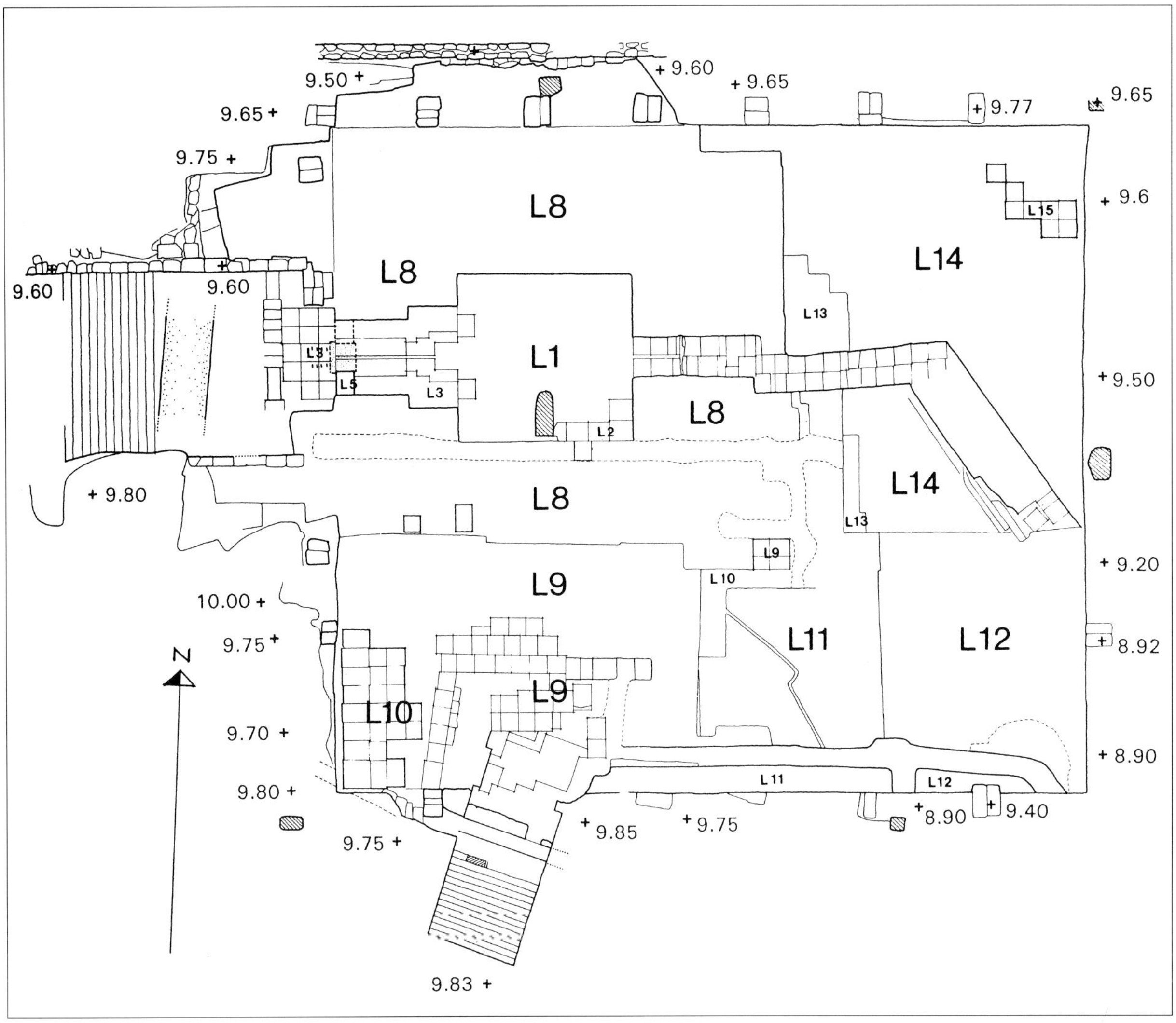

Fig. 1.55. Plan of the Quadrangle indicating the principal levels of the bedrock on which the foundations were laid.

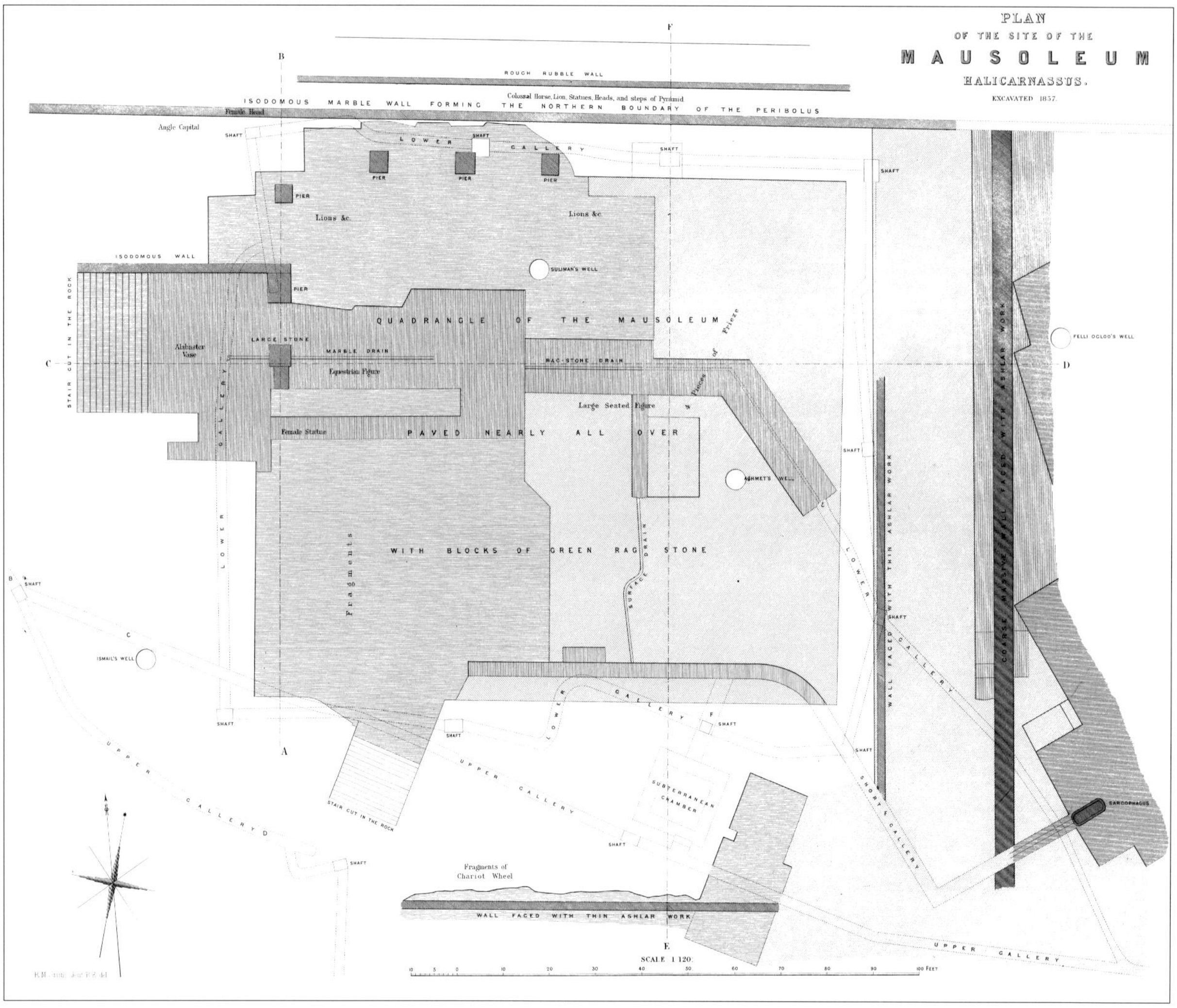

Fig. 1.56. Newton's plan of the Quadrangle (HD pl. iv).

Fig. 1. The site of the Monument re-excavated, 1:400.

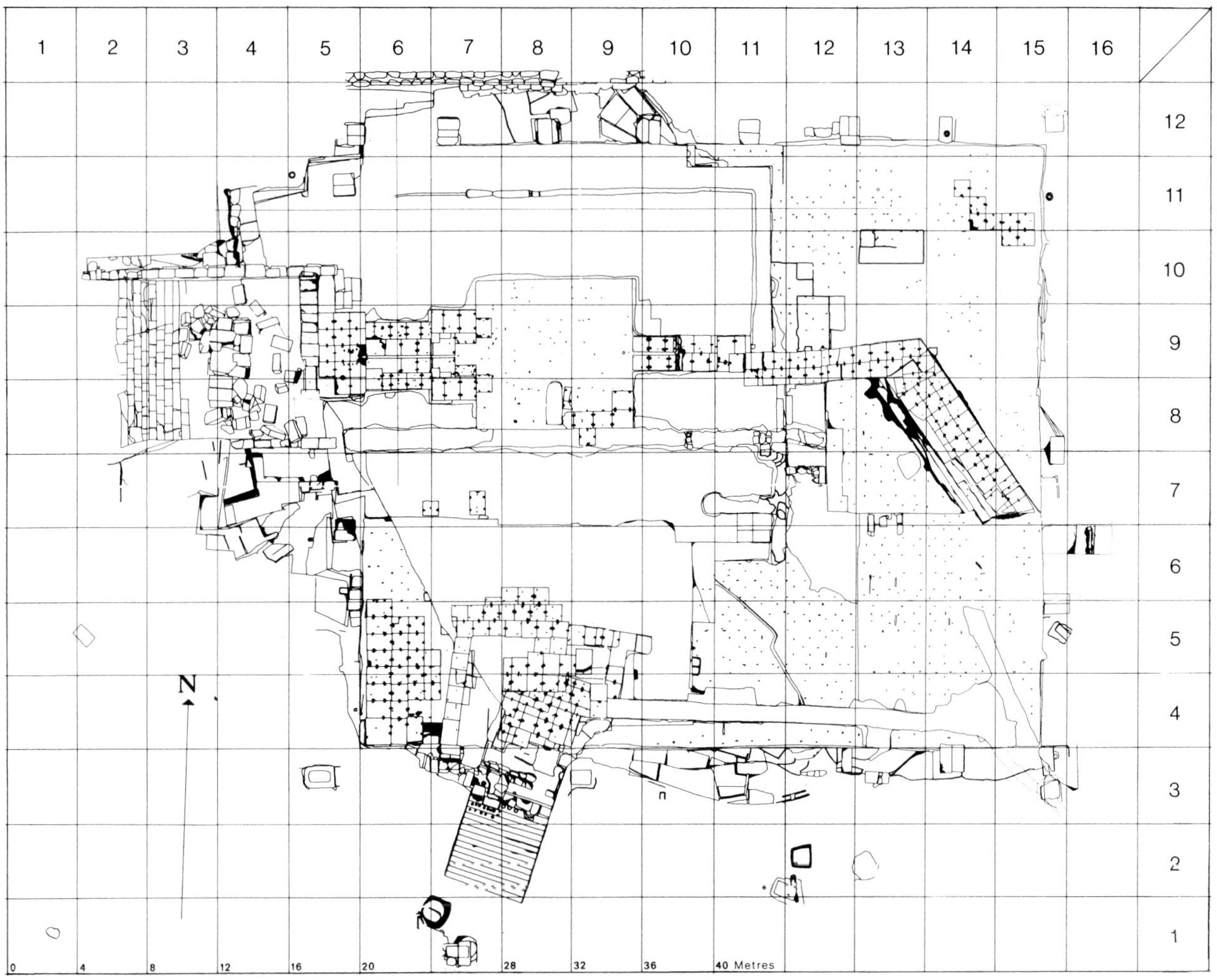

Fig. 1.57. Plan of the re-excavated foundations of the Maussolleion 1973 (western staircase only partly excavated). Reference system of 4 × 4 m squares indicated by superimposed gridwork of lines.

Fig. 1.58. Platform in the NE corner of the Quadrangle, looking SE. Note the pry-cuttings indicating the pattern in which the superincumbent foundation slabs were laid.

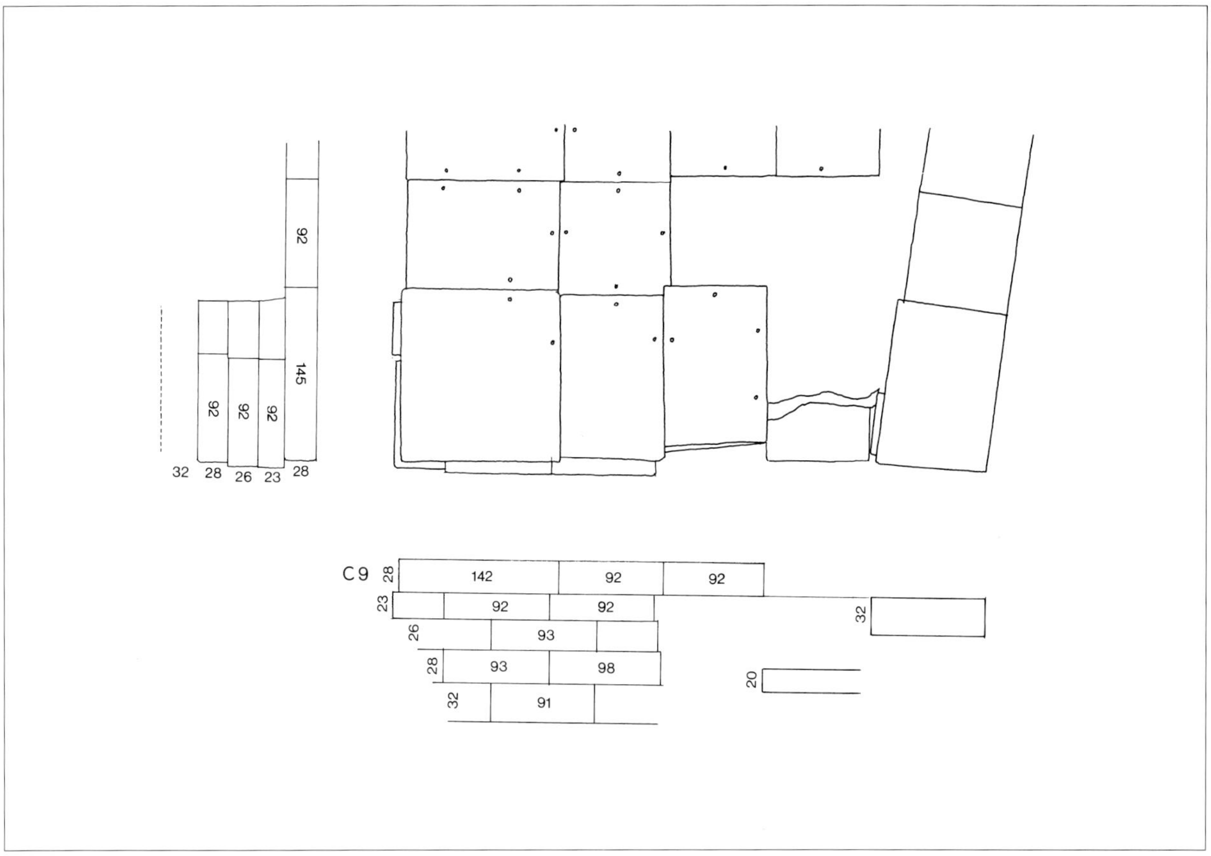

Fig. 1.59. Courses of foundation slabs at the SW corner of the Quadrangle filling out gaps in the bedrock underneath the first regularly laid course C9.

2. The drainage system around the Maussolleion ('Lower Gallery')

In one of the preliminary reports of the Danish expedition[12] the principal features of this system were described in the following terms:

"The so-called Lower Gallery surrounds the Quadrangle of the Mausoleum. It is man-high (with an average height of about 1.6 m) and flat-bottomed. The highest level of its bottom is found in the northwestern section, about 4.5 m above sea level. From this point it slopes very slightly towards the south and towards the east. The branches meet near the southeast corner of the Quadrangle in an outlet 3.95 m. above sea level, and this gallery must surely have functioned as a drain. Access to the gallery was provided by vertical shafts at varying intervals (10-15 metres), one at each corner and two more along the north, south, and east sides (L 1-10) [= S 1-10 in fig. 2.1]. For those who wanted to climb down into the galleries, cuttings were made in the sides of the shafts to facilitate footing.

"Newton's plan [fig.1.56 in the present volume] shows that there was some deviation in the course of the corridors between the shafts. It is obvious that when the direction of a gallery had been decided upon, shafts were sunk forming points of departure for teams of workmen penetrating in both directions, with the intention of meeting each other halfway. Should the course the workmen followed swerve, this would not become apparent until the teams had come close to each other. Between L6 and L7, for example, [= S9 and S10 in fig. 2.1] where a contraction of the gallery as well as an adjustment of the floor is found midway, traces of the pointed chisel show plainly that work had been going on from both sides. The dimensions of the gallery were apparently imposed by the necessity of providing adequate space for the workmen. At the point where the two teams met, therefore, an opening big enough to allow water to pass would be sufficient.

"L4 and L10 [= S4 and S6] were covered by large slabs of stone, one of which is still found in situ on top of L4. Like the Mausoleum foundations they consist of green lava but are more roughly worked. In most cases, the rock around the openings of the shafts had a ledge for the cover slabs, but grooves to drain rain water are nowhere to be seen. In principle, the shafts were used only while the galleries were being cut, but occasionally some of them may have served the purpose of dredging as well.

"From the tomb chamber of the Mausoleum, about 4.8 m. above sea level, drains can be followed both towards the west (the socalled "marble drain") and towards the east (the so-called "green stone drain"). The "marble drain" empties into the Lower Gallery,[13] where the latter crosses the landing of the western staircase. This section of the gallery is abnormally low and is covered by roughly worked slabs of green lava like those above the shafts L4 and L10 [= S4 and S6]. The "green stone drain" is constructed of foundation slabs laid in a deep and wide cutting in the living rock. The drain is about 15 cm wide and corresponds in height to two courses of slabs. The constructed drain takes a southeasterly direction and comes to an end just inside the eastern margin of the Mausoleum Quadrangle, where it empties into the shaft L10 [= S6] through a short gallery cut in the living rock."

The plan fig. 2.1 shows the parts of the system that have been investigated and measured by the Danish expedition: the north line between shafts S1 and S3; the entire west line apart from a few metres south of S1; the entire south line between shafts S7 and S10; and the southernmost part of the east line. However, to avoid confusion, L being elsewhere used to mean 'level', the shafts are here renumbered S1-10 following a clockwise course, in consequence of which the shaft missing between S1 and S10 (see below) will be S11.

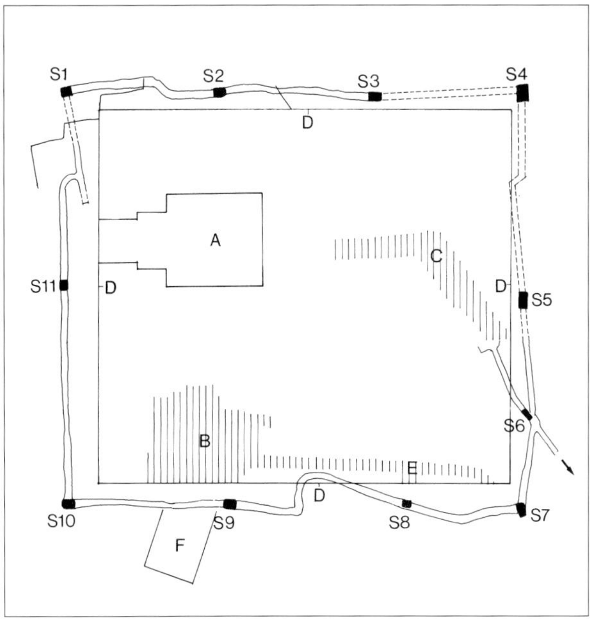

Fig. 2.1. Plan of the course of the Lower Gallery around the periphery of the Quadrangle (D) before the W staircase was cut and shaft S11 (hypothetically located) disappeared together with the upper part of the drain crossing the landing of the staircase.

Fig. 2.2. Drain coming from the tomb chamber and continuing eastwards towards shaft S6.

As already observed, the upper part of this section of the gallery must have been cut away when the western staircase was made. This conclusion is confirmed by additional observations p. 72 in the article:

"Immediately to the north of the landing of the western staircase may be observed an obvious result of miscalculation. From the shaft L1 [= S1] a blind alley extends as far as the north-eastern corner of the staircase. At this point there is a breach in the wall. Nonetheless, however, the gallery continues southwards for about one metre before stopping definitely. Apparently, therefore, the breach must have occurred while the staircase was cut (the gallery being already in existence)."

This estimate is convincing, but can be carried a bit further: the southward course followed from shaft Sl must have been abandoned when the workmen realized that it had taken a wrong direction. Presumably this happened when a team coming from the south was heard approaching. As it seems unlikely that the point of departure of the branch coming from the south could have been shaft S10 – if so, this branch would have had the extraordinary length of c. 28 m without deviating to any appreciable extent from the direction it must have been intended to follow – there must have been an intermediate shaft situated opposite shaft S5 at the middle of the east side of the Quadrangle.

This was probably placed immediately north or south of the south wall of the western stairwell. Under the wall itself there remains the lowest part of the pointed roof of the gallery (pl. E9). South of the wall, the rock is disfigured by cuttings due to quarrying activities (fig. 1.1). In this area, most of the upper part of the gallery has disappeared on account of the brittle composition of the bedrock. Presumably the quarry cuttings existed before the drainage system was cut.

The "marble drain" crossing the tomb chamber will be dealt with in another context (chapters 14, 17-18), and the problem of how the outflow passing through the eastern branch of the Lower Gallery was discharged from the Maussolleion Terrace will be taken up in connection with a discussion of the pre-Maussollan remains under the Quadrangle and south of it in a forthcoming volume (cf. chapter 24).

Evidently the Lower Gallery was planned to drain an area exactly the size of the Maussolleion, and there is no tangible evidence to suggest, let alone to prove, that a building of so impressive dimensions existed here before the Maussolleion was built. As the "marble drain" shows, the system was adapted to prevent groundwater from flooding the tomb chamber, and this may not have been its only purpose. Possibly groundwater rose to such a level in classical Antiquity that it had to be drained away to permit building on the site. If so, the establishment of a drain would have been the first practical step to be taken, once the position of the Maussolleion had been decided, and before the building operations proper could be initiated.

Since no definite indications of the existence of a structure preceding that of the Maussolleion can be observed, the likelihood is that the position of the tomb chamber and of the surroundings giving access to it had not yet been decided on when the drain was planned and cut.

3. The western staircase

This area has already been briefly described and commented on in connection with the publication of the sacrificial deposit excavated on the lower landing adjoining the entrance to the tomb chamber, but it remains to describe the complete architectural setting in detail (cf. pls. E4-6,12; figs. 1.2/5/6/9/47).

The stairway is c. 8.6 m wide and consists of 11 steps of bedrock rather coarsely cut, but averaging c. 24 cm in height and 44 cm in depth. In the areas adjoining the sidewalls of the stairwell, the steps are cut in the bedrock, whereas the intermediate steps are composed of separately cut slabs of the same material.(figs. 3.1-3) The lowermost part of the lower landing is cut in the soft strata of the bedrock (claystone). Its upper part and the lower part of the wall facing it on the north side consist of more solid strata (sandstone),[14] whereas the upper part of the wall is constructed of ashlar masonry of the same material, probably quarried in the neighbourhood.

The ashlars are laid in horizontal courses, but vary individually both in height and length. Obviously their size depended much on the particular structure of the strata from which they were quarried. Only the side facing the staircase is tooled as facade, while the back of the wall is left unfinished. Evidently it was to be covered by earth fill, and hardly intended even to be provisionally visible. Presumably it was filled up with the same light-coloured fill in distinction to the darker humus layers at the top, which is seen on Newton's photos of the plug-block figs. 10.5-6.[15]

Above the lower landing, the wall turns southwards at right- angles, assuming the form of a pillar c. 1.5 × 2.0 m in width and depth, and extending approximately as far as the pavement of greenish tufa in front of the tomb chamber (on this see below, chapter 8). Between the pillar's east side and the line marking the eastern margin of the pavement just mentioned and the entrance to the corridor there is a distance of c. 25 cm. On the interpretation of this discrepancy, see chapter 6, p. 52.

Of the south wall of the stairwell, the westernmost part is cut entirely in the bedrock (pl. E6). Just the gap between this and the line of the Quadrangle is constructed of ashlar masonry, which as in the north wall is laid in irregular courses and tooled as facade only on the side facing the stairwell.

The lowest course abuts on a spur of the bedrock projecting about 2 m from the Quadrangle line. On top of this rests the easternmost ashlar of the next course, which extends almost exactly as far eastwards as the easternmost ashlars of the north wall at the corner, where it takes the form of a pillar. Presumably, as in the case of the north wall, the south wall was reinforced by means of a pillar of rock-cut ashlars which abutted on the west facade of the tufa foundations south of the entrance to the tomb chamber. Possibly this structure had for the most part collapsed in the course of time, and there remained just a few ashlars in situ for the tombrobbers to clear away to make room for the vertical shaft from which they started cutting their mine (cf. below chapter 21).

Cuttings in the bedrock indicate the levels of the upper courses of masonry of the south wall now missing. The topmost cutting, at level 900, suggests that the complete height of the south wall may well have equalled that of the north wall as preserved at level 960. The two walls must therefore have formed a stairwell which rose at least c. 4.3 m above level 532 of the pavement in front of the tomb chamber.

It is hard to imagine which purpose this pit could have served, unless the fourth side was also closed by a wall and there was access from the lower landing to a subterranean room situ-

Fig. 3.1. The W staircase after its excavation (1977). The parts of the stairs cut in the bedrock are indicated by hatching. The line a-a marks the change in the bedrock from "sandstone" (left) to "claystone" (right).

ated east of the stairwell. However, since there is not the slightest indication that pre-Maussollan walls equalling the surviving walls in material and building technique ever existed, it seems most likely that the stairwell was built as a structure accessory to the foundations of greenish tufa of the Maussolleion proper: the latter must have been finished before the sidewalls of the stairwell were erected.

Similarly, the pillars built of ashlars of bedrock along the circumference of the Quadrangle (on which see below, chapters 4-6) were not bonded with, but abutted on the outside of the foundations. Considering the splendid craftmanship and the stones of high quality characteristic of the monument proper, one wonders why the accessory structures were built of the cheapest possible material. As a matter of fact, however, none of these structures was planned to be visible. The stairwell was backfilled when the tomb had been closed,[16] and hardly any of the pillars were visible above the levels up to which the highest of them are now preserved (cf. chapters 4-5).

Fig. 3.2. Photo from the British excavations showing the upper part of the W staircase exposed in the mine excavated along its north wall. A similar mine was excavated along the S wall, and the unexcavated earth between the mines is seen on the left. By courtesy of the Trustees of the British Museum.

Fig. 3.3. Photo from the British excavations showing the same part of the western staircase as in fig. 3.2. The unexcavated earth shown on the latter photo has been removed. By courtesy of the Trustees of the British Museum.

4. The pillars

Not including those built to buttress the side-walls that enclosed the western stairwell (cf. chapter 3), there were altogether 18 individually erected pillars along the periphery of the Quadrangle, counting clockwise from P1 at the NW corner via the NE, SE, and SW corners to P18 immediately south of P1 (fig. 6.1).[17]

The pillars P2-7 along the north side are placed at approximately equal intervals and opposite the pillars P10-15 along the south side. Though the three pillars on the west side, P16-18, are spaced at varying intervals, it may be of some significance that P17 and P18 are placed symmetrically on both sides of the entrance to

Fig. 4.1. Photo from the British excavations showing part of the Quadrangle at its NW angle. In the foreground on the left part of the N wall of the W staircase and its reentrant in front of the entrance to the tomb chamber. The staircase and the area around the plug-block are in the process of being back-filled. In the background the pillars P1-3. Compare pls. E1/5/12 and figs. 1.2/3/6. At the top of the picture are the garden walls of rubble masonry also seen on the photo fig. 4.3. By courtesy of the Trustees of the British Museum.

the tomb chamber, and that P16 is situated approximately opposite the only pillar on the east side, P8. P1 and P9 are placed at the NW and SE corners, respectively, while at the two other corners there was apparently no pillar.

All pillars were built on the bedrock immediately outside the line of the foundations, some resting on the bedrock at the edge of the foundation cutting (P1, P5-13, and P15), some in recesses cut for them in its vertical side (P16-17), and some on the bottom of the deep hollows that resulted from previous quarrying on both sides of the NW corner (P18, P2-4). On the lower landing of the south staircase a flattened area has been left on the bedrock, c. 120 × 140 cm, which would have sufficed to accommodate P14, provided that this was placed in accordance with the orientation of the adjacent foundation slabs, i.e. parallel to the oblique axis of the south staircase.

As will be shown below, the orientation of the pillars was hardly of any functional significance. What mattered was probably only the position of their centre. Though the pillars P12-13 have disappeared entirely, their existence can be concluded from cuttings in the bedrock for their bottom courses. Presumably none of the pillars is preserved to its original height.

Fig. 4.2. Photo from the British excavations. Judging from the altitude of the area in which the house in the middle and at the top of the photo is situated, the picture must comprise part of the NW angle of the Quadrangle and is looking NW in the direction of the slope of the Göktepe mountain. The house in the background on the extreme left may well be that of Hadji Nalban indicated on Newton's plan of the Quadrangle immediately W of the W staircase (HD pl. iv). The wooden gangway for wheelbarrows rising on the left appears to form a continuation of the one seen on the photo fig. 4.1. Below the wheelbarrow between two workmen standing on top of the bedrock on the right can be discerned the pillar P2, represented as on fig. 4.1 with a bunch of ropes on its top, while the top course of pillar P1 appears to peep out from a heap of rubble further to the left. By courtesy of the Trustees of the British Museum.

When excavating the pillars P2 and P3, Newton made the following observations:

"The irregular excavation in which the north piers were placed, was filled up with the same white soil which we found over the stair on the west ..."

"There can hardly be a doubt that all this excavation was filled in to the general level of the platform at the time of the building of the Mausoleum, and that the piers were made at that time for the purpose of supporting the soil more compactly."[18]

However, even if it be assumed that the pillars P2-4 and P18 might have had the purpose suggested by Newton (which from a technical point of view seems utterly unlikely), this hypothesis cannot account for the pillars that Newton failed to notice, in particular those placed on top of the edge of the foundation cutting, P1 and P5-13.

The reason why five courses are preserved of P2 and P3, while only one or two of the lowermost courses or none at all remain of the pillars placed along the top of the foundation cutting, is more probably that originally all pillars were carried to a uniform level above the Maussol-

Fig. 4.3. Photo from the British excavations showing part of the N side of the Quadrangle with pillars P2-5. Beneath P5 is seen the edge of the topmost platform of the levelled bedrock occupying the NE angle of the Quadrangle. Compare pl. E1. By courtesy of the Trustees of the British Museum.

leion Terrace and that the courses above the Terrace level were subsequently removed, whereas the courses below it were left intact, at least until the Hospitallers demolished the Maussolleion.

This hypothesis implies that the pillars were not intended to be permanently visible, but were erected to serve some provisional purpose, a conclusion which is supported by the fact that they were built of ashlars of the cheapest stone available, quarried from the solid strata of the bedrock on the site, and left undressed on the outside, no care at all being taken to give them a uniform and reasonably attractive look. What mattered was evidently not their appearance, but the solidity and stability of their construction. All joints, horizontal as well as vertical, are absolutely plane and fit as tightly as in the masonry of tufa or marble in the foundations or superstructure of the Maussolleion.

Moreover, as in the foundations of the peribolos wall also built of bedrock, congruence of transverse joints was systematically avoided.[19] In P3, for example, (cf. fig. 5.4) each of the four lowermost courses was composed of two ashlars some 60 cm wide and 130-140 cm long and alternately laid parallel to or at right-angles to the line of the foundations. This system resulted in a pillar, whose courses were alternately a little longer than wide or a little wider than long as seen from the same side: it was neither definitely square, having four equal sides, nor definitely oblong, but apparently assumed the form imposed by the dimensions of the available ashlars. Judging from the surviving remains, the pillars P4-5, 7-11, and 17-18 were constructed in much the same way.

A different principle of construction using three ashlars per course rather than two, the two of them being placed lengthwise beside one another, while the third was added at right-angles at their ends, is exemplified by P1 (the two lower courses), P2 (second and fourth courses), P6 (bottom course), and P15 (the two topmost courses). In consequence of this system, the pillar becomes definitely oblong, congruence of transverse joints being to some extent avoided by inverting the plan in every second course. Occasionally, a course may be composed of two or three ashlars of different width placed parallel to one another and at right-angles to the ashlars in the courses above and underneath (P2, fifth course).

To all appearances, precise scantlings of the ashlars used were not of any importance, provided that certain minimum dimensions (c. 120 cm) were properly maintained. Besides, using ashlars somewhat longer than prescribed would not have reduced, but added to the stability of the construction.

The pillars are preserved up to the following levels:

P1:	951	
P2:	915	(appr. 963 in Newton's day, cf. catalogue)
P3:	940	
P4:	746	(appr. 946 in Newton's day, cf. catalogue)
P5:	946	
P6:	936	
P7:	977	
P8:	892	
P9:	–	(lost, but cuttings for the lowest course survive)
P10:	941	
P11:	946	
P12:	–	(lost, but cuttings for the lowest course survive)
P13:	–	(do.)
P14:	–	(do.)
P15:	738	
P16:	939	
P17:	832	
P18:	822	

P7 reaches the highest level, 977, and the top level of the euthynteria course beneath the peribolos wall, 936, is also surpassed by the levels of P1, 3, 5, 9, 10, and 16, which range between 939 and 951, the maximum difference being only 12 cm. As a matter of fact, some of the pillars rise to one and the same level, so P3 and P10 (940/941), and P5 and P11 (946).

If our assumption that all the pillars reached the same level holds good, this level can hardly have been identical with the top level of P7, 977, for to reach this, supplementary courses as low as 26, 14, 36, and 31 cm, respectively, would have sufficed to complete P1, 2, 3, and 5, whereas the height of the surviving courses varies between c. 40 and 58 cm. It may be assumed, therefore, that originally P1, 2, 3, and 5 were at least two, and possibly three or even four courses higher, in which case they would have risen considerably above the euthynteria course of the peribolos wall, though precisely how much is a matter of conjecture.

As P3 covers part of the opening of the shaft S2, the pillars on the north side and presumably those on the other sides as well must have been built some time after the drainage system inaugurating the erection of the Maussolleion had been established.

The purpose of the pillars will be discussed in chapter 6.

5. Catalogue of the pillars P1-18

In his plan of the Quadrangle, Newton recorded only the pillars P2-4 and P18, but on some of his photographs of the Quadrangle under excavation (figs. 4.1-3) P1-5 are partly visible.

P1 *(figs. 1.10-11, 4.1, 5.1, 6.2, and pl. E1)*

The pillar rests on a platform levelled for it on the projecting bedrock adjoining the NW corner of the Quadrangle. Only the bottom two courses survive in situ. Both are c. 40 cm high and composed of two stretchers parallel to the periphery of the Quadrangle and a header at right-angles to it, the pattern in the upper course being inverted to avoid vertical joint congruence.

Top level as preserved: 951. The top course measures c. 110 × 155 cm in width and depth, respectively.

Unlike the pillars 2-7, P1 is placed with its longer sides parallel to the north line of the periphery. Possibly, therefore, it should be understood in relation to the west line. The pillar P9 was placed in a similar position at the SE corner of the Quadrangle. At the bottom of the rocky projection on which P1 stands are cuttings indicating the NW angle of the foundation courses C8-11, cf. fig. 6.2.

P2 *(figs. 1.10-12, 4.1-2, 5.2 a-b, 5.4 and pl. E1)*

Top level as preserved 915. As appears from a comparison with Newton's photo (figs. 4.1-3), this pillar was one course higher in his day. Judging from the photo, the height of the course now missing was approximately the same as that of the course underneath it, c. 48 cm. The top level of the pillar, as preserved at that time, was therefore c. 963. On top of it is seen on the photos figs. 4.1-2 (but apparently removed on the photo fig. 4.3) a bundle of the excavators' ropes.

Five courses survive measuring in height:

Course 1: c. 35 cm
Course 2: c. 51 cm
Course 3: c. 42 cm
Course 4: c. 41 cm
Course 5: c. 48 cm

To these should be added course 6: c. 48 cm high (conjectured from photo). Course 5 measures c. 125 × 140 cm in max. width and depth, respectively. As appears from fig. 5.4, congruence of vertical joints was systematically avoided.

P3 *(figs. 1.11-13, 4.3, 5.3 a-b, 5.4, and pl. E1)*

Top level as preserved 940. The pillar recently re-excavated is identical with the one shown on Newton's photos (figs. 4.1 and 4.3), the top of which is covered by earth not yet removed by the excavators. Five courses survive measuring in height:

Course 1: c. 41 cm
Course 2: c. 47 cm
Course 3: c. 50 cm
Course 4: c. 46 cm
Course 5: c. 58 cm

The top course measures c. 110 × 140 in max. width and depth, respectively. As appears from fig. 5.4, vertical joint congruence was systematically avoided. A mark in the form of an arrowhead is roughly incised on the front of the topmost course.

The marked tilt towards the S of the S side of the pillar appears to indicate that the part of the foundations on which it leant deviated correspondingly from the perpendicular.

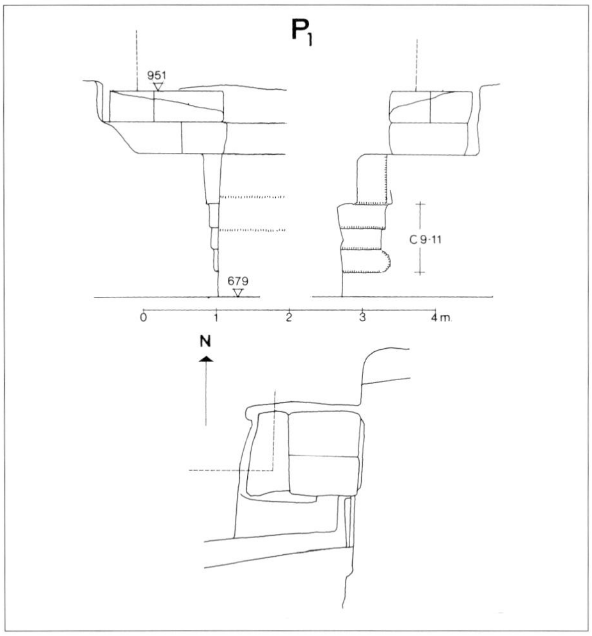

Fig. 5.1.

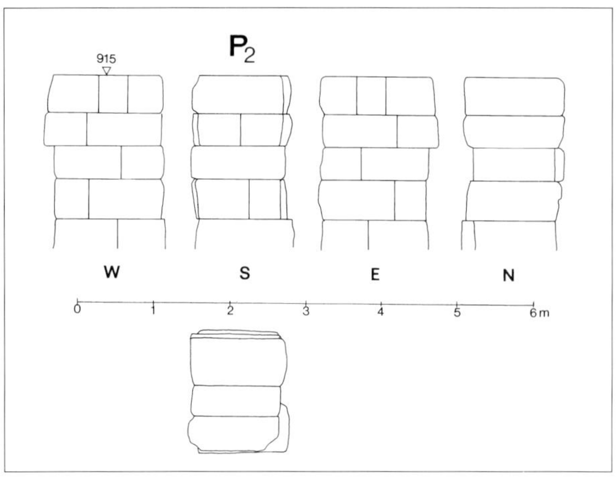

Fig. 5.2 a.

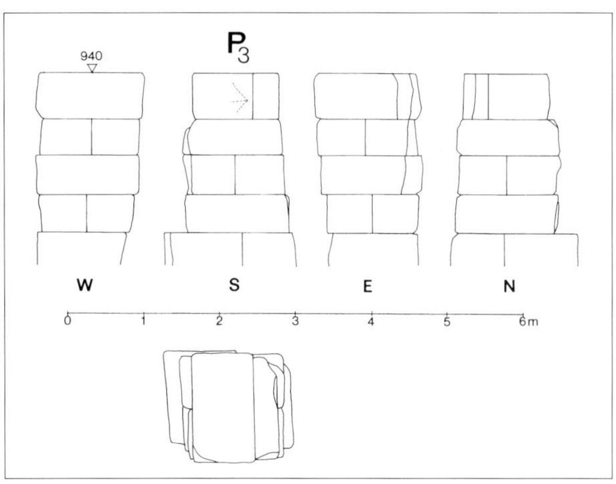

Fig. 5.3 a.

P4 (figs. 1.14, 4.3, 5.5 a-b, and pl. E1)

Top level as preserved 745. At present only the bottom course survives. C. 42 cm high, it consists of two slabs, and is c. 130 × 140 cm in max. width and depth, respectively. At the time of Newton, the pillar was much higher (fig. 4.3), at a cautious estimate approximately as high as P5, which reaches level 946.

The combined height of the courses now missing must therefore have been about 2

Fig. 5.2 b.

Fig. 5.3 b.

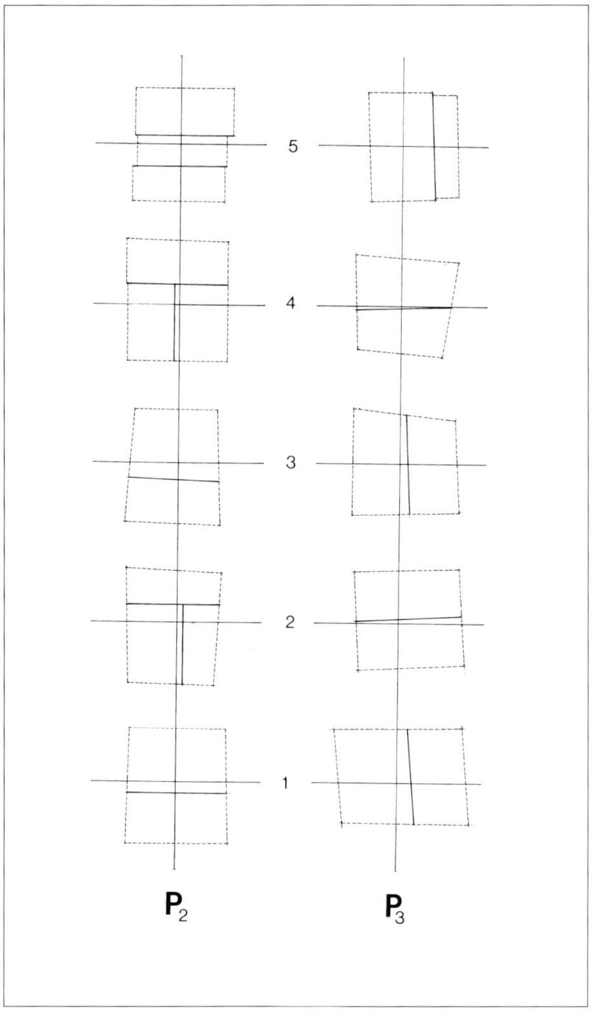

Fig. 5.4.

metres, equivalent to the four courses 2-5 of P3 (201 cm), i.e. there were altogether five courses inclusive of the surviving one.

The courses 5, 4, and 3 are visible on the photo, while the height of course 2 is conjectural. Fig. 5.5 shows a reconstruction of the pillar based on the details provided by the photo as combined with the dimensions of the surviving course. The courses 5 and 3 appear to have been approximately equal in height, course 4 a few cm lower:

Course 1: c. 42 cm
Course 2: c. 56 cm (conjectural)
Course 3: c. 50 cm (conjectural)
Course 4: c. 44 cm (conjectural)
Course 5: c. 50 cm (conjectural)

Like course 1, course 4 was subdivided by a vertical joint in the middle of the front.

P5 (figs. 4.3, and pl. E1)

Top level as preserved 946. The pillar rests on a platform levelled on top of the rock-cut edge of the Quadrangle. As at the time of Newton (cf. fig. 4.3), only the bottom course survives. C. 42 cm high, it consists of two slabs, measuring c. 120 × 130 cm in max. width and depth, respectively.

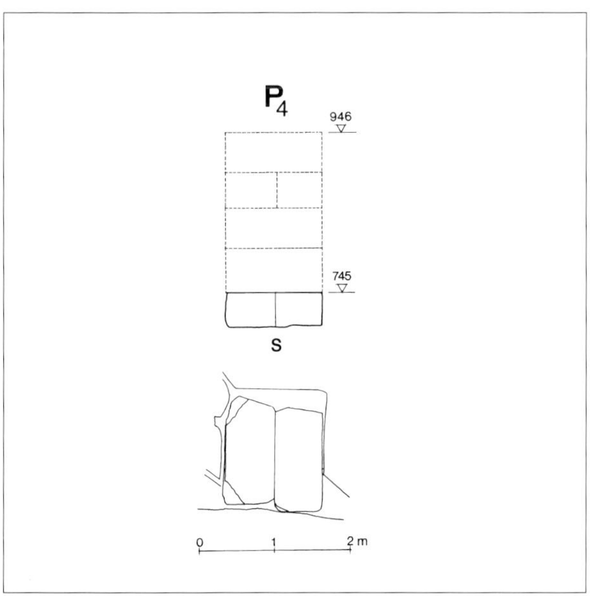

Fig. 5.5 a.

Fig. 5.5 b.

P6 *(fig. 5.6 and pl. E1)*

Top level as preserved 936. The pillar rests on the rock-cut edge of the Quadrangle. Only the bottom course, c. 41 cm high, survives. Consisting of three blocks, one laid parallel to the periphery of the Quadrangle, two at right-angles to it, it measures c. 120 × 150 cm in max. width and length.

Abutting on the left side of the pillar is a row of three rock-cut blocks, probably the remains of a rubble wall. Under the part of the pillar projecting from the edge of the Quadrangle was found a fill of chippings of greenish tufa, probably waste from the cutting of slabs for the foundations of the Maussolleion and possibly intended to add to the support of the block.

P7 *(fig. 1.17 and pl. E1)*

Top level as preserved 977. The pillar rests on the rock-cut edge of the Quadrangle. Remains of two courses survive, the lower c. 47, the upper c. 44 cm high. Immediately to the right of the pillar, the vertical side of the Quadrangle rises c. 80 cm, thus forming an angle into which ashlars belonging to the left side of the pillar are fitted. Presumably those of the right side were supplemented at the higher level, beginning with the third course.

For the irregular levels, cf. P15. It seems doubtful, however, whether the upper block is preserved in its original position.

P8 *(fig. 1.45 and pl. E2)*

Top level as preserved 892. The pillar rests on a platform levelled on top of the rock-cut edge of the Quadrangle. Only the lowest course is preserved, which is c. 40 cm high. It is composed of two blocks and measures c. 110 × 150 cm in maximum width and length, respectively. There being a distance of some 30 cm between the pillar and the line of the foundations on the east side of the Quadrangle, the pillar was probably erected independently of the foundations, cf. pillars P16-18 on the west side.

P9 *(pl. E3)*

On top of the edge of the Quadrangle at its SE corner at level c. 890 are traces that must indicate the outline of the bottom course of a pillar now lost. This course appears to have consisted of two blocks and to have measured c. 150 × 160 cm in max. width and length, respectively.

P10 *(fig. 1.48 (background) and pl. E3)*

Top level as preserved 941. The pillar rests on a platform levelled on top of the edge of the Quadrangle. The surviving course is c. 44 cm high, is composed of two blocks, and measures c. 140 × 160 cm in max. width and length, respectively.

P11 *(fig. 1.37 (background) and pl. E3)*

Top level as preserved 946. The pillar rests on a platform levelled on top of the edge of the Quadrangle. Half of the bottom course survives, c. 40 cm high, and c. 60 × 140 cm wide and long, respectively.

P12 *(pl. E3)*

On top of the edge of the Quadrangle, opposite P5 on the north side, is a platform at level 876 and 170 × 150 cm in max. width and depth, which may well have accommodated a pillar. The anterior part of the platform was probably widened by means of a block placed in a cutting at level 834.

P13 *(pl. E3)*

On top of the edge of the Quadrangle, opposite P4 on the north side, are two platforms of irregular form at levels 885 and 927, respectively, which are c. 2 m in width and c. 1.70 m in depth and may well have accommodated a pillar.

P14 *(pl. E3)*

If a pillar opposite P3 on the north side existed, it must have stood on the rock-cut landing at the bottom of the southern staircase adjacent to the foundation slabs for the Maussolleion, as indicated in fig. 6.1.

Fig. 5.6.

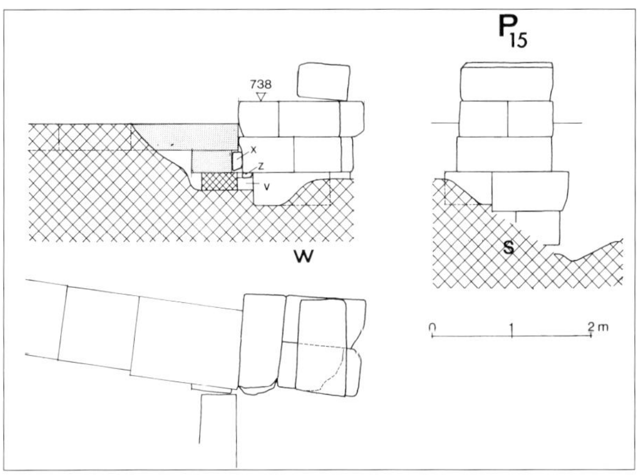

Fig. 5.7.

Fig. 5.8.

P15 *(fig. 5.7 and pl. E3)*

Top level as preserved 738 (not including a c. 45 cm high displaced block, probably belonging to the next course and indicating a top level of 783). The pillar is built on an irregular configuration of the bedrock, and is partly encased in masonry which will be described in connection with Zahle's study of the southern staircase. The bottom level of its lowest course is at 562. The sides most easy to approach are those facing W and S (fig. 5.7). On these sides the pillar consists of four courses in situ which have the following heights:

Course 1: c. 42 cm
Course 2: c. 48 cm
Course 3: c. 43 cm
Course 4: c. 43 cm
(course 5: c. 45 cm high is not in situ)

Course 4 measures c. 122 × 154 cm in max. width and length, respectively. Where the pillar courses 3-4 abut on the foundation courses C7-8, small pieces of marble or limestone have been inserted in the gaps between them (v-x-z), presumably for the sake of appearance or to give an impression of stability. It was apparently the intention that the pillars should abut on the foundations and receive some support from them, and it can hardly be doubted that the foundations had been laid before the pillar was built, for the inverse operation would have been awkward to handle, from a practical point of view.

P16 *(fig. 5.8 and pls. E3, E4)*

Top level as preserved 939. The innermost part of the three lowest courses of the pillar rested on a c. 70 cm deep recess cut in the side of the Quadrangle. The lowest course is c. 50 cm high and measures c. 110 cm in width. The next course was composed of two blocks, one of which, c. 39 cm high, survives in situ. A c. 48 cm deep cutting provided a footing for the northernmost part of the third course, which was c. 37 cm high, while the following courses rested entirely on top of the edge of the Quadrangle.

Judging from the remains, the maximum

width of the courses now missing may well have been c. 120 cm, while their maximum depth is purely a matter of conjecture. Judging from the distance between the pillar and the line of the foundations, c. 15-20 cm, the pillar did not abut on the foundations, but was free-standing.

P17 (pl. E4)

Top level as preserved 832. The distance between the pillar and the line of the foundations on the west side of the Quadrangle is some 50 cm. Evidently, therefore, the pillar could not have abutted on the foundations. The surviving blocks from the two bottom courses rest on platforms cut in the bedrock. The lower one is c. 42 cm high and c. 78 cm wide; the upper one, composed of two blocks, is c. 48 cm high and c. 112 cm wide, while the blocks measure c. 110 and 115 cm, respectively, in length. The pillar was therefore almost exactly square in plan.

P18 (fig. 1.8-11 and pl. E4)

Top level as preserved 822. The pillar could not have abutted on the foundations, to which there was a distance of some 30 cm.

Three courses survive, each consisting of two blocks, alternately laid cross-wise to avoid congruence of vertical joints. The courses have the following heights:

Course 1: c. 31 cm
Course 2: c. 54 cm
Course 3: c. 44 cm

The max. dimensions of the top course are c. 120 × 120 cm.

6. Features of the superstructure deducible from the surviving foundations and pillars

Although the obvious intention was to lay the foundations in a gridwork system of perfect regularity, the slabs actually laid and still in position at the SW and NE angles of the Quadrangle are only approximately orthogonal and vary slightly in side length, as the following examples will demonstrate:

	length	width
NE angle	91.5 cm	89.5 cm
	90.5	90
	88.5-89	87.5
	91	87-88.5
	90-91	89.5
	90	89
SW angle	93	91
	97.5	96.5
	92.5	89.5

The consistent use of slabs of exactly the same size and orthogonal form would evidently have simplified the technical procedure of laying them, in terms of time and manpower, and the reason why a different approach was chosen in the cases just mentioned was hardly that the workmen did not know the square or were not familiar with its practical application.

More likely, the anomalies observed were due to some extent to inaccuracy in the layout of the ground plan, which became apparent to the builders when the extensive foundation courses above the levelled bedrock were to be laid. It must then have been realized that the periphery of the foundations had not been laid out at angles that were perfectly orthogonal (see further below). In consequence of this lack of precision, as can be shown on the basis of the meticulously accurate drawing of the ground plan recorded by the architects of the Danish expedition (see the folded plate), the SW and NE angles of the ground plan were in fact slightly obtuse, while the NW and SE angles were correspondingly acute.

The deviation of the shorter sides of the periphery from a line perpendicular to the longer sides amounts to c. 25 cm (fig. 6.1). On a perfectly orthogonal foundation slab 90 × 90 cm wide, the same degree of deviation would have equalled about 8 mm, i.e., sufficient to require adjustment on at least two of its sides to make them fit the adjoining slabs in the gridwork. Possibly the workmen were at a loss how to solve the problem and resorted to the method they were used to when dealing with polygonal masonry: to shape each joint individually in precise conformity with the joint it was intended to fit.

The orientation of the numerous pry-cuttings surviving on the surface of the levelled bedrock in the easternmost part of the Quadrangle shows that the rows of foundation slabs along the longer sides of the periphery were placed exactly parallel to these and that therefore the necessary adjustment had to be made along the periphery of the shorter sides.

The surviving evidence for the form of the ground plan can be summed up as follows:

West side

The line of the foundations facing W must have extended between the SW corner defined by the foundation slabs in situ, and the vertical cuttings in the bedrock indicating the outline of the foundation slabs at the NW corner (figs. 1.8, 5.1, 6.1-2 and pls. E1, E4). This line coincides very nearly (but for an interval of about 5 cm) with the east side of the pillar built to buttress the north wall of the western staircase, which undoubtedly abutted on the Maussolleion foundations (cf. above p. 39). The gap may well be due to the uneven surface of the foundations, as this

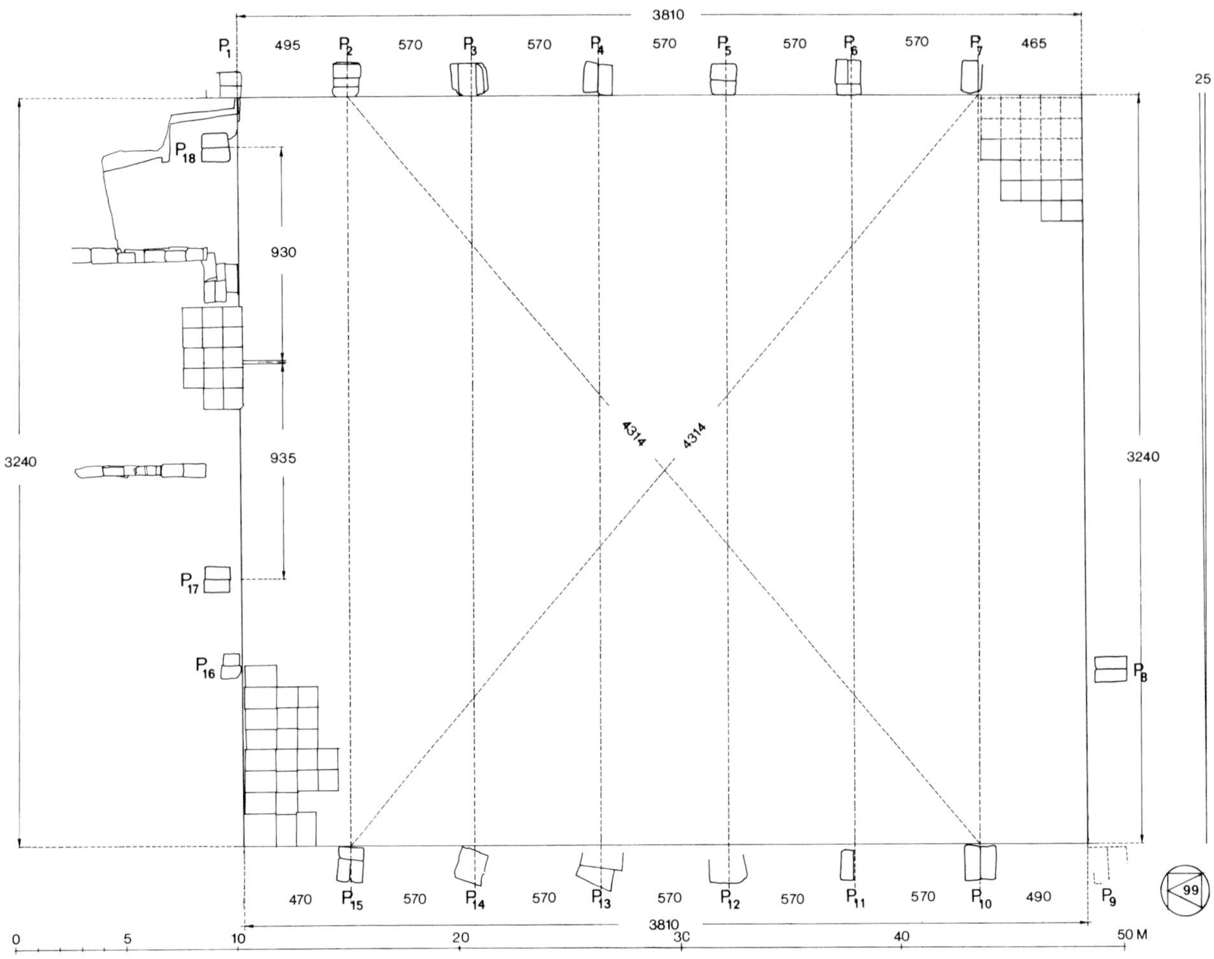

Fig. 6.1. Reconstruction of the foundations of the Maussolleion. While the reconstructed periphery has the form of a slightly oblique-angled parallelogram (max. deviation from the right-angle c. 25 cm), the pillars on the N and S sides appear to have been placed exactly opposite one another, the diagonal lines connecting P2 with P10, and P7 with P15, respectively, being of equal length.

is illustrated by the variously projecting foundation courses in situ at the SW corner (fig. 1.59).

From the line connecting the SW and NW corners to the front of the masonry adjoining the S side of the plug-block, which at the time of Newton was preserved to a height of five courses (figs. 10.5-6), is a distance of about 20 cm (cf. above, fig. 3.1). Presumably it took the form of a recess corresponding in length to the platform in front of the entrance to the tomb chamber and flattened to make the plug-block fit. The facades of the two slabs nowadays surviving in situ are not merely quarry-faced, but point-chiselled, and their lower edge is bevelled in the same way as the rock-cut ashlars of the walls enframing the W stairway (figs. 1.26-27, pl. E12).

East side

The east side of the foundations is indicated by the easternmost row of foundation slabs from course 14 still in situ at the NE corner of the Quadrangle (figs. 1.16-17). Cuttings on the vertical rock-cut side of the Quadrangle at the SE corner (pl. E2) show that the courses C11 and C12 abutted on it, whereas the following courses C13 and C14 have left no traces.

Presumably, therefore, the latter courses were not contiguous to the side of the Quadrangle, but kept at a distance from it of possibly some 10-15 cm.

If this is assumed, the north and south sides of the foundations had the same length, c. 38.10 m.

North and south sides

These sides are delimited by the pillars P2-7 on the north side and P10-15 on the south side. The south sides at the top of the pillars P2, P5, and P6 are almost exactly on a line and appear to provide the most reliable basis for a definition of the north side of the foundations.

On the south side, only the pillars P10 and P15 are sufficiently well preserved to be used as fixed points for the a reconstruction of this side of the foundations. Judging from these indications, the distance between the two rows of pillars measured across the Quadrangle was c. 32.4 m.

The circumference

According to the observations above, the circumference of the building at the level of the foundations must have been 2 × 32.4 + 2 × 38.1 m = 141.0 m. If it is assumed that the euthynteria course of the superstructure was set back a few centimetres from the line of the foundations, say 5 cm, the maximum circumference of the superstructure at its lowest level must have been 5 × 8 = 40 cm shorter than that of the foundations, i.e. c. 140.6 m.

Since the circumference of the Maussolleion specified by Pliny as 440 feet should probably be understood to refer to the superstructure at its bottom level, the foot unit implied must have been 140.6:440 = 0.32 (0.3195) m.[20] This is almost precisely the roughly estimated unit of 32 cm on which my tentative transcription of metric dimensions of architectural marbles from the superstructure of the Maussolleion has been based.[21]

Converted into foot units of 32 cm, the shorter and longer sides of the circumference would have measured c. 101 and c. 119 feet, respectively. Pliny's figure could therefore not have resulted from adding up 100 feet on the shorter and 120 feet on the longer sides,[22] and may well have been an approximate estimate taking into account only measurements in feet and ignoring dactyls.

Among features of the ground plan reflecting dimensions in the superstructure should possibly also be reckoned the pillars placed along the periphery of the Quadrangle. As already stated (above, chapters 4-5), the length and width of each individual pillar vary in each individual course. It is therefore impossible to define its centre except in approximate terms.

At all appearances, however, the pillars along the longer sides of the Quadrangle were spaced at equal intervals, when they were laid out, and if an axial spacing of c. 570 cm is supposed to underlie the distribution, all the axes in both rows of pillars will be found to lie very close to what the eye will perceive as the approximate middle of each pillar, or perhaps rather as its centre of gravity. Even an axial spacing just a couple of centimetres shorter or longer than the one of c. 570 cm will be found to apply less convincingly, and increasingly so from the middle of each series towards the pillars at both ends, 2, 7, 10, and 15.

In a preliminary report[23] I have suggested the possibility that the north and south rows might have been used to support scaffoldings. It may be doubted, however, whether the soft and brittle bedrock would have been considered sufficiently solid for such a purpose, and the pillars would probably have been spaced too far apart to provide a stable footing for scaffoldings of the requisite height for a building as tall as the Maussolleion. Besides, stones could have been lifted to any level, where required, by means of movable cranes working on top of the building itself, as it rose course upon course.

The spacing of the pillars, on the other hand, may well have been related to the dimensions of the colonnade of the Maussolleion, for the axial spacing of the columns was probably somewhat shorter on the longer sides of the building than on its fronts, where it measured c. 300 cm,[24] and may well have equalled half the axial pillar spacing.

This would not necessarily imply that the pillars were built primarily to indicate the positions of column axes. It may have been their foremost purpose to define a level independent of the building itself, which also might serve as a basis for laying out a number of distinctive features of its ground plan. It may be assumed that the top course of the pillars was made of stone of a solid structure not susceptible to breaking,

Fig. 6.2. Cuttings in the bedrock for the NW angle of the foundations (cf. pls. E1 and E4).

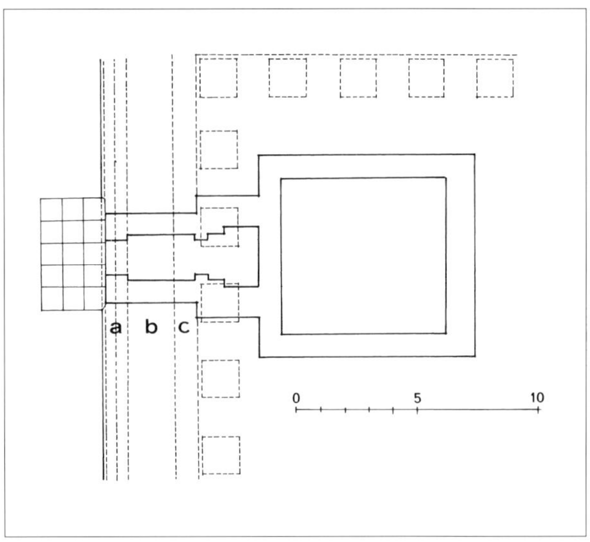

Fig. 6.3. Plan of the colonnade of the Maussolleion superimposed over the plan of the sepulchral compartments.

a: crepidoma at the foot of the podium.

b-c: sculpture bases around the podium.

and providing a surface suitable for the incision of guide lines, for which purpose a foundation slab of tufa of the usual dimensions, c. 90 × 90 × 30 cm, would have sufficed.

Incised transverse lines on the slab could have marked the axis of every second column on the longer sides. Incised on the pillars P2, P7, P10, and P15, the axes of the four angle columns would have been particularly important, since they would have fixed the position and orientation of the colonnade in relation to the ground plan of the lower part of the building.

The intermediate pillars P3-6 and P11-14 could have served to indicate levels on the basis of which it would be possible to work out a curvature of the euthynteria course and the crepidoma.[25] The distance between the pillars could have been spanned by long rulers like those referred to in the Lebadeia inscription, which were at least twenty feet long, six dactyls thick, and half a foot high, i.e. no less than six and a half metres in length, and 12 × 16 cm in section.[26] Rulers of such dimensions must have had the form of wooden beams. In Lebadeia they were used to ensure that the surface of the pavement described in the inscription would become perfectly plane.[27]

If the axial distance on the basis of which the pillars on the longer sides were spaced reflects the axial spacing of the columns in the colonnade on top of the monument, these spacings must be assumed to equal integral numbers of dactyls.

The following possibilities may be considered:

570 cm = 285" (foot = 32.0 cm); axial column spacing = 142.5".

570 cm = 286" (foot = 31.9 cm); axial column spacing = 143".

7.5" goes 19 times into 142.5" and 20 times into the middlemost axial column spacings on the fronts, 150", thereby securing modular compatibility, and is equivalent to half the basic module 15" traceable in several parts of the superstructure.[28] As 143" is a prime number not divisible by any other integer than itself and the number 1, it comes short of satisfying requirements like those fulfilled by the alternative of 142.5 dactyls.[29]

The pillars on the N and S sides appear to have been placed exactly opposite one another, the diagonal lines connecting P2 with P10, and P7 with P15, respectively, being of equal length (fig. 6.1). The abovementioned deviation from a precisely orthogonal system observed in the lay-out of the foundations must therefore have been corrected before the superstructure was erected. If it had been maintained, it would have complicated the building procedure immensely. However, surviving corner blocks from various parts of the superstructure are in fact exactly orthogonal.[30] The N and S rows of pillars may therefore be confidently related to the plan of the superstructure rather than to that of the foundations.

Apart from the fact that P17 and P18 on the west side are placed exactly symmetrically with respect to the axis of the tomb chamber, and that P18 is situated approximately opposite P8 on the east side, there seems to be no evidence suggesting which function or functions these pillars were intended to serve. If they had been meant to assume a permament function, as for example that of supporting sculptures or other objects of artistic attraction that were to be seen along the foot of the superstructure, it is hard to understand why such a poor material as the bedrock was used instead of some of the nearly 200,000 slabs of solid tufa which went into the foundations of the Maussolleion.

Among dispositions in the layout of the ground plan of the Maussolleion at the level of its foundations reflecting distinctive features in its superstructure should possibly also be reckoned the plan of the sepulchral compound. While the sidewalls in the corridor are c. 90 cm thick, those in the anteroom are about 30 cm thicker. This difference may be due to calculations on the part of the architects. As fig. 6.3 demonstrates, the vault of the anteroom was charged not only with part of the enormous weight of the podium on which the columns rested, but also with the weight of two columns and the pyramid structure they supported, while above the corridor rested only the bases for free-standing sculptures around the podium.

Similar considerations may have induced the builders to make the east wall in the tomb chamber c. 30 thicker than the other sides, perhaps the fact that the podium was wider on this side, which therefore would be exposed to a particularly forceful lateral thrust, should the individual courses of foundation slabs constituting the core of the building happen to be dislocated in consequence of an earthquake.[31]

The architects must have been aware of the risk, for the foundation slabs had only clamps to secure their attachment to the neighbouring slabs, but no dowels to prevent them from rocking or sliding sideways independently of the courses below and above. This shortcoming may well have contributed to the destructive factors that eventually brought about the complete disintegration of the Maussolleion.

7. The situation of the foundations of the Maussolleion with regard to its surroundings

The topmost foundation course surviving inside the Quadrangle, which is situated within its NE quarter, reaches level 890 (L15, cf. pl. E2). Pry-cuttings on top of this course testify that there was at least one additional course of foundation slabs above it, which was staggered half a slab-width in relation to the course underneath. The average height of the topmost foundation courses in situ being c. 30 cm, the first, second, and third courses above level 890 may be assumed to have reached approximately levels 920, 950, and 980, respectively.

Figs. 7.1-2 illustrate the consequences of placing tentatively the bottom and top of the euthynteria course of the Maussolleion at levels 950 and 980, respectively (compare the levels indicated in the drawing Poul Pedersen (1991) I, fig. 86 (= our fig. 1.55):

On the east side, the rock surface near the NE corner of the Quadrangle at levels 950 and 960 will cover a maximum of 10 cm of the height of the euthynteria course, while near the SE corner at level 890 two courses of foundation slabs will be open to view.

On the W part of the S side, and on the W side at levels 975-985, the rock will rise to levels between 5 cm below and 5 cm above the top of the euthynteria course, and only at the point where it rises to level 1000 will it encroach on the bottom step of the crepidoma – that is, if seen at a distance.

In this arrangement, the topmost course of pillar P7, which reaches level 977, will be almost exactly flush with the top of the euthynteria course of the Maussolleion, i.e. will not encroach on its crepidoma, and this may be the reason why it was not removed after the monument had been finished.

At the north side, the top of the euthynteria course of the peribolos wall (at level 936) will be placed 14 cm below the bottom level 950 of the euthynteria course of the Maussolleion. This implies that a pavement connecting the two structures without exposing the building's topmost foundation course must have been flush with a level c. 14 cm above the euthynteria of the peribolos wall, thus covering the lower part of its toichobate (fig. 7.1).

However, a pavement made of stone slabs could not have been placed at a lower level than 965, which is the top level of the highest eminence of the natural bedrock in the passage north of the Maussolleion,[32] and would therefore cover the lower part of the bottom course of ordinary ashlar masonry in the peribolos wall (i.e. the one resting on its toichobate).

In actual fact, there is not the slightest indication in the form of cuttings along the foot of the peribolos wall suggesting that a pavement made of stone slabs was ever planned, let alone existed. Besides, if it had existed, the edge of the bedrock along the periphery of the Quadrangle could not have been left in its natural state at levels ranging between c. 890 and 1000, but must have been flattened to form a solid base for the adjoining pavement slabs.

It is not, of course, impossible that a pavement was actually planned. From a modern point of view, it would have had the advantage of concealing the appearance of courses of foundation slabs beneath the superstructure. However, the need of such a disposition may not have been felt equally urgent in Antiquity. Compare, for example, the Parthenon on top of the Acropolis rock, which rests on several courses of foundation blocks under the three-stepped stylobate, the topmost ones of which must have been fully open to view on the south and east sides of the building.

Poul Pedersen has conjectured that the rocky eminence of the Quadrangle might have been enclosed by the terrace walls of andesite ashlars discovered by Newton along its east and south sides, and partly rediscovered in the

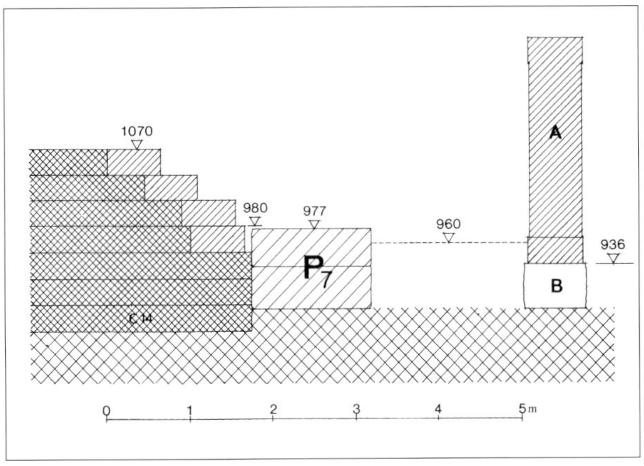

Fig. 7.1. Top of the euthynteria course of the Maussolleion hypothetically indicated at level 980 and seen in relation to pillar P7 and to the euthynteria course (B) of the N enclosure wall (A).

trenches P10 and P11 at the recent excavations.[33] The date of these walls, in particular that of its southern branch, is a matter of dispute, and the issue cannot be dealt with properly in the present context, since it implies a discussion of several other more or less problematic remains situated in the area south and east of the Quadrangle (cf. chapter 24).

It may be argued that even if the walls were built before the Maussolleion was constructed, they might have been reused and raised to a level flush with the bottom of the monument.

As a matter of fact, however, none of the trial trenches excavated by the Danish expedition in various places on the Maussolleion Terrace west and south of the Quadrangle has revealed the slightest trace of a pavement. The only remains that may be interpreted as evidence of a paved terrace were discovered by Newton and Biliotti in the area immediately south of the ashlar wall that according to Poul Pedersen's suggestion might have formed the south side of the platform on which the Maussolleion stood.

In his diary, Biliotti reports the following observations:[34]

After having identified the ashlar wall (diary 31st March and 1st April 1865) he discovers "a row of green stone slabs running N. and S. for about 25 feet. Some of these slabs measure 1' thick and 4' square, some less. – Towards the E. similar slabs have been discovered by Mr Newton, which are still visible on the same level. They formed perhaps a pavement which if prolonged towards the N. would join the Quadrangle nearly in the middle."

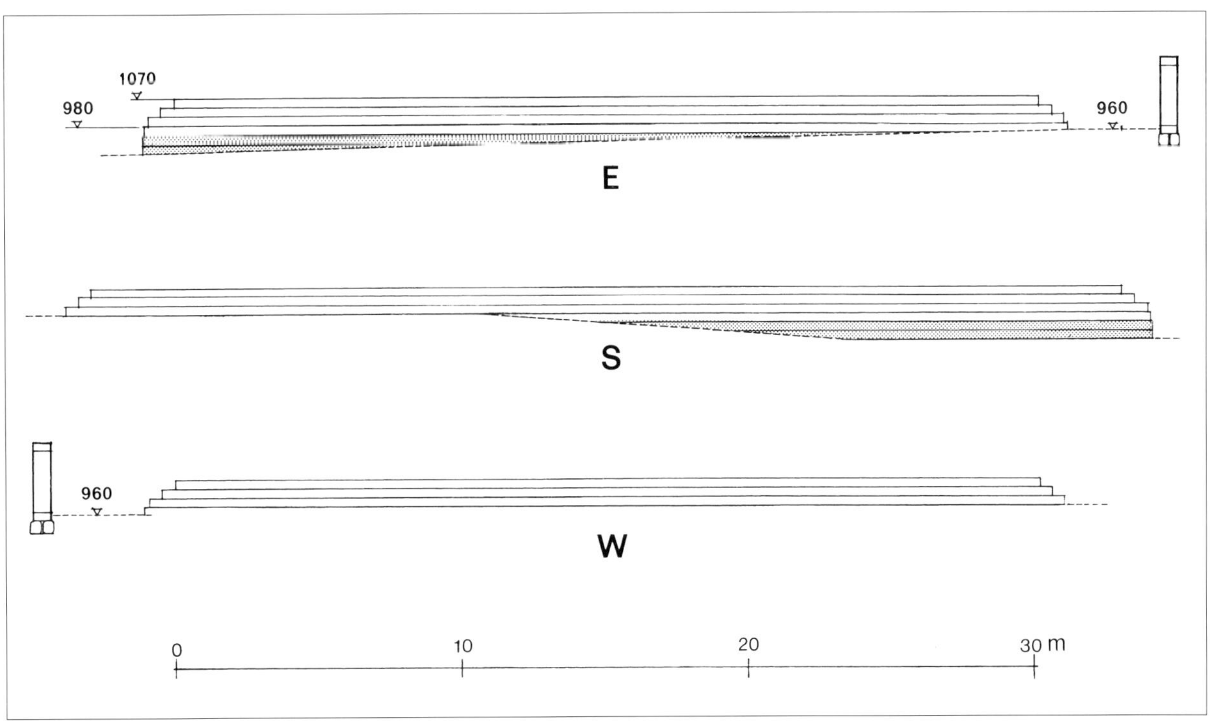

Fig. 7.2. Foundations, euthynteria course, and crepidoma reconstructed in accordance with the height indications on fig. 7.1, and seen in relation to the levels of the bedrock adjoining the building on its E, S, and W sides.

On May 4th Biliotti observes in the NW corner of Mehmeda's property "extending for a few feet the continuation of the pavement with green stone slabs discovered by Mr Newton."

On May 25th "some slabs of green stone are met here and there. They no doubt belong to the pavement already found in different spots, they being at the same level with them."

On the following day, the excavators "meet again green stone slabs always at the same level, and dig round them. They rest either on the rock, or on the artificial platform made of fragments of rock."

The approximate positions of the slabs mentioned by Biliotti are indicated in Poul Pedersen's sketch, fig. 85 in part I of his publication of the Maussolleion Terrace.

To all appearances, Biliotti's conclusion that the slabs of green stone which he discovered must belong to a pavement was largely deduced from the fact that they were found at the same level. As reported on March 1st, some of the slabs measured 4' square, i.e. c. 120 × 120 cm, and were therefore considerably larger than the standard size of slabs used in the foundations of the Maussolleion (c. 90 × 90 cm),[35] while other slabs were smaller. At any rate, their dimensions must have differed so much that they did not conform to a grid pattern comparable to the system used in the laying of the courses of foundation slabs in the Maussolleion. Judging from the absence of further specifications, this was probably also true in general terms of the slabs that turned up at subsequent diggings in the same area.

Apart from the information that some of the slabs were found lying in a row "for about 25 feet" (i.e. less than 8 metres long) nothing is said to corroborate Biliotti's assumption that they might be part of a pavement "which if prolonged towards the N. would join the Quadrangle nearly in the middle" or to suggest that they were distributed in a regular pattern appropriate to the laying of an extensive pavement.

In the tomb chamber of the Maussolleion and its corridor there was a course of foundation slabs underneath the marble pavement, whereas the pavement composed of standard-size foundation slabs in front of the entrance to the tomb chamber (chapter 8) was not supposed to be permanently visible, but served the provisional purpose of providing a solid base for the plug-block, from which this could be pried into position by means of pry-cuttings cut in the surface of the pavement.

Evidently, pry-cuttings cut in the soft bedrock could not have resisted the pressure of the crowbars needed to push the colossal plug-block forward.

Judging from this evidence, a pavement covering the Maussolleion Terrace would most likely have been composed of slabs of marble placed on top of a foundation course of tufa slabs of the standard size (c. 30 × 90 × 90 cm) laid in a regular grid pattern.

If the tufa slabs observed by the British excavators had been laid in connection with the erection of the Maussolleion, the adjoining terrace wall of bedrock (andesite) must have been visible as well. However, in masonry clearly related to the Maussolleion, ashlars quarried from the bedrock were apparently not used except for structures not meant to be permanently visible, such as the pillars and the subterranean parts of the monument hidden by earth fill (chapters 3-5).

Judging from the comparative evidence, therefore, it seems doubtful whether the remains interpreted by Biliotti as parts of a pavement, and the terrace walls enframing the south and east sides of the Quadrangle, should be seen as contemporary with the Maussolleion. Until this issue is definitely settled – which will be difficult to achieve without supplementary excavations – hypotheses are the only possible way of approaching the issue:

The excavated evidence suggests the possibility that after the Maussolleion had been erected, the enclosure was left in a dilapidated state and never suitably adapted to match the standards of the monument. It is not even certain that the walls of the enclosure on its south and west sides were finished.[36] Presumably attention was paid primarily to the perfection of the east side facing the market square and the north side extending along the principal thoroughfare of the city.

If it had been the intention that the great expanse of the enclosure should serve the practical purpose of accommodating spacious monumental structures relevant to sepulchral requirements such as a stadion for gymnastic competitions or a racecourse for horseracing, the absolute absence of architectural remains in situ attributable to structures of that type and size, and the poor occurrence of scattered blocks that might have come from them, would seem to preclude that such an intention was ever carried into effect.[37]

It seems more likely, therefore, that apart from providing a convenient position for the monument, the area parcelled out for the prospective Maussolleion was intended to remain unbuilt.

Using the term ALSOS (cf. note 37), Poul Pedersen appears to suggest the possibility that the Maussolleion might have had the character of a grove in which Maussollos was worshipped as a god, and that the monument was his temple. It is perhaps conceivable that, as suggested by me, the Maussolleion might have been "an institution combining hero-cult with deification".[38] To all appearances, however, there could not have been a proper cella with a cult image within the colonnade of the building,[39] and no finds suggesting the existence of an altar before its east front were reported by the British excavators.

Alternatively the enclosure could have been planned by analogy with the oriental type of park called PARADEISOS that served as hunting-ground for the Persian kings and grandees and was imitated in the satrapies of Asia Minor. The dedication of a paradeisos might have been seen as particularly appropriate to hero-worship and therefore perfectly consistent with the sacrificial deposit on the lower landing of the W staircase.[40]

Not a few paradeisoi are mentioned by Xenophon:

Several were situated at Daskyleion in the Propontis. In some of them, surrounded by walls, were wild animals of various kinds.[41]

At Kelainai in Phrygia, Cyrus had a palace and a large paradeisos full of wild animals[42] "in which he used to hunt on horseback wherever he wished to give himself and his horses exercise". Through the middle of this paradeisos flowed the Maeander river.

Where Greek mercenaries encamped beside the city of Sittake not far from Babylon, they saw a large and beautiful paradeisos "thickly covered with all sorts of trees".[43]

These descriptions may give an idea of what the Maussolleion enclosure might have been designed to contain, and what it might eventually have looked like at the time of Maussollos' death.

It would have been a comparatively easy task to cover the area with a variety of trees, which in later times might have been cut down and replaced by vegetable-producing kitchen gardens, few traces being left of the original arrangement.

The enclosure might also have been planned to keep wild game of different sorts available to hunters, but to prevent the animals from escaping, the surrounding walls would of course have had to have been erected to their full extent.

However, it might not have been intended to serve as a hunting-ground for Maussollos while he was still alive. More likely, it was meant to be at his disposal in his underworld existence.

On the west front of the Maussolleion facing what was by far the most extensive part of the enclosure, comprising almost 18,000 sq.m., the colossal sculptural groups depicted a hunting party, probably with Maussollos in the middle, while the groups on the opposite side facing the market square appear to have referred to Maussollos' official activities in his capacity as satrap and founder of the new city state of Halikarnassos.[44]

The continuous course of the north peribolos wall at a uniform level throughout the entire length of the enclosure should probably be understood to imply that a terrace based on earth fillings flush with the top of the euthynteria course at level c. 936-940 (cf. Pedersen [1991]9) was planned to form an approximately plane surface covering almost the whole area.

On this background, the immediate surroundings of the Maussolleion, where natural configurations of the bedrock rose to slightly higher levels, might have added favourably to the architectural prominence of the monument. According to the level 950 hypothetically estimated for the bottom of the euthynteria course of the Maussolleion (cf. above), the distance between this and the general terrace level at c. 936 was only some 14 cm. This would have left a maximum of half the height of a foundation slab visible below the euthynteria course of the monument on both sides of the SE corner (cf. fig. 7.2), which gap could easily have been covered up completely by means of earth fill, or low shrubs.

Seen from the outside, the most conspicuous feature of the enclosure, apart from the Maussolleion, would in that case have been trees rising perhaps as high as five or even ten metres above the enclosure wall (see drawing below). According to Poul Pedersen's calculations based on a statistic analysis of the surviving blocks from the north side, the wall measured c. 2.56 m in height.[45]

If Artemisia's death intercepted her efforts to finish the Maussolleion, and funds for the completion of the project were no longer available, the part of it most likely to have been left unfinished would presumably have been the terrace on which it stood. Possibly trees remained to be planted. At any rate, it must have taken several years before they reached the height they were expected to attain. Alexander may have seen them as full-grown at his arrival at Halikarnassos in 334 BC.

Alternatively this was what the founder had visualized that the innermost surroundings of his monument should eventually look like, which does not make much difference, provided that the principal viewpoint on which the hypothesis is based can be sustained.

If the Maussolleion terrace had been completely finished, all remains of previous buildings rising above the euthynteria course of the north peribolos wall ought to have been demolished, but what remained of the foundations of bedrock ashlars some 37-46 m due south of the Quadrangle (building F) was not removed, although it rose to a level about 70 cm above the euthynteria course of the peribolos wall.[46]

My hypothesis implies that both the remains of building F and the retaining walls south and east of the Quadrangle are pre-Maussollan and must have been built to serve functions related to the use of the site as a cemetery before it was cancelled to make room for the Maussolleion. These walls may have confined a platform based on the eminence of the rock where the Maussolleion was later to be placed, and giving entry to the tombs accessible from the south staircase and its lower landing. In those days, access to the platform must have been from the west or north, possibly from a road following the same track as the 15 m wide boulevard that was later established along the north wall of the Maussolleion terrace.

On the history of the site in Pre-Maussollan times, cf. below, chapter 24.

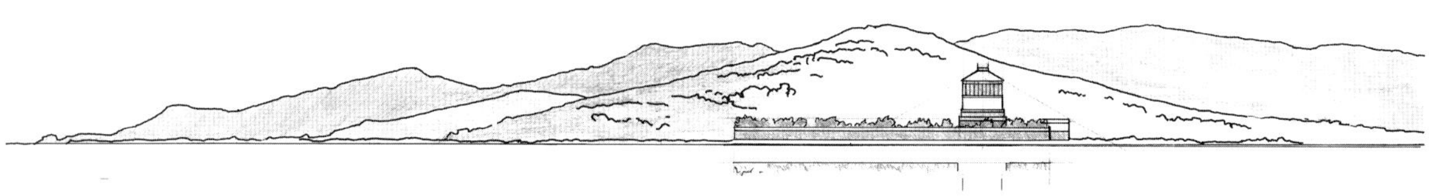

8. The platform in front of the entrance to the tomb chamber

The rectangular platform is composed of three rows of five blocks of the standard size (87.0-91.5 cm square and c. 30 cm thick) and of the greenish tufa characteristic of the slabs used in the foundations of the monument proper. The slabs were connected with one another by means of clamps, one across each joint, while along the margin of the platform they rest in a rock-cut rebate in the bedrock (it would have been pointless to fasten dowels in the fragile bedrock). One corner slab is missing, but its former existence is proved by clamp holes.

Since the slabs of the easternmost row are laid almost precisely on a line flush with the west side of the corridor, they were probably the first to be placed. In the following two rows, slabs varying a little in side length were used, thus causing the west margin of the platform to form a broken line, which the slabs covering the drain were laid to fit (fig. 3.1).

As the drain branching off towards the tomb chamber passes under the platform, this was clearly a feature planned in connection with the Maussolleion, as also suggested by the use of foundation slabs. Evidently the purpose of the platform was not to embellish the entrance to the tomb, but to form a solid basis for the plug-block while this was being moved into position.

This is indicated by two series each of four 8-10 cm long and c. 7 cm deep pry-cuttings cut in the top surface of the platform (fig. 8.1). The pry-cuttings also make it clear that before being displaced, the plug-block must have been lowered vertically into a provisional position on the platform by means of heavy lifting gear (on which, see further below, and fig. 17.2).

Part of the middlemost slab of the platform closest to the entrance and of the slab adjoining it towards the south have been roughly chiselled away, whereby the drain was exposed to view. Most of this area was covered by the plug-block which in its final position projected 30-34 cm from the line of the foundations, and it seems unlikely that any device connected with the drain and worth extracting for its metal value could have existed in such a place.

More probably the cuttings must be ascribed to efforts of grave-robbers who tried to find a way of extracting the plug-block from its position in front of the corridor, attempts which have also left traces on the plug-block itself (cf. chapter 11).

Fig. 8.1. Pavement of foundation slabs in front of the entrance to the tomb chamber. Note the two series of cuttings that were used to pry the plug-block (seen overturned on the left) into position.

9. The bronze grating said to have covered the drain crossing the western staircase

According to Newton, a bronze grating now in the British Museum (reg.no. 1857.12-20.348) was somehow connected with the drain of the Maussolleion.[47] It is a rectangular piece of bronze plate measuring c. 45 cm in length and 23.4 and 25.4 cm, respectively, in width at the ends. Near the larger end is a circular, c. 2.5 cm deep depression c. 19.5 cm in diameter, which is pierced by concentric rows of holes, each of which measures 5-6 mm in diameter (fig. 9.1).

The piece was not hammered, but cast in a mould in which the holes were made with a pointed tool. The part in the middle is broken, apparently due to physical force rather than to corrosion. The bronze plate has an average thickness of 3.5 mm and is curved in longitudinal section to a maximum depth of about 1 cm, as if somebody had trodden on it.

Undoubtedly it was intended to function as a strainer, but Newton's description of the position in which it was found is far from clear (HD 142-3):

"On the eastern side, a drain issuing from under the paved area of the Quadrangle at the point marked epsilon in the Plan (pls. iii-iv), flows into the eastern gallery, and on the western side, another drain passed out of the building, at beta, as has been already stated [cf. HD 98].

This drain, found in position, flowed under the great stone [i.e. the plug-block], emptying itself into the gallery through a bronze grating inserted in the covering slab of pavement."

Judging from this passage, the strainer was found at the point where the branch coming from the tomb chamber joins the drain crossing the lower landing of the western staircase, i.e. at beta in Newton's plan. However, to make sense, Newton's description must imply that the bronze grating was inserted vertically in the joint between the west margin of the platform described in chapter 8 and the adjoining covering slab of the drain, and that it was its purpose to prevent foreign matter in the drain from clogging and obstructing the passage in the branch.

However, as recent experiments have shown, the drain would have been too narrow to permit the insertion of the strainer in such a position. Besides, it may be doubted that the piece was made for the purpose attributed to it by Newton. The concave bottom of the perforated circular area indicates that it was intended not merely to strain out but also to collect undesirable matter contained in the fluid passing through it, exactly like the strainer in a modern kitchen sink.

Evidently, therefore, it was to be placed in a horizontal position, the fluid to be sieved issuing from a vertical conduit placed perpendicularly above the strainer. There would not, however, have been any obvious way of fitting it into the drainage system of the Maussolleion, unless it was adapted to an outlet in the marble pavement of the tomb chamber, and anyway the purpose of the blank part of the piece apart from the sieve is difficult to explain.

Judging from Newton's interpretation of its purpose, it was probably found near the drain crossing the lower landing of the western staircase, though perhaps not in its original position. Possibly it had been discarded as unfit for use because of the broken sieve, and had been thrown as garbage into the pit left by grave-robbers who had attempted to clear away the plug-block at the entrance to the tomb chamber (cf.chapter 10).

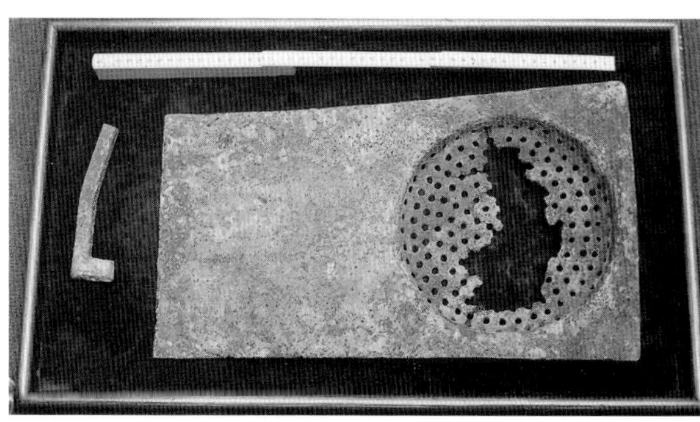

Fig. 9.1. Bronze grating in the British Museum, reg.no. 1857,12-20.348.

10. The plug-block that closed the entrance to the tomb

The plug-block, of greenish tufa like that of which the foundation slabs were made, measures 208.7 cm in height (figs. 10.1-4). Its back, the side that was inserted in the opening which gave access to the corridor, measures in width c. 138 cm below and c. 134 cm at the top. This side as well as the two sides adjoining it are smoothly dressed.

The front of the stone, which is 30-34 cm deep and roughly tooled with the pointed chisel, projects 3.5-5.5 cm on both sides, thus attaining a uniform width of c. 145 cm. In all probability the projection was also carried along the top of the stone but disappeared when this was cut away by grave-robbers (cf. below).

Newton, who discovered the block still in situ, gives the following information (HD 96ff., cf. Appendix 2):

"It is worthy of note that the great stone east of the staircase rested on two slabs of white marble, to which it had been carefully adjusted in the following manner ... In the great stone, bronze dowels were fixed, corresponding with bronze sockets let into the marble slabs. The accompanying cut [HD 97] shows one of these dowels within a bronze collar, which was fixed in the great stone with lead. Doubtless it was intended by the architect that, on lowering this stone, the dowels should drop out of their collars into the sockets below; but, whether through accident or fraud, they appear to have remained in the collars instead of descending into the holes to which they had been fitted.

This may be seen on examining the ends of these dowels, which are united all around the edge to the collars by a strong patina ...

It is to be observed that these slabs [i.e. those under the plug-block] were the only marbles belonging to the edifice which were found in posi-

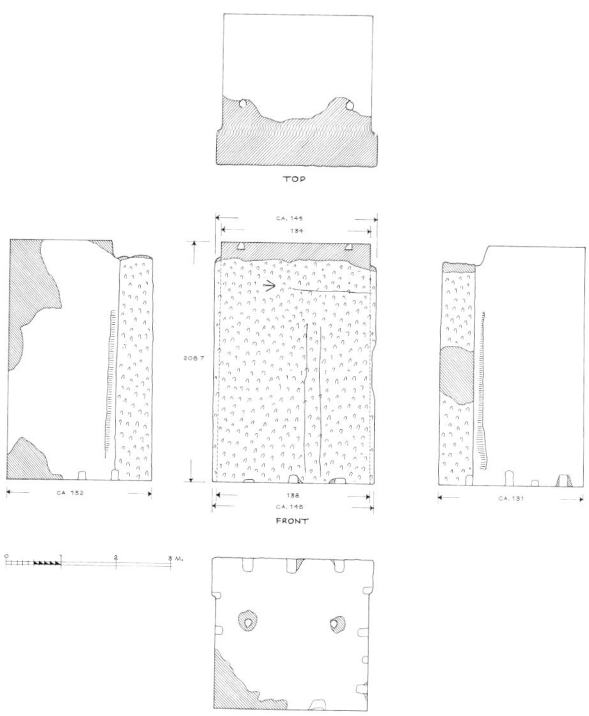

Fig. 10.1. Plug-block of greenish tufa (Jeppesen (1976) 48, Abb.1).

Fig. 10.2. Plug-block, bottom.

Fig. 10.3. Plug-block, right side, bottom on the left.

Fig. 10.4. Plug-block, front. Note the part cut away from its top reaching as far as the dowels.

Fig. 10.5-6. Photos from the British excavations showing the plug-block in the position in which it was found, on fig. 10.5 seen from the inside, looking NW, on fig. 10.6 seen from the outside, looking SE. Note five courses of foundation slabs on the S side of the plug-block, the top of the uppermost course being flush with the platform of bedrock on which the officer stands (fig. 10.6), and part of the marble pavement projecting under the plug-block (fig. 10.5) at the feet of his bearded companion. By courtesy of the Trustees of the British Museum.

Fig. 10.6.

tion; and it is to be presumed that they would not have escaped the spoilers of the Mausoleum, had it not been for the difficulty of displacing the immense stone placed upon them, – a difficulty which we only overcame by the application of two screw-jacks."

Newton does not seem to have observed that originally similar bronze sockets had been let into the top of the plug-block. Evidently these had been removed by grave-robbers in an attempt to establish the depth of the plug-block and to make it possible to remove it, and are now lost.

While the breaks seen on the rear part of the left side and on the back of the block were in all probability due to damage done to the stone during the demolition of the monument by the Hospitallers (they are clearly visible on Newton's photos, figs. 10.5-6), other traces of damage must have resulted from attempts of robbers to force their way into the tomb chamber.

On the front of the block, 1.5-2.5 cm deep lines have been incised with the chisel, one horizontal and two vertical ones, by means of which the robbers may have hoped to trace veins in the structure of the stone that would permit them to cleave it (fig. 10.4). They also probed with long chisels along its sides behind the projecting front edge. Rows of chisel marks testify to these activities, which must have taken place before the foundations were dismantled by the Hospitallers; whether still in Antiquity or later cannot be made out (fig. 10.3).

On the uppermost part of the front is a small flattened area, on which is incised a mark consisting of three strokes fanning out from the same point (fig. 10.4). The mark must have been carved before the western stairwell was filled with earth, or at a time when grave-robbers had left the block partly accessible, or alternatively after the Maussolleion foundations had been completely uncovered by the Knights. It cannot be distinguished on Newton's photo fig. 10.6 where the front of the block is shaded. The mark will be discussed in connection with similar marks found on other stones excavated on the site of the Maussolleion in a forthcoming volume.

The sockets and dowels extracted by Newton from the bottom of the block, and the corresponding sockets that were let into the two slabs of marble pavement referred to by Newton are now in the British Museum, the latter still incorporated in two corner-pieces sawn off from the slabs. The following description of these items will supplement the details recorded by Newton.

11. Collars and dowels from the bottom of the plug-block in the British Museum

Reg.no. 1857.18-20.354 (fig. 11.1 b).

Collar in the form of a c. 9 mm thick cylindrical tube (interior diameter c. 36 mm, length 95 mm) inside which is a dowel of circular section as long as the collar and c. 34 mm in diameter. On the outside, the collar has three longitudinal ribs of square section, probably for the purpose of securing a better hold of the molten lead in which it was fastened.

Reg.no. 1857.18-20.355 (fig. 11.1 a).

Collar and dowel similar to no. 354, but not necessarily cast from the same moulds. Part of the lead with which the collar was fixed to the stone still adheres. On the outside of the collar is engraved the letter P (rho), and possibly additional letters are hidden underneath the surviving remains of lead.

The report of a technical examination of these pieces undertaken by the Research Laboratory in the British Museum (March 1986) provides the following information:

"Qualitative X-ray fluorescence analysis showed that they are both of leaded tin bronze, which is quite usual for Hellenistic [sic] castings.

"The outer cylinder of the plugs is one casting with the ribs. The turning marks on the outer face of the cylinder were almost certainly turned on the original wax model before the ribs were added to complete the wax pattern. The many casting holes in the metal would have engaged the chisel leaving distinctive marks if turning of the metal had been attempted after casting. One of the inner cylinders (reg.no. 355) has fresh lathe pip marks at either end and this may have been cleaned up on the lathe after casting."

That the collars reg.nos. 354-55 were in fact removed from the bottom of the plug-block (those let into the top of the block must have been removed by the robbers chiselling away its anterior edge) is in keeping with the depths of the holes in the plug-block, which amount to 95 and 100 mm, respectively.

Fig. 11.1. Two collars for cylindrical dowels extracted from the bottom of the plug-block by Newton, BM reg.nos. 1857.18-20.354-355.

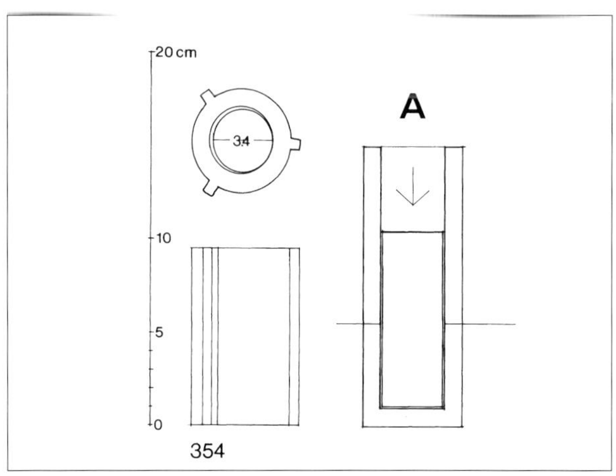

Fig. 11.2. On the left, collar no. 354 and the cylindrical dowel found to have stuck in it; on the right, drawing illustrating the system that permitted a dowel provisionally contained in a collar in the bottom of the plug-block to descend into a similar collar in the pavement underneath (cf. chapters 11-12).

12. Two sawn-off corners of pavement slabs with collars still in position

(BM cat.nos. 990-991, Mausoleum Room Guide A 29-30)

Fig. 12.1. Two sawn-off corners of pavement slabs of white marble with collars still in position, BM cat.nos. 990 and 991.

Cat.no. 991, red number 121 (figs. 12.1-3).

The slab is 17 cm high and measures c. 23 and 28 cm, respectively, along the preserved lateral joints which are carefully flattened with anathyrosis. The underside is roughly dressed, partly with the toothed chisel. On the smooth top surface, the centre of the collar is indicated by two incised lines a and c crossing each other at right-angles parallel to the joints, at a distance of 90-93 and 175 mm, respectively, from the edge.

Parallel to, and at a distance of 18 mm from the latter line, is incised a third line b whose purpose is not apparent (cf. no. 990). The collar has an interior diameter of 35 mm and resembles closely the collars from the bottom of the plug-block (figs. 11.1-2), except that, in distinction to these, it is closed at the bottom end, its interior depth being 45 mm.

Its complete length cannot be measured, but is probably about 55 mm, which accords with the depth of the collar holes preserved on top of the plug-block (55 and 60 mm, respectively): with an interior depth of 45 mm, each lower collar was dimensioned to hold about half of the 95 mm long dowel planned to descend into it from the corresponding upper collar which retained the upper half of the dowel (cf. fig. 11.2 A).

Cat.no. 990, red number 116 (figs. 12.1-3).

This piece shares several characteristics with no. 991. The height of the slab and the dimensions of the collar and of the dowel are the same; and once again, a third line b is incised parallel to and at a distance of 18 mm from the one marking the centre of the dowel, a. Obviously the two pieces must derive from a common context, but exactly how they were placed in relation to each other and to the plug-block can be concluded only from a study of the composition of the pavement from which they came (see below).

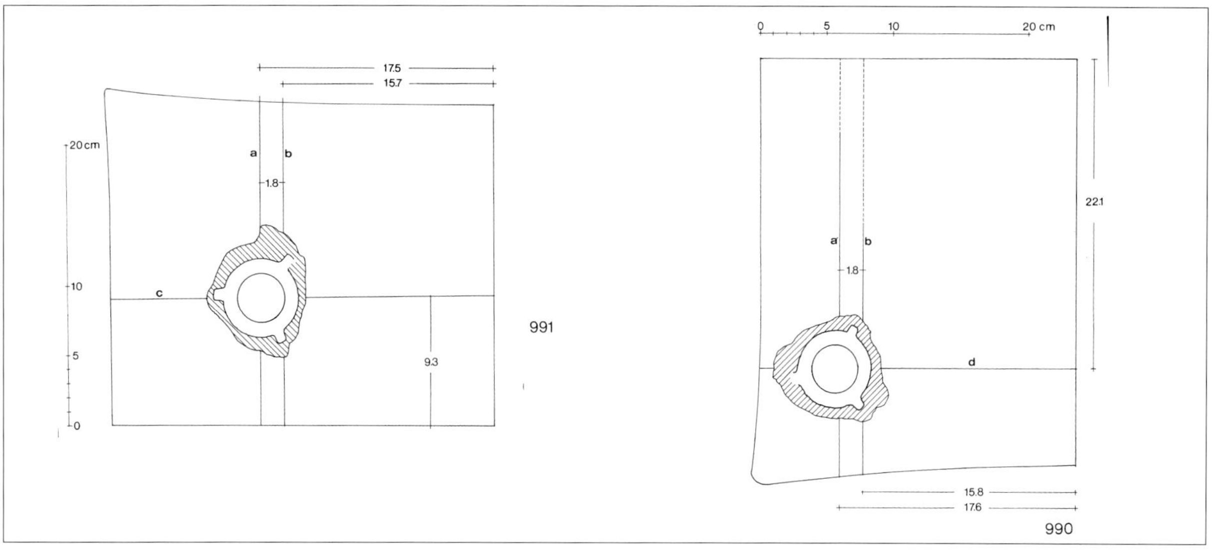

Fig. 12.2. Collars let into and construction lines incised on top of the pavement sections BM cat.nos. 990 and 991.

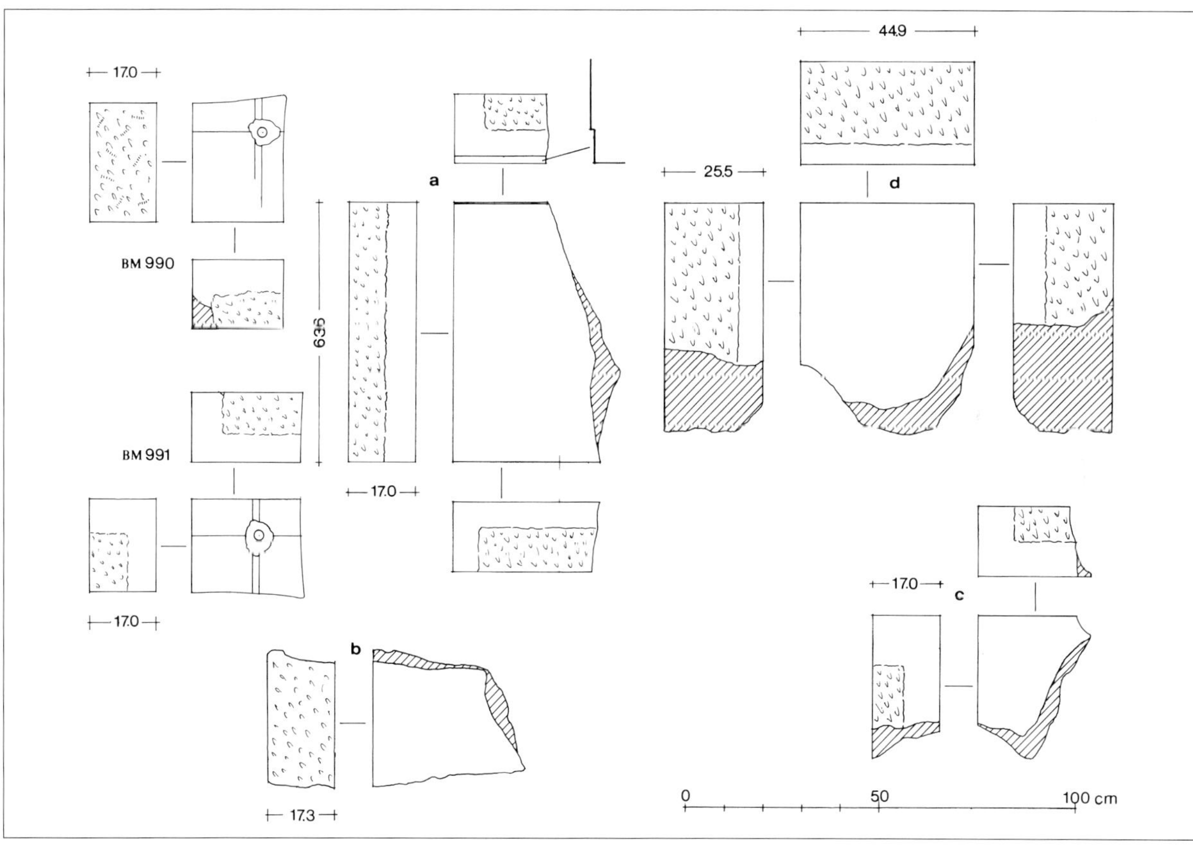

Fig. 12.3. Fragments of pavement slabs of white marble, a-c from the corridor, d presumably from the anteroom. On the left, side views of the sawn-off corners fig. 12.2.

Fig. 11.2 A illustrates how the ingenious dowel-and-collar system was devised to function:

On top of the plug-block and in the marble pavement on which this was to rest were inserted collars of the shorter type, and in the bottom of the plug-block and of the lintel above it collars of the longer type, in which the dowels were contained before falling into their sockets.

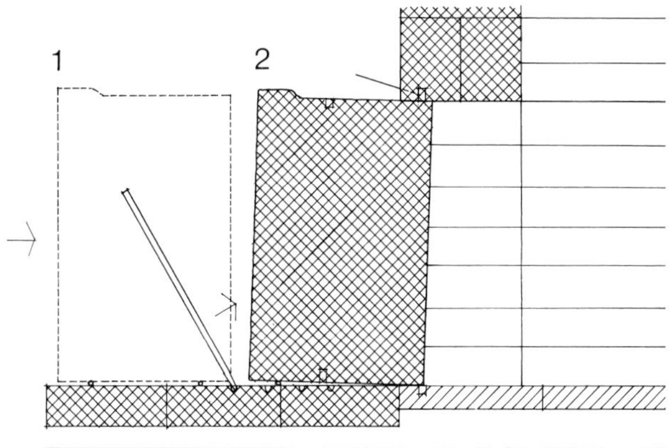

Fig. 12.4. Diagram illustrating procedure likely to have been followed while shifting the plug-block into position (cf. main text for explanation).

If the device was to work properly, the four dowels must fall simultaneously, two above and two below, but considering the primitive technical equipment available, it is hard to imagine how this could have been successfully achieved.

As a matter of fact, the lower dowels were found to have stuck in their upper collars, while it is no longer possible to conclude whether or not the upper dowels worked as planned.

It must have been the purpose of the bevels cut along the lower edge on all sides of the plug-block except the back (where they would have disfigured the inside of the corridor, cf. Newton's photo fig. 10.5 and figs. 10.1-4) to secure the hold of a system of ropes with which the block could be lowered into its initial position on the pavement in front of the tomb chamber (cf. fig. 17.2). This conclusion is confirmed by the absence of a lewis-hole on top of the block.

The two series each of four pry-cuttings on the pavement already mentioned (above, chapter 8) demonstrate that the plug-block was shifted into its final position by means of crowbars, but the distance between the first pair of pry-cuttings and the entrance to the tomb implies that the block must have projected about 20 cm into the door opening before the crowbars were used (fig. 12.4):

The block having been moved as close to the opening as possible by means of a couple of iron rollers, it must be assumed, the foremost roller was removed, thus permitting the lower edge of the block to rest on the pavement while being pushed further ahead, and the upper edge to pass immediately underneath the bottom of the lintel. When the remaining roller had been removed, and the block was resting entirely on the pavement, it could be shifted into its final position by means of the pry-cuttings.

During this procedure precautions would have had to be taken to prevent the dowels from falling out of their collars until they had been placed exactly above their sockets. As the lower pair of dowels were 95 mm long (cf. fig. 11.2), they would have remained safely in their collars while the stone was being shifted, provided that the diameter of the rollers was small enough (say some 30 mm at the most) to prevent them from falling out.

The upper pair of dowels would have had to be kept suspended by means of a special device, perhaps in the form of a metal rod inserted in a hole in the lintel, which, when extracted, would permit the dowel to descend into its socket.

13. The foundations around and above the plug-block

As already observed (above, p. 52), the foundations along the platform in front of the entrance to the tomb chamber seem to have been reduced to form a c. 20 cm deep recess. Of this part of the facade there survived in Newton's day on the right side of the plug-block (as seen on his photos, figs. 10.5-6) five courses measuring altogether c. 1.47 m in height, the topmost of which was flush with the surface of the bedrock at level L678/679, cf. figs. 1.3, 26, 27, pls. E4, 6, 12.

Of these courses, the bottom two were found still in position at the recent excavations. The lower one is 28.2-30.5 cm, the upper one 27.0-28.3 cm high. The sides facing the landing of the staircase are tooled with the pointed chisel, but have bevelled edges dressed with the toothed chisel emphasizing the horizontal joints. The opposite sides, on which the south wall of the corridor abutted, are dressed with anathyrosis.

The masonry above the plug-block must have been supported by a lintel of extraordinary capacity which is likely to have equalled a number of foundation courses in height (two at the least).

14. The corridor

As the two surviving courses of masonry framing the plug-block on its south side already referred to were fastened with clamps to the ashlars of the wall facing the rock-cut south side of the corridor, this was evidently built of courses of the same thickness and of the same material, the greenish tufa.

The masonry north of the plug-block must have been constructed in the same way, which supposition is supported by a shallow rebate in the rock-cut north face of the corridor (pl. E5). This indicates that the lowest visible course (i.e. the one immediately above the marble pavement of the corridor) was c. 30 cm high.

The rock-cut bottom of the corridor is covered by two longitudinal rows of c. 32 cm high foundation slabs of tufa, between which runs the drain. This space is confined by two additional rows of slabs laid at a higher level – the bottom courses of the side-walls – and forming, as it were, a 1.82-1.84 m wide, 2.74 m long, and 17 cm deep depression, inside which was laid a marble floor of the same thickness.

The slabs of the surviving bottom courses of the side-walls are between 83 and 92 cm long, and pry-cuttings and dowel holes testify that the upper courses were composed of slabs of much the same dimensions staggered half a slab-length and laid in an approximately isodomic arrangement.

The marble pavement consisted of three longitudinal rows of slabs, the middle one covering the drain (fig. 14.1 a-b). This division is indicated by six pry-cuttings related to the longitudinal joints, while two can be referred to a transverse joint approximately in the middle of the corridor. A more precise specification of the dimensions in length and width can be given for the slabs on which the plug-block rested, fragments of which survive. One fragment is preserved in situ under the projecting piece of wall adjoining the south side of the plug-block, while a corner fragment (a) belonging to the same slab was found somewhat displaced, but very near its original position. This piece seems to have been placed on a line with another corner fragment (c) still in situ at the north side of the corridor.

If the fragments a and c are combined with the two sawn-off corner fragments in the British Museum already described (chapter 12), the collars in them will be placed exactly where they should to fit the dowels in the bottom of the plug-block, when this was in position. In this arrangement, the double incised line would have been used to specify the position of the dowel in the direction in which the plug-block was to be shifted. Some uncertainty or inaccuracy in measuring out the relevant distance may have induced the mason to abandon the line he had first incised, in favour of one 18 mm farther towards the east.

It remains to account for Newton's statement that the plug-block "rested on two slabs of white marble" (HD 96, see Appendix 2). As already demonstrated, there must originally have been an intermediate slab between the two carrying sockets for the dowels; and as a matter of fact this is clearly visible on one of Newton's photos taken before the plug-block was removed (fig. 10.5 = HD pl. viii,1). Judging from this evidence, the piece now missing was placed on the axis of the drain and measured about 53 cm in width.

The corridor must have been at least as high as the plug-block, i.e. c. 208 cm, and as will be shown below, the double-door of marble which closed the entrance to the anteroom may well have had precisely or approximately the same height.

Like the anteroom, the corridor was probably roofed with a corbelled vault constructed of foundation slabs projecting from the longer sides and meeting one another along the longitudinal axis (fig. 17.3 b).

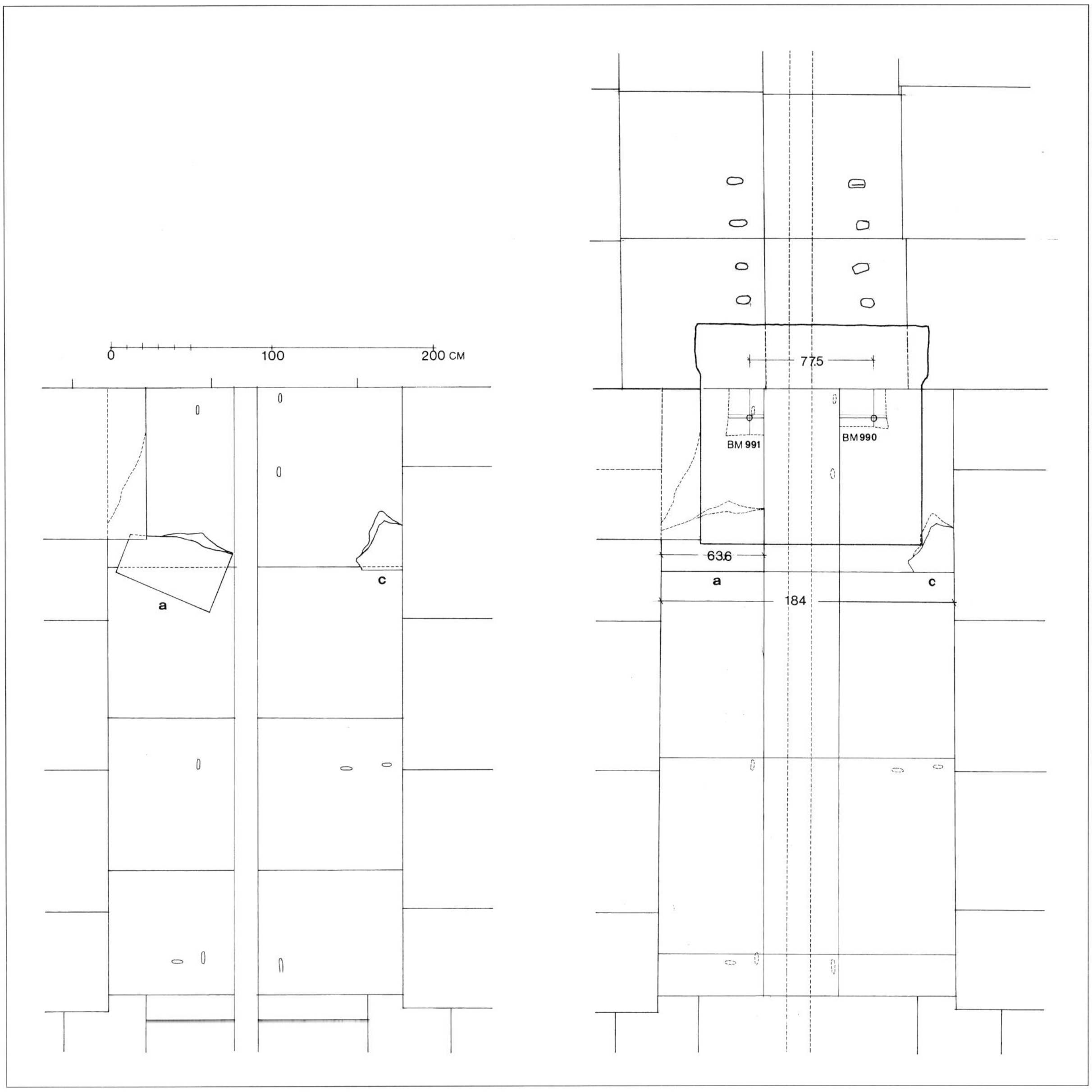

Fig. 14.1.

a Plan of the course of foundation slabs in the corridor with pry-cuttings indicated, and fragments of the pavement found in situ.

b Plan of the pavement in the corridor reconstructed in relation to the position of the collars underneath the plug-block, cf. Newton's photo fig. 10.5.

15. The double-door of white marble, summary of the evidence for its reconstruction

At the entrance to the anteroom, the marble pavement of the corridor was delimited by two c. 54 cm wide blocks of greenish tufa projecting c. 23 cm from each of the side walls (fig. 17.1). It can hardly be doubted that they must be interpreted as foundations for projecting wall sections, between which was inserted a 138 cm long threshold of white marble supporting a doorway of the same material.

Several fragments have been found on the Maussolleion site, both by Newton and by the Danish excavators, which can be attributed to a double-door of white marble fitting the dimensions of the passage just described.

Its reconstruction rests primarily on the evidence of four fragments in the British Museum (catalogued below A-D), while ten more (E-N) were recovered during the recent excavations.

Of the latter, four (E, G, J, L) were found in square 7/9 which comprises the anteroom and the adjoining part of the tomb chamber (fig. 1.57), and one (F) in square 9/9 in the rear part of the tomb chamber, while H, I, K, M, and N have been identified through re-examination of the many thousands of battered pieces which were provisionally set aside during the excavations for later identification and registration.

The fragments in the British Museum were not given individual registration numbers until 1972. They are not mentioned in any of Newton's reports, and their find spots are therefore unknown. The red numbers of the cases in which they were packed: 128, 129, 136, 138,[48] do not give any direct indication of their provenance, except that possibly the two pieces in cases 128 and 129 (A and D) were packed at the same time and had been found not far from each other.

In the Mausoleum Room Guide (p. 71, A.28) fragments B and C are correctly identified in the following terms:

"Two fragments of marble door with hinge; the pivot of the hinge has fitted into a bronze socket; the point of the pivot is cup-shaped, and must have worked on a ball within the socket."

Geoffrey Waywell's suggestion, that they were somehow connected with the chariot on top of the monument, must be rejected,[49] cf. the descriptions given in the catalogue, chapter 16.

Stable isotopic ratio analyses of fragments A, B, C, D, E, F, G and I undertaken by the Technical Laboratory in the British Museum (BMTL)[50] and by Professor Norman Herz (NH) at the Department of Geology at the University of Georgia to whom I am much obliged, have provided the following plots:

	delta^{13} C	delta^{18} O
A (NH)	4.88	-2.64
B (BMTL)	4.65	-2.37
C (NH)	4.83	-2.49
D (NH)	4.87	-2.59
E (NH)	4.612	-2.887
F (NH)	4.746	-2.533
G (NH)	4.649	-2.471
I (NH)	4.737	-2.674

After these samples had been analysed, fragments E and I were discovered to fit each other (cf. the catalogue). Their figures demonstrate, therefore, that within one and the same piece of marble, delta C and delta O plots may vary between 4.612 and 4.737 (0.125) and between -2.674 and -2.887 (-0.213), respectively.

This conclusion is confirmed by the plots for fragments D and F which vary between 4.746 and 4.870 (0.124) and between -2.533

and -2.590 (0.057), respectively, for points of similarity in their shape indicate that these fragments must come from one and the same door-leaf (cf. catalogue).

Judging from the range of the delta C plots, all the samples may have come from one and the same door-leaf, and although the range of the delta O plots, -O.517, is considerably wider, both sets of plots lie within the limit defining Ephesian marble[51] and do not necessarily suggest that the two door-leaves were made of different types of marble, or that the surviving fragments came from both door-leaves, although the statistical probability is that they did.

A stable isotopic ratio analysis can provide a technically reliable definition of a given sample, but will not account for all variations in the geological composition that may occur in the marble piece from which the sample is taken. If the plots of a number of samples from different fragments vary to a striking extent, these are not likely to come from one and the same piece of marble, but even if the plots are exactly the same, they do not automatically indicate a common provenance.

On examining the fragments in Bodrum and comparing them with one another, I came to the conclusion that the marble they are made of does not differ much in appearance and may be described in general terms as being composed of densely deposited whitish, about half a mm thin layers alternating with 2-3 mm thick, slightly darker layers of a greyish-yellowish tinge.

A reconstruction of the double-door in the Maussolleion must, however, be based primarily on the conclusions that can be drawn from a study of details of form and workmanship of the individual fragments (cf. figs. 15.1-3):

Where the two door-leaves met in the middle of the doorway and overlapped each other, they were differently shaped, and obviously the fragments deriving from this part of the doorway, D and F, belonged to one and the same door-leaf.

Parts of the rounded side of the door-leaf, semicircular in section, which abutted on the rebate behind the door-jamb, are represented on fragments A and E/I.

The maximum thickness of the door-leaves, where they met, is 110-111 mm (fragments D and F), inclusive of the recessed panels on both sides.

The panel on the front side, which is also represented on fragments A, G, and E/I, measures between 12 and 14 mm in depth, while the shallower panel on the back, which is also to be seen on fragments B, D, F, G and E/I, is only 8-8.5 mm deep.

The thickness that can be measured between the panels varies between 87 and 90.5 mm (fragments D, F, G, and N).

On the front side, the panels were delimited by vertical fillets which were 34 mm wide along the door posts (fragments A and E/I), and 47 mm wide in the middle, probably on both sides of the line along which the door-leaves met (fragments D and F).

The fillets were decorated with separately turned knobs of marble in imitation of nail-heads of metal, which were fastened in circular holes (preserved on fragments A, D, and F), and similar knobs were used to embellish horizontal cross-ties connecting the vertical fillets (fragments G and E/I).

The diameter of the holes for the knobs on the central fillets and on the cross-ties is around 16 mm, their depth 13-15 mm (fragments D, F, G, and E/I), and around the hole on fragment G is a concentric corrosion line indicating the outer diameter of the knob itself, which was c. 33 mm.

These measurements agree perfectly with the dimensions of three separately turned knobs that have been found during the recent excavations (fragments O-Q). A fourth piece of precisely the same form, R, is considerably smaller, 20 mm in maximum diameter, and can be ascribed to a lateral fillet, cf. the dimensions of the hole and the concentric trace indicating the outline of the knob on fragment A.

All the knobs were made of a white, very fine-grained and homogeneous type of marble, which differs strikingly from the marble of which the door-leaves were made.

On fragment F are traces of a circular piece of metal c. 100 mm in diameter, which probably served as handle and may have been modelled in the form of a lion's head.[52] This was anchored in a hole cut through the stone by means of a long iron spike which, as indicated by traces of rust, was bent at right-angles on the back of the door-leaf.

Since the particulars of the surviving fragments bear a strong resemblance to the details of a double door of marble found in a tomb excavated in 1976 in the neighbourhood of Bodrum (Yokusbasi) and reconstructed in the Bodrum Museum of Underwater Archaeology, and to similar double-doors from tomb chambers at Milas (see below, Appendix 4), it may be plausibly assumed that the door-leaves in Maussollos' tomb had cross-ties both at the top, in the middle, and at the bottom, and that each of these were decorated with three rows of knobs.

This would imply that each door-leaf was subdivided into two panels, probably both on the front and on the back, i.e. that there were altogether eight individual panels and just as many individual approximations to accuracy in measuring out the appropriate thickness between front and back panels. It is not surprising, therefore, that variations amount to as much as four millimetres.

As far as the evidence goes, it is perfectly compatible with the supposition that the pattern according to which the knobs on the door-leaves from the Maussolleion were arranged was in principle exactly the same as on the door-slabs found elsewhere at Bodrum and at Milas:

(1) Each cross-tie was decorated with two rows of three knobs, between which was a third row of four knobs.

(2) The vertical distance between any two of the rows with four knobs was subdivided by knobs placed on the vertical fillets on both sides of the panels, into equal spacings.

(3) The spacings opposite the lower panels might be considerably larger than those opposite the upper panels, the lower panels being usually higher than the upper ones.

On the above-mentioned doors, (cf appendix 4) the knobs are cut in the surface of the door-leaf, and on one and the same door they are uniform in size and shape (semispherical or ellipsoid in section).

What makes the doorway from Maussollos' tomb appear outstanding in craftmanship on the background of the comparative evidence so far available is the care that was taken to ensure perfect homogeneity of the knobs by having all of them turned on a lathe and by using marble of exquisite quality for this particular purpose. Unparalleled, to my knowledge, is also the use of knobs of smaller size on the vertical fillets along the door-posts in distinction to the larger ones on other parts of the door-leaf.

According to the reconstruction proposed in figs. 15.1-3, there must have been 18 knobs of the smaller and 66 of the larger size, in the proportion 3:11. This figure comes close to the ratio 1:3 based on the surviving number of knobs, one of the smaller, and three of the larger size.

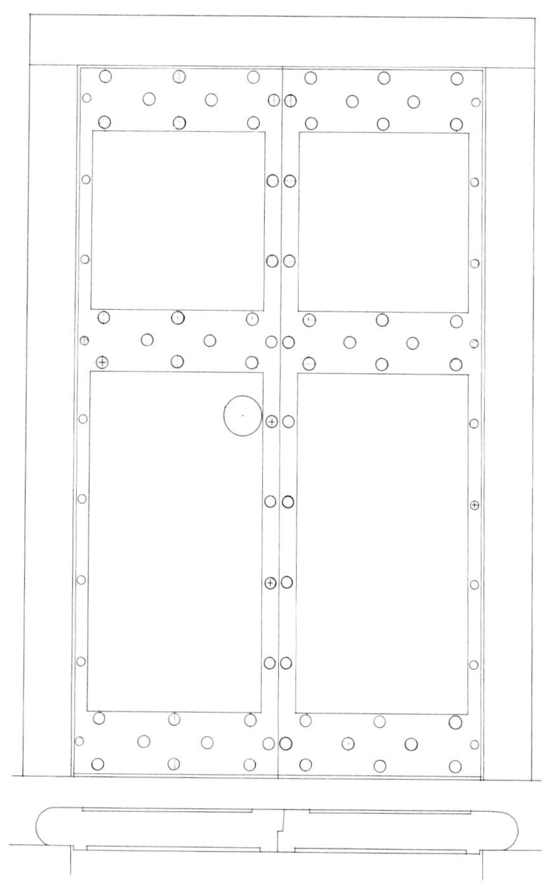

Fig. 15.1. Front elevation of double-door of white marble reconstructed on the basis of the fragments positioned in figs. 15.2-3.

The reconstruction includes the following hypothetical features for which there is no evidence:

(1) The pressure of the masonry above the doorway was probably relieved by means of a beam of tufa level with the beam above the plug-block and corresponding to courses C8-9.

(2) The door posts are supposed to have been 13 cm wide, and the lintel 22 cm high, inclusive of a c. 9 cm high cornice.

(3) The threshold may have risen to a level of c. 3 cm above the pavement of the corridor, and the door opening is estimated to have been c. 184 cm high and 112 cm wide.

(4) Due to their thickness, the door-leaves were probably so heavy that they had to be supported by wheels running in rails let into the pavement of the anteroom.

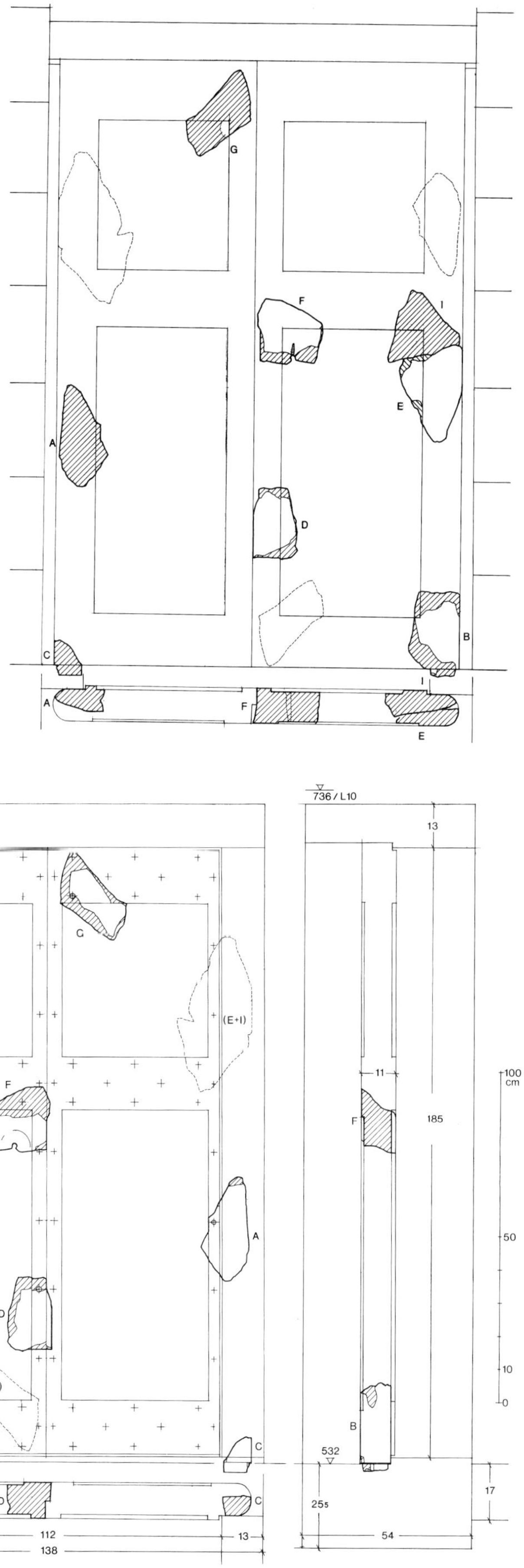

Fig. 15.2-3. Double-door of white marble reconstructed on the basis of the fragments A-G and I (cf. chapters 15-16), front and back elevations, and sections.

16. Catalogue of door fragments A-R

All fragments are made of white marble of the composition described above in general terms. The veins run parallel, or approximately parallel, to the tooled surfaces.

A. *BM 1972.5-22.19, red number 129*

Find-spot not recorded. Anterior part of the rounded side of a door-leaf including part of a recessed panel, 12.5 mm in depth, which is bordered by a plain fillet, 34 mm in width. In the middle of this a hole 13.5 mm in diameter and 17 mm deep has been drilled. Around the hole is a fine concentric line 22 mm in diameter which indicates the outline of a turned knob that was fixed in the hole (cf. fragment G). While the plane surface is finely smoothed, the rounded surface has been tooled with the claw chisel. Less than a quarter of the semicircle survives, but at a cautious estimate its full diameter was about 10 cm.

The back has been broken. Thickness as preserved (not including the fillet) c. 7 cm, length c. 32 cm.

B. *BM 1972.4-17.7, red number 136*

Mausoleum Room Guide 71, A 28; Waywell (1978) cat.no. 655; Walker/Matthews (1997) 52, Table 1 no. 22. Find-spot not recorded. Fragment of a door-leaf including the semicircular side that abutted on the door-post, and having at the end a round projection, c. 82 mm in diameter, to which was fastened a cylindrical or semi-spherical covering of bronze fixed with molten lead, in all probability one of the pivots on which the door-leaf turned. Traces of lead and green bronze patina remain around the base of the projection, and on one side is a small cutting which presumably held a rib cast with the bronze covering and preventing this from rotating independently of the door-leaf.[53]

A

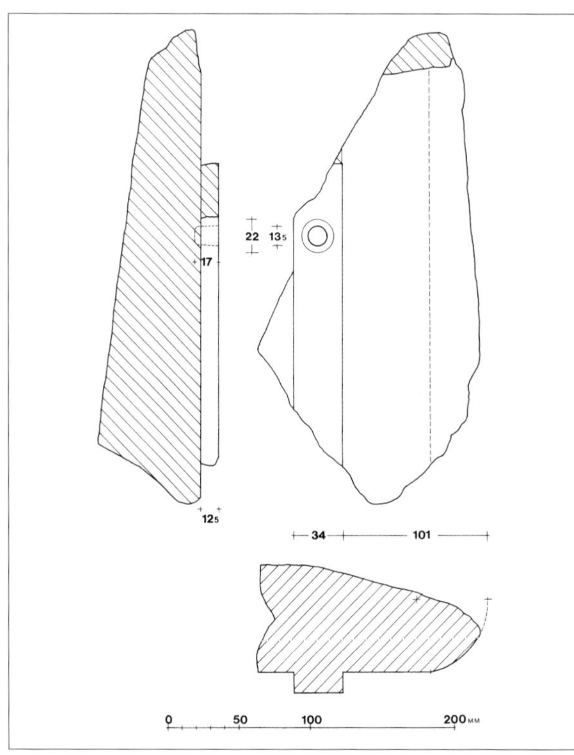

A

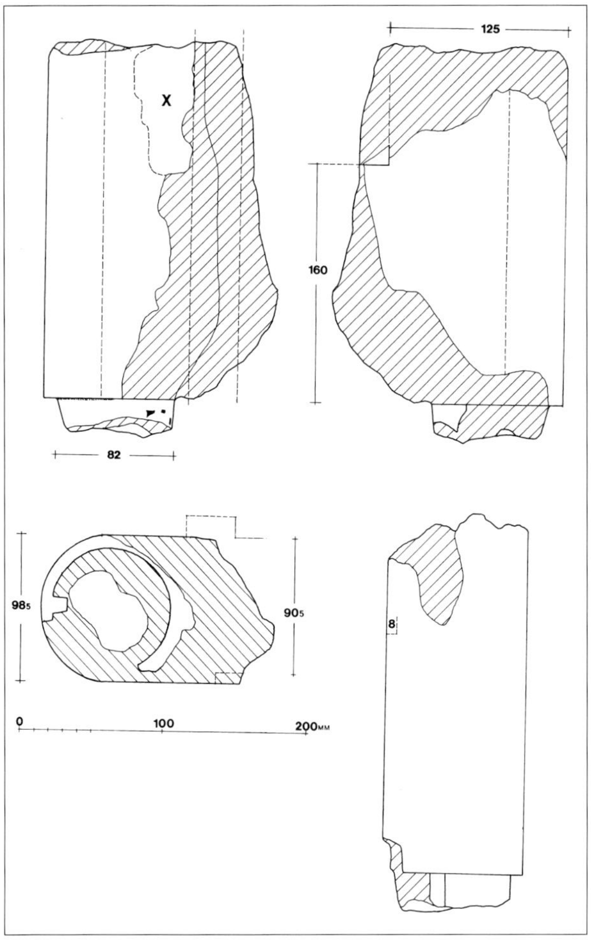

B

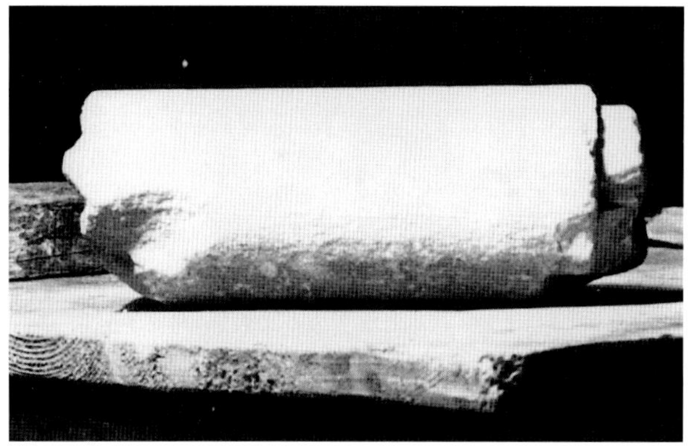

B

B

The top of the projection is broken along the edge, but preserved in the middle, where it has the form of a roughly chiselled hollow, there being nowhere the slightest trace of wear due to rotation. The original height of the projection may well have equalled that preserved on fragment C, 32 mm. Both sides as well as the semicircular part between them have been dressed with the claw chisel.

The piece measures 98.5 mm in thickness, and on one side of it is preserved the corner of an 8 mm deep panel, both features confirming its attribution to the double-door of Maussollos' tomb: the panel must be the shallow one on the back of the door-leaf (cf. fragments D and E/I), while the other side is so battered that the cross-tie and the vertical fillet originally bordering the panel have disappeared entirely. A claw-chiselled area at × must have reached approximately as far as the vertical edge of the fillet.

As for the pivotal function of the piece and the question whether it came from the lower or the upper end of a door-leaf, cf. below in connection with the description of fragment C.

C. *BM 1972.4-17.8, red number 138*

Waywell (1978) cat.no. 656. Find-spot not recorded. Fragment of a door-leaf including half of the semicircular side that abutted on the door-post, and half of a round projection, 82 mm in diameter and 32 mm in height, to which was fastened a cylindrical covering of bronze fixed with molten lead. Traces of brownish and greenish patina remain around the base of the projection.

As on fragment B, there is a small cutting on the side of the projection. However, the projection is not rounded along the edge, but truncated at right-angles with the claw chisel. There

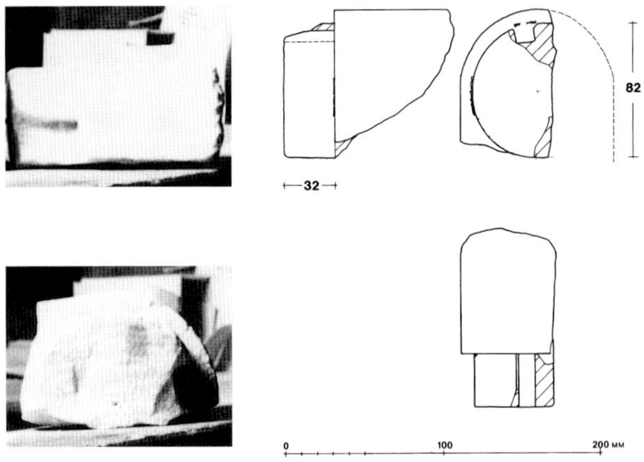

C

is no trace of wear due to rotation. The semicircular surface has been tooled with the claw chisel (interstitial distance c. 2.5 mm). The original thickness of the door-leaf must have been around 10 cm, and it can hardly be doubted that it came from the same doorway as fragment B, though not necessarily from the same door-leaf.

Low cylindrical projections like the those on fragments B and C are preserved at both ends of the well-preserved door-leaves from the "School Yard Tomb" at Milas (Appendix 4, fig. 28.9). Judging from comparative evidence, therefore, our fragments may have come from either end of the door-leaves to which they belonged. Since the bronze covering is missing on both fragments, the problem cannot be settled definitely, but it may be argued that the truncated projection on fragment C seems better suited to fit a position at the top than at the bottom of a door-leaf.

D. *BM 1972.5-22.1, red number 128*

Find-spot not recorded. Comprising part of the innermost vertical edge of a door-leaf, this fragment has a rebate, angular in section (also seen on fragment F), into which must have fitted a corresponding profile cut along the edge of the adjoining door-leaf. On the front side is a 47 mm wide fillet bordering on a 12 mm deep recessed panel. In the middle of the fillet is a 14 mm deep circular hole, 16 mm in diameter, in which was fastened a turned knob, cf. fragments A, F, G, and E/I. On the opposite side is an 8 mm deep recessed panel. The thickness of the door-leaf between the panels is 90 mm, cf. fragments B, F, G, and E/I (thicknesses between 87 and 90.5 mm).

Overall width and length c. 23 × 14 cm.

D

D

D

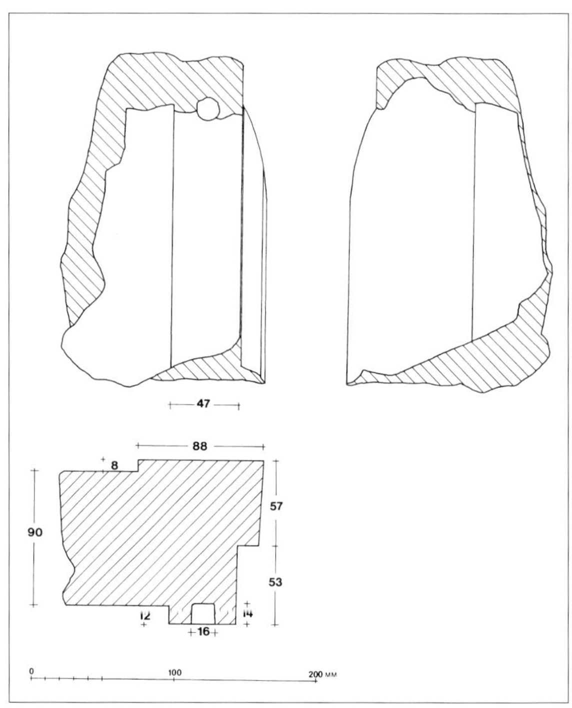

D

E/I. *Bodrum, Quadrangle*

The piece is composed of two fragments:
E: XO 13, found in square 7/9 comprising the anteroom and the adjoining part of the tomb chamber.

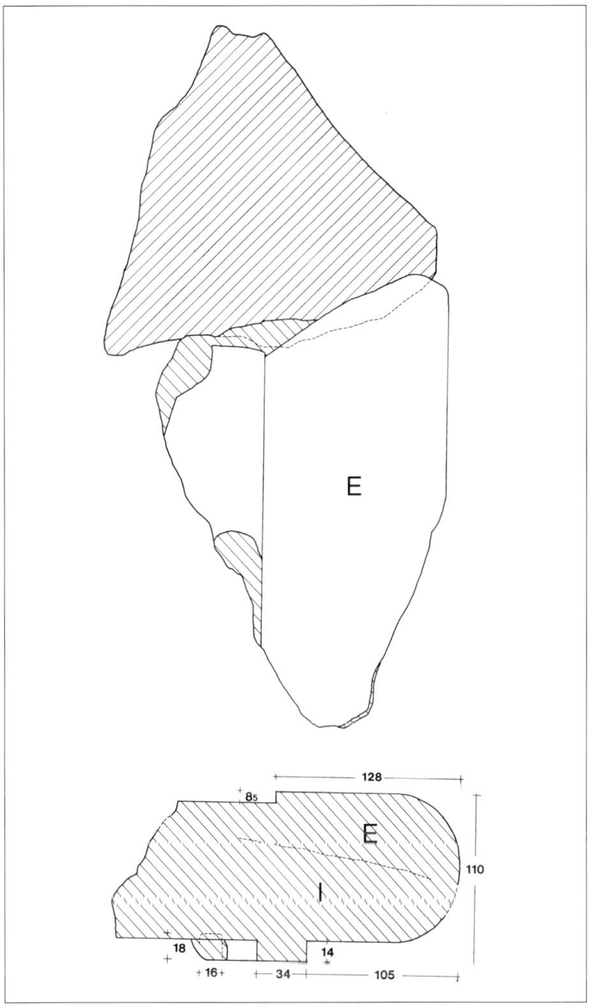

E

I: XO 17, find-spot not recorded, identified by scrutiny of nondescript fragments.

Part of door-leaf including the semicircular side that abutted on the door-post. On the front is a 34 mm wide fillet which joins a cross-tie at the same level, thus defining the corner of a 14 mm deep recessed panel. Near the edge of the cross-tie is a circular hole, 18 mm deep and 16 mm in diameter for the insertion of a turned knob, cf. fragments A, D, F, and G.

On the back is an 8.5 mm deep recessed panel. While the panels are perfectly smoothed, the rounded surface is tooled with the claw chisel. It measures in diameter c. 96 mm.

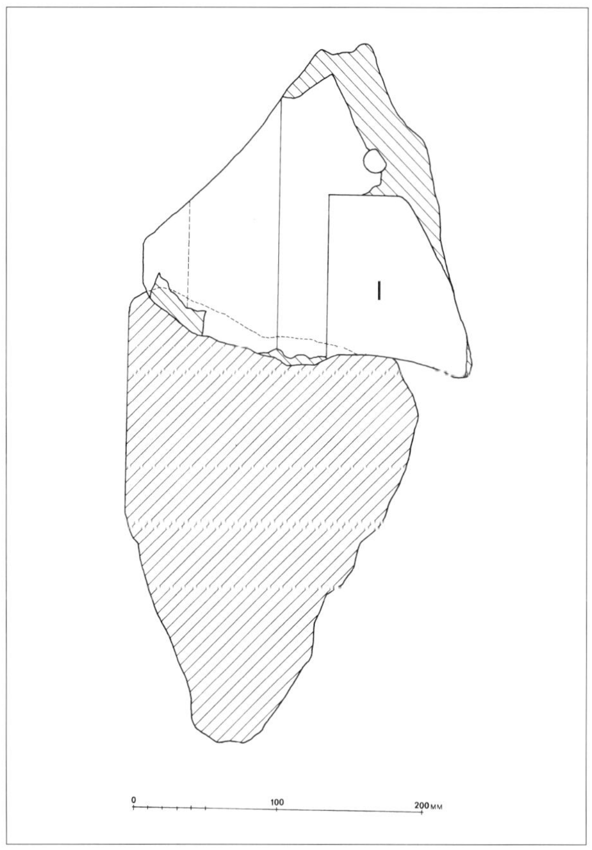

E/I

E/I

I

I

I

I

I

Overall dimensions:
E: c. 30 × 20 cm
I: c. 23 × 22 cm
E+I: c. 46 × 23 cm
E+I: reconstructed thickness incl. of the panels 110 mm (cf. fragment F)

F. *Bodrum, Quadrangle*

XO 10. Found in square 9/9 comprising the easternmost part of the tomb chamber.

In section, this fragment is strikingly similar to fragment D and must come from the same door-leaf. On the front side is a 47 mm wide fillet bordering on a 12.5 mm deep recessed panel. Along the fillet runs a rebate angular in section and exactly similar to the one on fragment D, but partly broken. At the lower end of the fillet as preserved survive part of a drilled hole for the insertion of a turned knob like the one on fragment D.

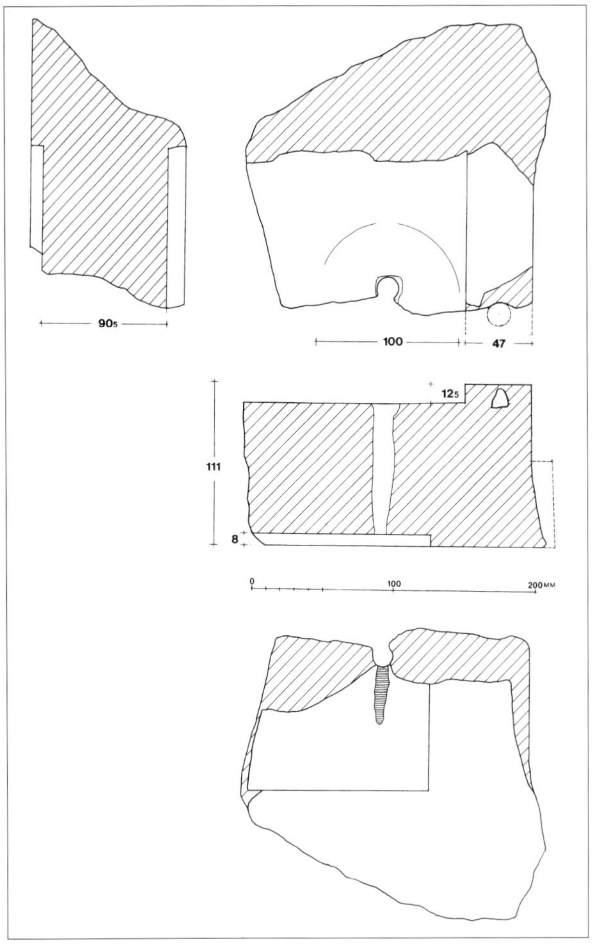

F

F

F

F

F

F

F

The piece is perforated by a roughly cut hole (not drilled). Around this is seen on the front side traces of corrosion indicating a concentric circle c. 100 mm in diameter, while on the back is the rust-stained imprint of an iron nail, presumably one of the bent points of a bifurcated spike by means of which the missing metal object on the front was fastened. This was probably a handle, possibly in the form of a ring suspended in the jaws of a lion's head cast in bronze. On the back is the corner of an 8 mm deep recessed panel dressed with a fine claw chisel, while around it has been used a coarser claw chisel.

Overall dimensions ca. 20 × 22 cm.

G. *Bodrum, Quadrangle*

XO 18. Found in square 7/9 comprising the anteroom and the adjoining part of the tomb chamber.

On the finely smoothed front face bordering a 14 mm deep recessed panel has been drilled a slightly conical hole c. 16 mm in diameter and 15 mm deep. Around this can be distinguished traces of a concentric circle c. 33 mm in diameter which indicate the outline of a turned knob of the larger type that was fixed in the hole, cf. fragments D and F.

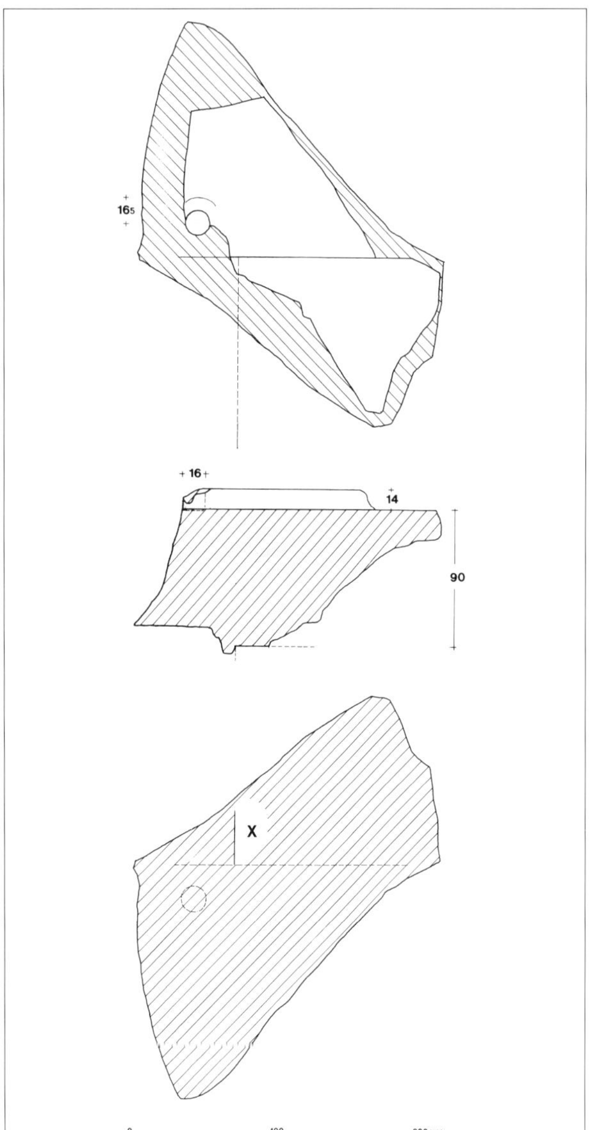

G

G

G

G

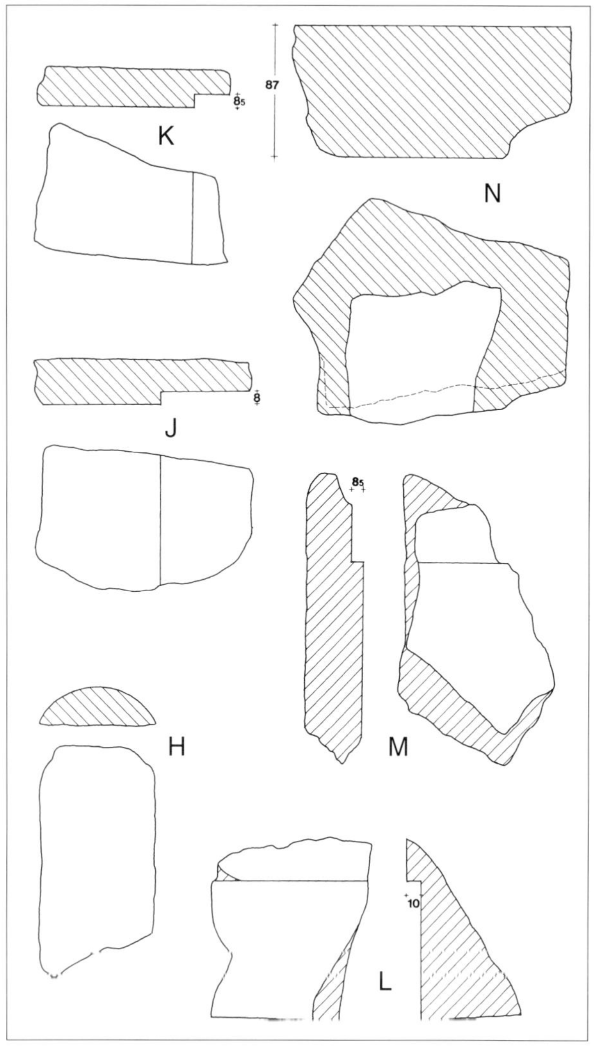

On the badly battered opposite side, the edge of a recessed panel (depth not preserved) which follows a direction at right- angles to that of the panel on the front face is preserved.

The fragment must come from one of the cross-ties.

Overall dimensions c. 21 × 26 cm.

H. *Bodrum, Quadrangle*

Find-spot not recorded, identified by scrutiny of nondescript fragments.

Only what may be part of the rounded side of a door-leaf which is tooled with the claw chisel is preserved. About half the outline of a semicircle survives, and judging from this, the full diameter was approximately 10 cm, cf. fragments B and E/I.

Overall dimensions c. 15 × 8 cm.

I. *see E/I*

J. *Bodrum, Quadrangle*

XO 2. Found in square 7/9 comprising the anteroom and the adjoining part of the tomb chamber.

Part of recessed panel 8 mm in depth, which is smoothly dressed, while the surface around it is claw-chiselled. Broken on all the other sides.

Overall dimensions c. 15 × 9 × 3 cm.

K. *Bodrum, Quadrangle*

Find-spot not recorded, identified by scrutiny of nondescript fragments.

Part of recessed panel 8.5 mm in depth. The adjoining surface has been dressed with a fine claw chisel. Broken on all the other sides.

Overall dimensions c. 13 × 8 × 2.5 cm.

L. *Bodrum, Quadrangle*

XO 12. Found in square 7/9 comprising the anteroom and the adjoining part of the tomb chamber.

Part of recessed panel 10 mm in depth dressed with a fine claw chisel, possibly from the back of a door-leaf. Broken on all the other sides.

Overall dimensions c. 12 × 11 × 8 cm.

M. *Bodrum, Quadrangle*

Find-spot not recorded, identified by scrutiny of nondescript fragments.

Part of recessed panel, 8,5 mm deep, and of adjoining cross-tie dressed with the claw chisel (interstitial distance 1.5-2 mm). Broken on all the other sides.

Overall dimensions c. 19 × 11 × 4 cm.

N. *Bodrum, Quadrangle*

Find-spot not recorded, identified by scrutiny of nondescript fragments.

Part of door-leaf between the bottoms of the panels, thickness 87 mm (cf. the thicknesses measured on fragments B, D, F, G, and E/I: 90-90.5 mm).

One side is perfectly smooth, the other tooled with a fine claw chisel.

Overall dimensions c. 19 × 15 cm.

O. *Bodrum, Quadrangle*

Found in the cavity in the rock-cut bottom of the tomb chamber, cf. chapter 22.

Of white, very finely-grained marble turned on a lathe.

Round knob, ellipsoidal in cross section, 22 mm high and 31 mm in diameter. It was mortised by means of a round, slightly conical tenon, 10.5 mm high and 16 mm in max. diameter, into a hole of the same diameter bored in a fillet or cross-tie in one of the door-leaves, cf. fragments D, F, and G.

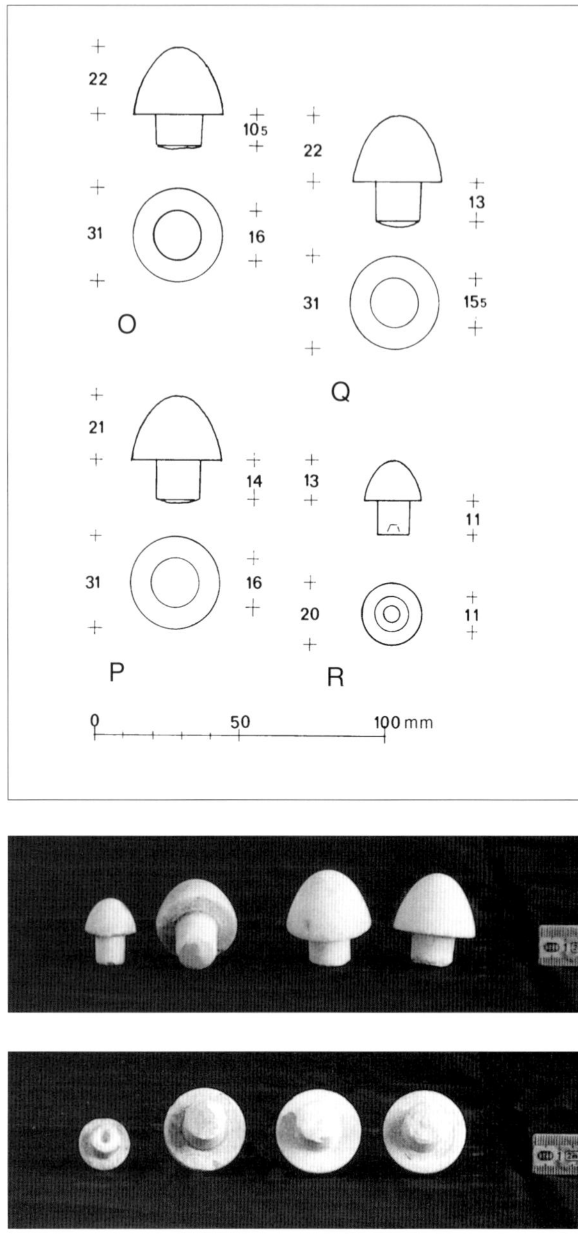

O-R

P. *Bodrum, Quadrangle*

Found in the cavity in the rock-cut bottom of the tomb chamber, cf. chapter 22.

Of white, very finely-grained marble turned on a lathe.

Round knob like O and Q, 21 mm high and 31 mm in diameter. The tenon is 14 mm high and 16 mm in max. diameter. Traces of red paint survive on the underside of the knob around the tenon. Possibly the fillet or cross-tie, on which the knob was to be placed, was painted red all over, while the knob itself remained unpainted; alternatively, and perhaps more likely, the knob except the tenon was completely painted before being fastened in order to avoid staining the surface around the knob, which was not to be painted.

Q. *Bodrum, Quadrangle*

Found in the cavity in the rock-cut bottom of the tomb chamber, cf. chapter 22.

Of white, very finely-grained marble turned on a lathe.

Round knob like O and P, 22 mm high and 31 mm in diameter. The tenon is 13 mm high and 15.5 mm in diameter.

R. *Bodrum, Quadrangle*

Found in the cavity in the rock-cut bottom of the tomb chamber, cf. chapter 22.

Of white, very finely-grained marble turned on a lathe.

Round knob like items O, P, and Q, but considerably smaller, only 13 mm high and 20 mm in diameter. The tenon is 11 mm high and 11 mm in max. diameter, and at its end is a fresh pip mark for the lathe on which the knob was turned. Knobs of this size were used to adorn the lateral fillets, cf. fragment A.

17. The anteroom and its connection with the tomb chamber

Underneath the threshold of the doorway separating the corridor from the anteroom, the bottom of the drain declines steeply before continuing eastwards at a c. 45 mm lower level, i.e. level 478 on which the lowest course of foundation slabs in the anteroom and the tomb chamber is based.

Apparently Newton did not excavate this part of the corridor and therefore believed that what he called "the marble drain" passed out of the building on the west side and "flowed under the great stone [i.e. the plug-block], emptying itself into the gallery through a bronze grating inserted in the covering slab of pavement" (HD 142-3).

However, as shown above (chapter 9), the arrangement Newton visualized can only have existed in his imagination. Evidently the purpose of "the marble drain" was not to drain off ground water from the tomb chamber into the W branch of the Lower Gallery, but quite the opposite: as in the corridor, the drain passed through the anteroom and across the tomb chamber under a pavement of marble towards the point at the middle of the east wall where it can still be seen to continue further east (fig.2.2).

In addition to the foundation slabs surviving in situ in the anteroom, three more were found lying in the neighbourhood (marked with crosses on the plan fig. 17.2). Judging from the height of the foundation course for the side walls of the anteroom, wich measures between 24.8 and 25.5 cm, this was probably equivalent to the thickness of the marble floor covering the space between them. As a matter of fact, this is the height of a block of white marble that was found in square 8/9, i.e. in the middle of the tomb chamber (fig. 12.3, d).

Measuring 44.9 cm in width, it is broken in length (length as preserved c. 57 cm). Its top surface is smooth, but strongly corroded – it must have been exposed to weathering over a long period after the departure of the Hospitallers in 1522. It is characterized as a pavement slab by having anathyrosis only along the top edges (width 5-8 cm), but none along the vertical edges of the block, just as the foundation slabs underneath it.

The underside has been flattened with the claw chisel. Judging from pry-cuttings on top of the foundation course, the marble pavement in the anteroom was composed of transverse rows of slabs, four of which measured c. 45 cm in width, i.e. just the width of the surviving slab.

Behind the doorway, the width of the corridor, 184 cm, was maintained to a depth of 66 cm. Altogether the anteroom was 2.34 m deep and 240 cm in maximum width, i.e. approximately quadratic in plan.

The conclusion that this area was not merely an open recess incorporated in the tomb chamber, but had the form of a separate room for which the designation "anteroom" would have been perfectly appropriate, can be based on the following arguments:

Fig. 17.1. Reconstructed plan and longitudinal section of the sepulchral complex.

- a Approximate level of euthynteria course and crepidoma (one course lower than suggested above in figs. 7.1-2).
- b Plug-block.
- c Corridor.
- d Drain vents.
- e Double-door of white marble.
- f Anteroom.
- g "Une porte fort basse" (de la Tourette) reconstructed in the form of a low passage through one of the lower panels of a monumental doorway moulded in stucco on both sides of the wall (cf. the front elevations figs. 17.3, and 17.5-6).
- h-k Stuccoed decoration in low relief tentatively reconstructed on the basis of de la Tourette's description: columns (h), base with statues (i,j), and frieze (k).
- m Artemisia's sarcophagus.
- n Ossuary containing Maussollos' bones.
- o Levels of euthynteria course, toichobate, and upper masonry of the northern enclosure wall.

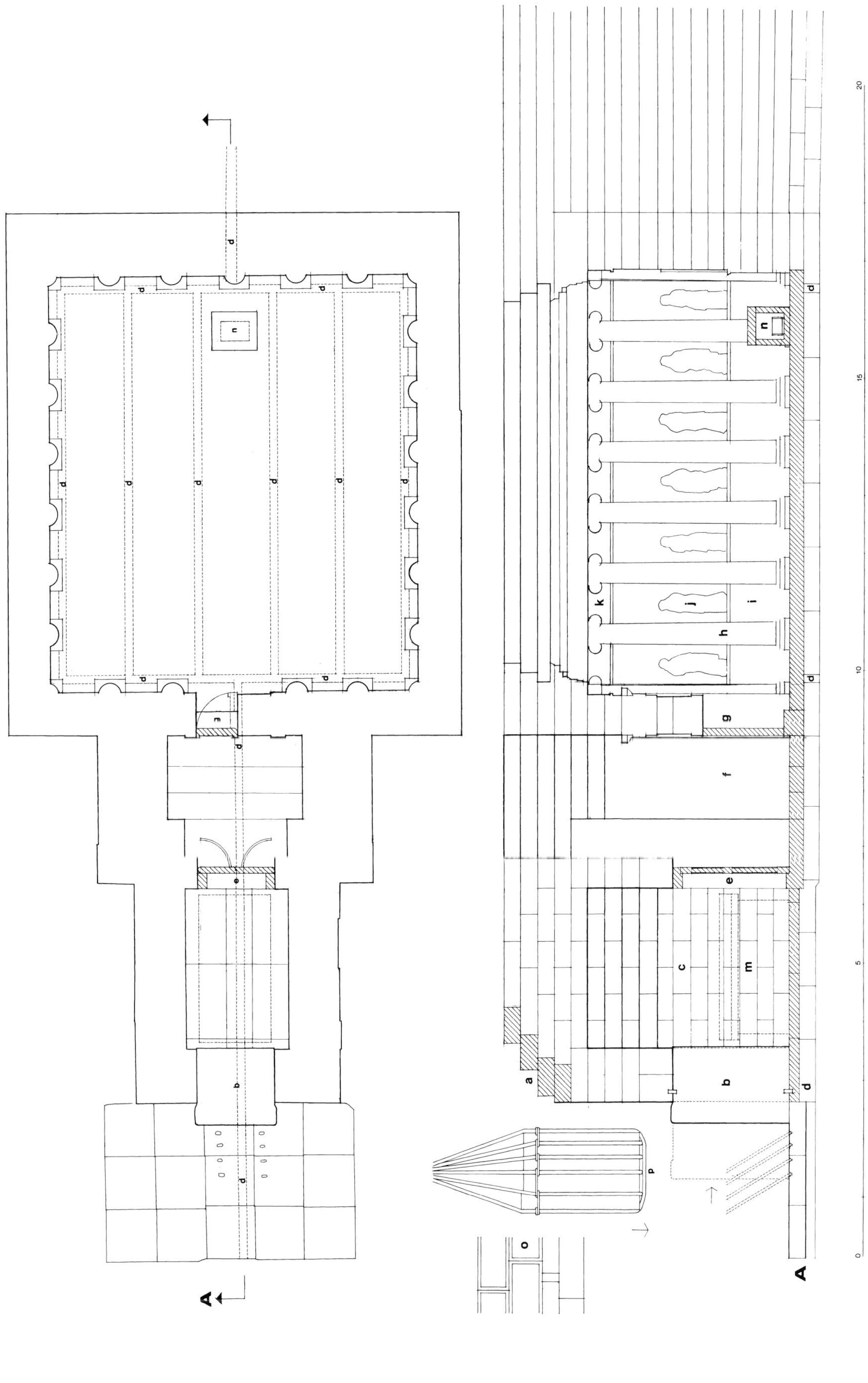
A
A
a
b
c
d
e
f
g
h
i
j
k
m
n
o
p
0
5
10
15
20

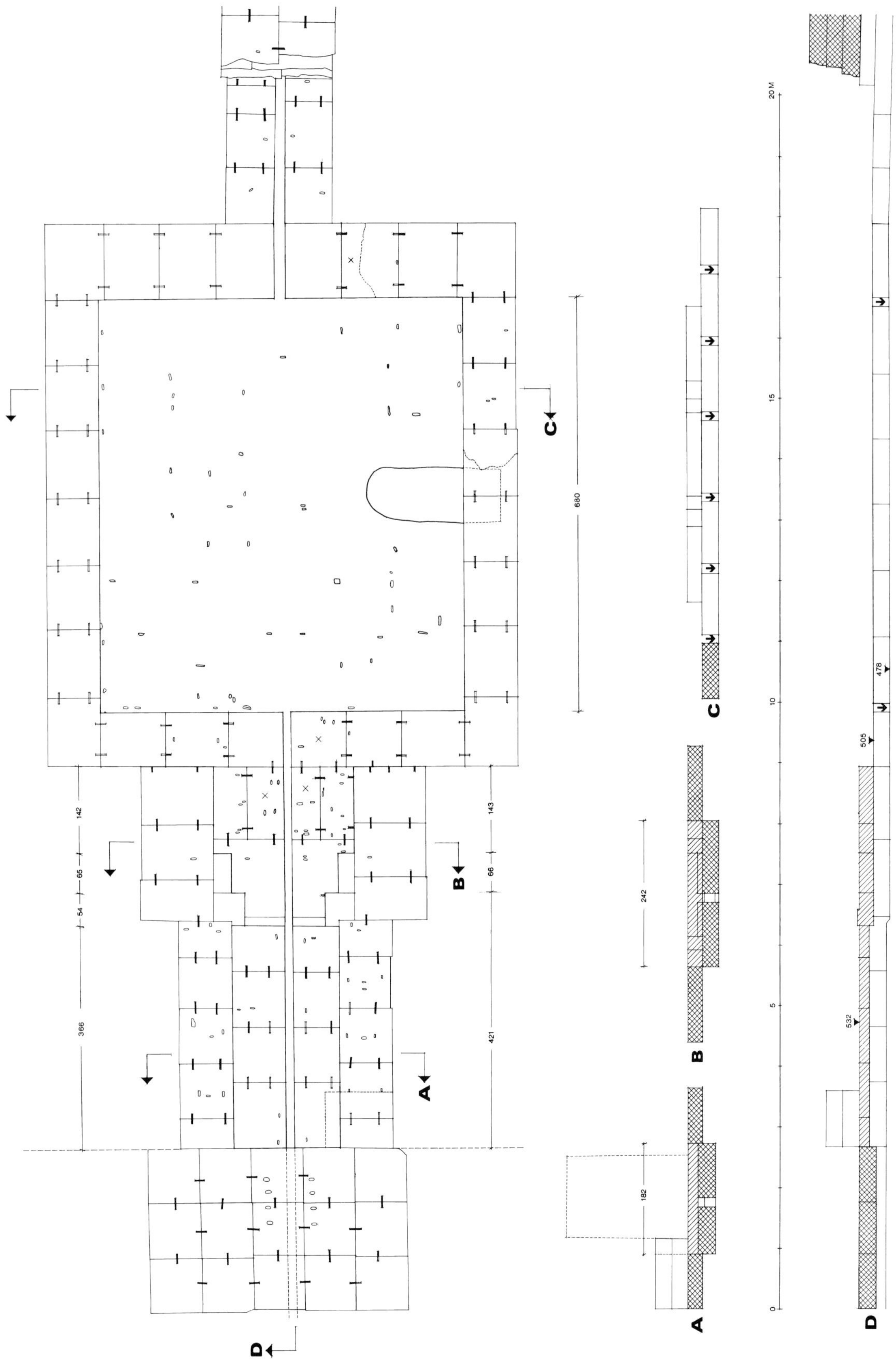

Fig. 17.2. Courses of foundation slabs of greenish tufa in corridor and anteroom and under the walls of the tomb chamber, reconstructed on the basis of slabs surviving in situ (cf. folded plate in the back of the book). Those marked with a cross were found near their original positions, but not in situ. The cross-section C indicates the drain vents assumed to have been left open between the rows of foundation slabs under the pavement of the tomb chamber.

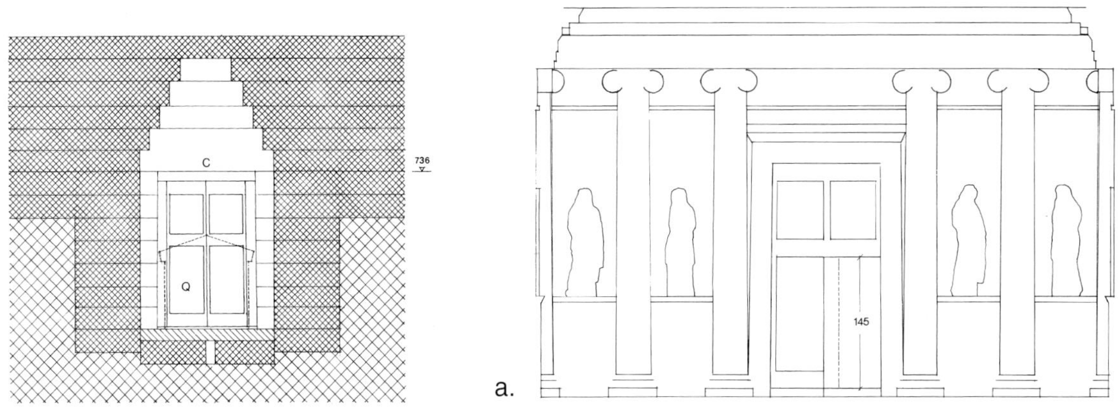

b. a.

(1) The foundation course which supported the wall of the tomb chamber on its south, east and north sides was continued unbroken (interrupted only by the drain) along its west side.

(2) According to the account of de la Tourrette (see Appendix 3), the tomb chamber was decorated on all sides (tout autour) with columns in low relief (en demy-bosse); and from the tomb chamber there was access to a kind of anteroom through a very low doorway (une porte fort basse, qui conduisoit à une autre, comme antichambre).

c.

Since there were no rooms on the three other sides of the tomb chamber, this doorway could only have been the one that gave access to the tomb chamber from the corridor; and being remarkably low, it could hardly have been identical with the doorway at the end of the corridor which, as the fragments show, must have had a height permitting people of normal stature to pass through without difficulty (above, chapter 15).

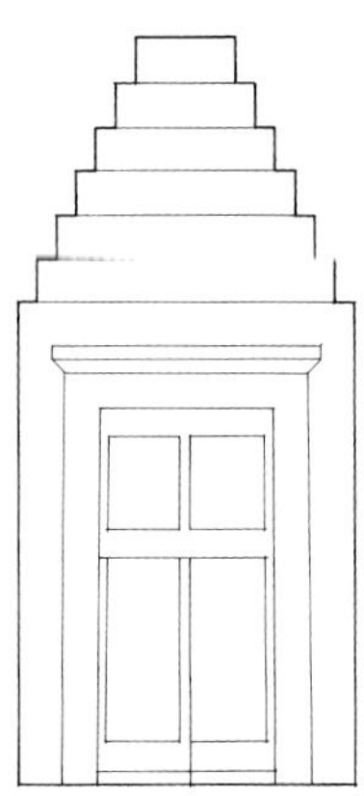

d.

The reason why de la Tourette found the exceptionally low proportions of the opening between the anteroom and the tomb chamber

Fig. 17.3.
a Reconstructed elevation of the W wall of the tomb chamber (note the low passage through the lower panel of the moulded doorway).
b Cross-section through the corridor, looking E.
c-d Cross-sections through the anteroom, looking W (c) and E (d).

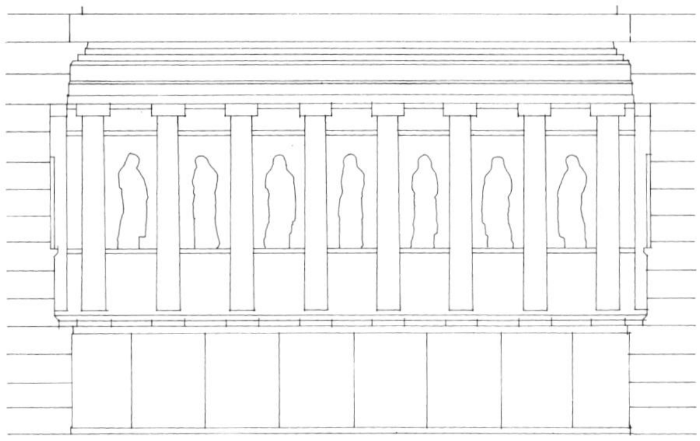

Fig. 17.4. Alternative reconstruction of the stucco decoration in the tomb chamber based on the interpretation of de la Tourrette's description.

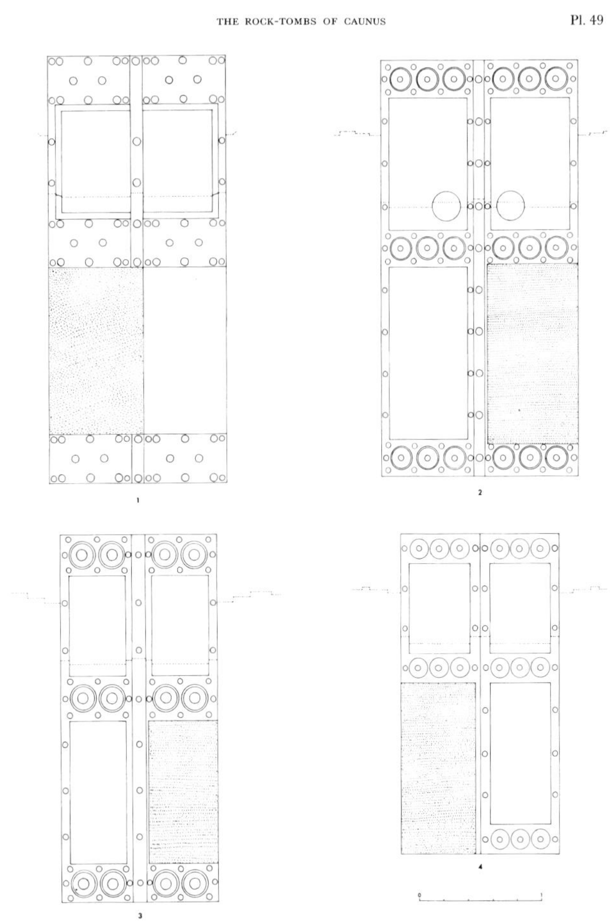

Fig. 17.5. Rock-cut sham doorways with a passage through one of their lower panels. From monumental tombs at Kaunos (Roos (1972) pl. 49).

worthy of note was probably that they struck him as surprisingly small as compared to the impressive dimensions of the tomb chamber itself which he correctly characterized as "a beautiful, large, square room" (une belle grande sale carree). Measuring c. 6.25 × 6.80 m in width and length, it was indeed remarkably large, even larger than any of the royal Macedonian tomb chambers,[54] and a height matching these dimensions could hardly have been less than between 3.5 and 4 metres.

A door-opening suited to an architectural framework of these proportions must have been at least some 2.5-3 m high, while "a very low door opening" would have had to be considerably lower than the average height of people in the 16th century (presumably about 1.6 m), i.e. hardly higher than about 1.4 m. However, fragments of a marble doorway of the monumental size would have been easily distinguishable both from those of the smaller doorway actually identified (chapter 16), which all conform to a uniform scale, and from fragments of a doorway as small as the one described by de la Tourrette.

Offerings and other objects relevant to the sepulchral services, it is true, might have been deposited in the lateral niches on both sides of the anteroom, but it could hardly have been the only or the principal purpose of screening off an antechamber at the end of the corridor to make room for such requirements, for these were amply satisfied on the lower landing of the western staircase just outside the entrance to the tomb.[55]

More likely, the construction of a separate anteroom was dictated primarily by the necessity of providing more space both in width and height at the end of the corridor than this afforded in itself (it may not have been higher than the plug-block, i.e. c. 208 cm): there must, after all, have been a monumental doorway leading into the tomb chamber, which required a greater width and height than the corridor would allow room for, and which therefore motivated the erection of a partition wall pierced by a passage (the double-door) that would give access both to anteroom and tomb chamber.

Fig. 17.7. Foundation slabs in the anteroom, looking NW and SW.

However, the monumental doorway was not necessarily made of marble and constructed like a true doorway, but may well have had the form of a sham door moulded in stucco and painted like the rest of the architectural decoration of the tomb chamber (on this see chapter 18); and possibly the low passage mentioned by de la Tourrette was provided by leaving an opening as large as the lower panel in one of the fictitious door-leaves. It may be assumed that the doorway was represented in its entirety not only inside the tomb chamber (fig. 17.3, a), but also on the side facing the anteroom (fig. 17.3, d).

If it is estimated that it was c. 2.60 m high and 2.25 m wide, the opening in the lower panel would have measured c. 66 cm in width and 145 cm in height (fig. 17.6, in which a door-leaf working on pivots is suggested).[56] Actually such a solution was chosen in some of the rock-cut monumental chamber tombs at Kaunos of which a selection is shown in fig. 17.5.[57]

These doorways measure 125-159 cm in width and 246-330 cm in height. The 55-75 wide and 110-138 cm high openings must have been cut primarily for the purpose of permitting craftsmen to hollow out the tomb chamber, but since the openings were eventually closed by a removable slab of stone (sliding or working on pivots), it was obviously the intention that they should remain accessible to relatives or personnel attending to sepulchral services, thus allowing them to get in and out while performing their task.

It may be conjectured that the opening into Maussollos' tomb chamber was used for similar purposes in the period that passed between the death of Maussollos and Artemisia's demise two years later,[58] when the tomb was sealed by the plug-block, and its entrance closed for good.

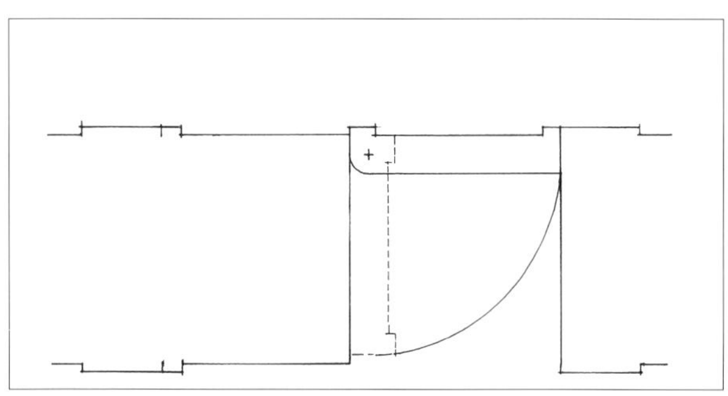

Fig. 17.6. Tentative reconstruction of the marble door with which the low passage through the stuccoed doorway leading into the tomb chamber could be closed.

18. The tomb chamber

Of the foundation slabs, on which the walls of the tomb chamber were built, two survive in situ on the west side, on either side of the anteroom, while one of the missing slabs was found lying very near its original position (marked with a cross in the plan fig. 17.1). At the SE corner of the tomb chamber, there remain, in addition to the corner piece, one slab on the east side, and two slabs and part of a third on the south side. Those on the west and south sides are 90-92 cm wide, and 95 and 108 cm, respectively, in length, those on the east side 122 cm wide and 100 cm long.

The slabs are connected with one another by means of clamps, but at the sides facing inwards, i.e. towards the interior of the tomb chamber, they have no anathyrosis, nor are there any clamps by means of which they could have been fastened to the slabs forming the foundation course between the walls.

Instead, these sides have been smoothly dressed with the pointed chisel all over, much like the sides of the drain passing through the corridor and the anteroom. The drain must therefore have branched off in both directions along the periphery of the tomb chamber before turning off at right-angles at the middle of the east wall (fig. 2.2).

The fragment of a foundation slab found lying near the cavity at the middle of the south wall (seen in figs. 1.18-21, 24-25) measures 121.5 cm in width and has anathyrosis and two clamp holes, while the other sides, preserved to a length of c. 56 and 42 cm, respectively, are smoothly dressed like the sides of the drain. Probably, therefore, it should be attributed to the row of 122 cm wide slabs of which the east wall was composed and is marked with a cross on the plan fig. 17.1).

In the rock-cut bottom of the tomb chamber are many pry-cuttings indicating the pattern of the foundation slabs that formed the foundations of the marble pavement. The cuttings that were used for shifting slabs in the direction from south to north, or vice versa, are grouped in lines subdividing the space between the south and north walls into five rows each about 120 cm wide, which means that there must have been a row in the middle that prevented the drain coming from the anteroom from continuing in the same direction across the tomb chamber.

This conclusion is supported by the observation that a pry-cutting that was used for prying a slab in the direction from east towards west (or vice versa) is situated precisely opposite the drain coming from the anteroom (marked with an arrow on the plan fig. 17.1).

Because of the fragile surface of the rock, some of the pry-cuttings are partly effaced and not a few may have disappeared entirely. Judging from what remains, however, it may be plausibly assumed that there were altogether four intermediate branches across the tomb chamber in addition to the drains along the walls (fig. 17.2). Apparently, efforts were made to drain off effectively ground water oozing out from the bedrock, and possibly precautions were taken even to prevent moisture from seeping up between the joints of the pavement slabs by capillary action. On groundwater conditions in the Maussolleion area in Antiquity see below, Appendix 1.[59]

Like the corridor and the anteroom, the tomb chamber was built inside a cutting in the bedrock. Measured from the bottom of the cutting, the vertical sides facing west, north, and east are almost precisely 2.00 m high. The south side is preserved to a maximum height of merely about 50 cm, its upper part having been cut away when grave-robbers made a mine passing just outside the tomb chamber (chapter 21).

The lower part of the rock-cut sides, rising to a height between c. 1.0 and 1.3 m, consists of bedrock of a relatively solid geological composition, the surface of which is so well-preserved that traces of the pointed tools used to flatten it can be observed. At higher levels the original surface has disintegrated, and along the upper edge of the cutting much of the material has crumbled away (pls. E5,a-o; E6,a-e; E8,a-h; E9,a-b; E10,a-d).

It is evident that in the lower area the surface was in some places dressed to accommodate the individual ashlars or courses of masonry facing the inside of the cutting. Traces of two courses of masonry flush with the slabs preserved in situ on the south side of the plug-block in its original position can be traced on the rock-cut south side of the anteroom, where there is a horizontal cutting at level L5 (pl. E6). Similar cuttings can be seen on the rock-cut north side of the corridor, opposite the plug-block at level L4 (pl. E5); on the north side of the tomb chamber at level L3 (pl. E5); on the east side of the tomb chamber at levels L3 and L4 (pl. E10); on its west side at levels L3 and L5 (E9, north of the anteroom), and at L7 (south of the anteroom), where there is a distinct c. 33 cm high cutting indicating the bed and left side of a slab from course C7, visible on the photo fig. 1.28, cf. pl. E9.

It can hardly be questioned, therefore, that the seven lowest wall courses of the tomb chamber and of the anteroom were adjusted to match the courses of the foundation slabs in the corridor and were equally sized. It is tempting to infer from this evidence that they were made of the same material, i.e. the greenish tufa.

Besides, to ensure structural stability sufficient to counteract the enormous pressure of the corbelled vault and of the weight transmitted to it from the superincumbent masonry, the wall courses above the top level of the rock-cut sides of the tomb chamber (at level c. 678) must have been bonded with the courses of foundation slabs of greenish tufa behind them that formed the solid core of the monument.

Evidently, when the grave-robbers came across the back of the tomb chamber's south wall while digging their mine, they did not suspect that this piece of masonry could be associated with the tomb chamber. Presumably, therefore, it did not look in any way different from the foundation courses visible on the outside of the monument at the spot where they had sunk the shaft from which they drove the tunnel.

There would not have been any point in using a precious material like marble for the walls, unless they were intended to produce an impression of splendour, and in that case the masonry would most probably have been constructed in imitation of the sophisticated ashlar masonry typical of monumental buildings and also exemplified in the stucco decorations of the first Pompeian style and its predecessors.

Above all, the lower part of the wall would have been faced with a dado in the form of a high orthostat course, and regular courses of ashlar masonry would have been reserved for the main zone above the string course crowning the dado. On the other hand, considering the lavish decoration of the outside of the monument, it is hard to believe that the walls of the tomb chamber could have been left entirely blank and that no care was taken to disguise the aesthetically unattractive character of the stone of which they were built.

According to de la Tourrette's report (see Appendix 3), the tomb chamber was richly decorated, and the details of the description suggest the possibility that the walls were covered with painted decorations in stucco. Nothing is said in the report to suggest that there were any columns standing between the walls, i.e. in positions where they might have helped support the roof. On that issue, the surviving remains of the floor are equally inconclusive: there may or may not have been intermediate columns or pillars.

But even if such supports had existed, beams of very impressive dimensions must have been placed on top of them to sustain the weight of the superincumbent masses of foundation courses, and no remains of pillars or beams that might have been used for such a purpose have been identified on the site. Barrel vaults of the type used in Macedonian tombs, it is true, were capable of carrying mounds of a considerable height, but these were much lower than the Maussolleion and not of stone, but of earth.

The use of barrel vaults may well have been in its beginnings at the time when the Maussolleion was built, but the capacity of the barrel vault could hardly have been as thoroughly tested as to recommend its employment above the tomb chamber of the Maussolleion. Besides, being rather useless for the construction of fortifications in the Castle, the wedge-shaped ashlars of a barrel vault would probably have been left lying on the site. However, no remains of blocks of that particular shape have turned up during the recent excavations.

In all probability, therefore, the tomb chamber, its anteroom, and its corridor were all roofed with corbelled vaults composed of foundation slabs projecting from the courses that constituted the core of the monument, and were not necessarily different from these in any respect.

A similar arrangement based exclusively on the evidence of de la Tourrette was suggested by Edmund Oldfield,[60] who also drew attention to the corbelled vaults roofing the square tomb chambers in 4th century tumuli at Pantikapaion.[61] In the Kul-Oba, for example, the tomb chamber measures c. 4.25 × 4.40 m and is covered by a vault consisting of seven courses of c. 40 cm high steps overlapping each other, as they ascend to a small central opening, which is covered by a single flat stone.

Corbelled vaults roofed the tomb chambers in some of the earliest Egyptian pyramids,[62] were widely used in the Minoan/Mycenaean epoch, and also locally known at Halikarnassos, as attested by the roofing of the tomb chamber inside a monumental tumulus near Torba a few miles north of Halikarnassos.[63]

19. The sarcophagus lid of white marble, summary of evidence for its reconstruction

"Within the north-west angle of the Mausoleum" Newton found two fragments "of the lid of a marble SOROS,[64] with a low pedimental roof, and chiselled with much care"; and it seemed to him "not unlikely that they formed part of the SOROS in which the body of Mausolus was found by the Knights" (HD 114). The same pieces are described as no. 1 in a list of finds that "may possibly be remnants" of the treasures "which the Sepulchral Chamber of Mausolus probably contained when first opened by the Knights" (HD 263).

In the Mausoleum Room Guide, 63, no. 158, Newton gives the following description:

"The corner of the lid of a white marble SOROS, mentioned [HD] p.114. This terminates at one end in a fine joint, showing that the lid was made of several pieces of marble. The lower face of the marble has evidently been adjusted with great nicety to the SOROS which it covered. The letter A is cut upon this lower face: throughout the Mausoleum, the relative position of the several mouldings and other subordinate members of the Order was, in like manner, indicated by letters.

The chiselling of the surface of this marble lid is so like that of the architectural marbles found in situ that I have no hesitation in ascribing it to the period of the Mausoleum. With it was found a fragment similarly chiselled, which probably belongs to the same SOROS."

On the basis of these descriptions, the two fragments can be identified as the two parts of which the restored corner piece now carrying the reg.no. 1972.5-22.12 was put together. There are no visible joins that fit, but it seems likely that part of the breaks now covered by plaster do in fact join each other. At any rate, the external dimensions and mouldings are exactly the same on both fragments.

In actual fact, however, the letter A is cut on top of the sloping surface representing the roof of the lid, and not, as Newton recorded (cf. above), on the bottom of it, for this was adjusted to fit the receptacle underneath.

The piece will be described in detail as fragment a in the catalogue below. With this can be associated three fragments recently excavated, b-d, one of which was found in square 9/5.[65] Identified by me in the Hospitallers' Castle at the harbour of Kos in 1986, fragment e evidently comes from a sarcophagus lid of exactly the same type and size as the one exemplified by the fragments from Bodrum.

The marble of which fragments b, c, and d were made can be described in much the same terms as the fragments E/I, F and G from the double-door of marble (cf. chapter 16), i.e. as being composed of densely deposited thin, whitish layers alternating with thicker, slightly darker layers of a greyish-yellowish tinge.

A stable isotopic ratio analysis of these fragments and fragment a carried out under the supervision of Professor Norman Herz gave the following results:

	delta^{13} C	delta^{16} O
Fragment a	4.54	-1.60
Fragment b	4.38	-3.26
Fragment c	4.37	-2.87
Fragment d	4.46	-2.97

The delta C plots range between 4.54 and 4.37 (difference 0.17), the delta O plots for fragments b, c, d between -3.26 and -2.87 (difference -0.39),[66] while the delta O figure for fragment a, -1.60, is only about half as big as the figures for the other fragments.

From the analysis of the door fragments E

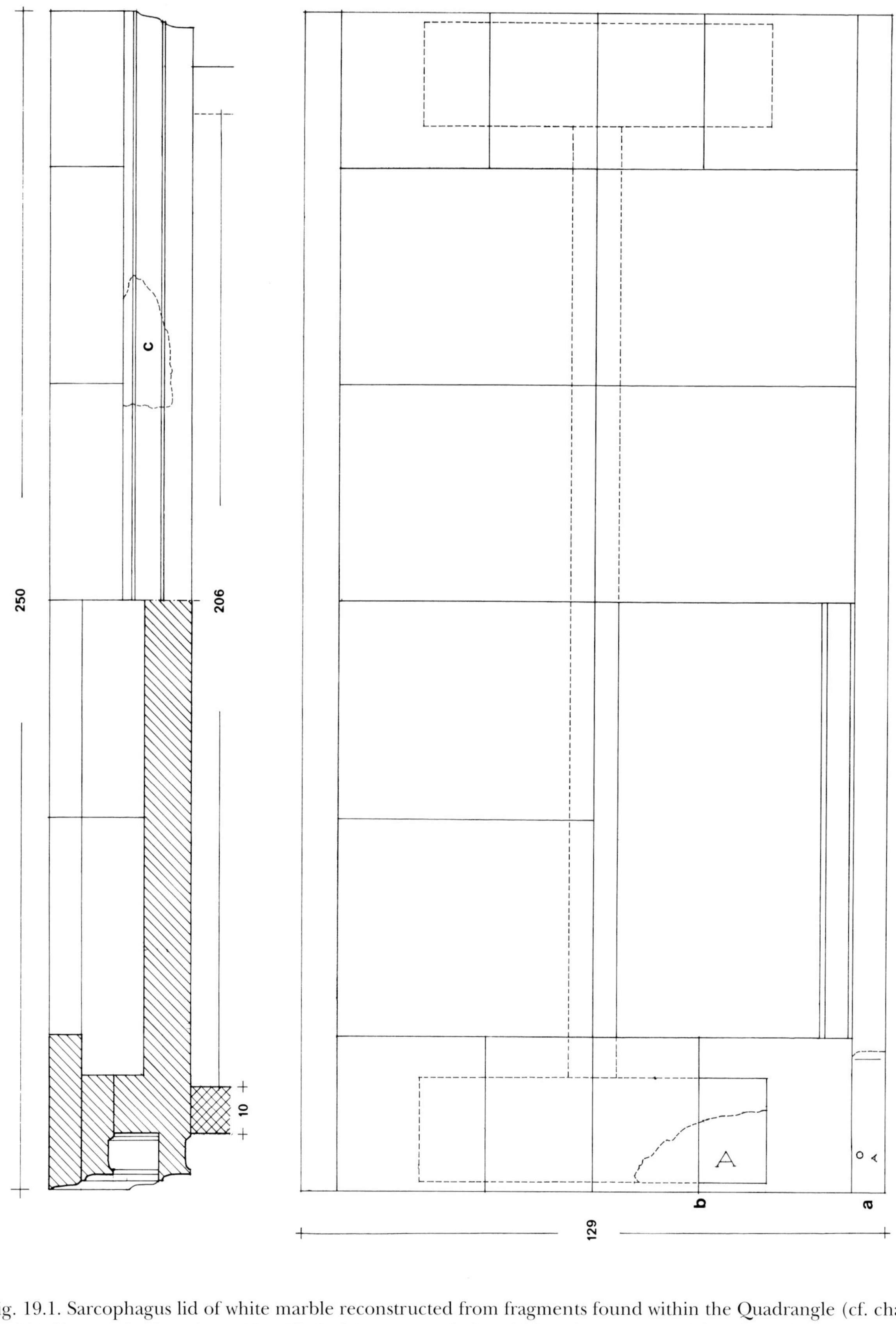

Fig. 19.1. Sarcophagus lid of white marble reconstructed from fragments found within the Quadrangle (cf. chapter 20). No remains have been identified of the receptacle for which a cheaper material such as a locally quarried limestone may have been used. All maximum dimensions are conjectural, but in keeping with current standards (cf. Appendix 4).

and I which can be shown to fit each other in one of their breaks (above p. 81), plots as different as 0.125 and -0.213 (for delta C and delta O plots, respectively) may occur within one and the same piece of marble.

Consequently, as the differences between the plots of fragments c and d are only 0.09 and -0.10, respectively, they may well be assumed to come from the same piece of marble, while the high delta O plot of fragment b, -3.26 suggests that this was of a different piece of marble of almost the same composition, but possibly obtained from a different part of the same quarry. In actual fact, the marble of fragment b is evidently of a finer quality than that of c and d.

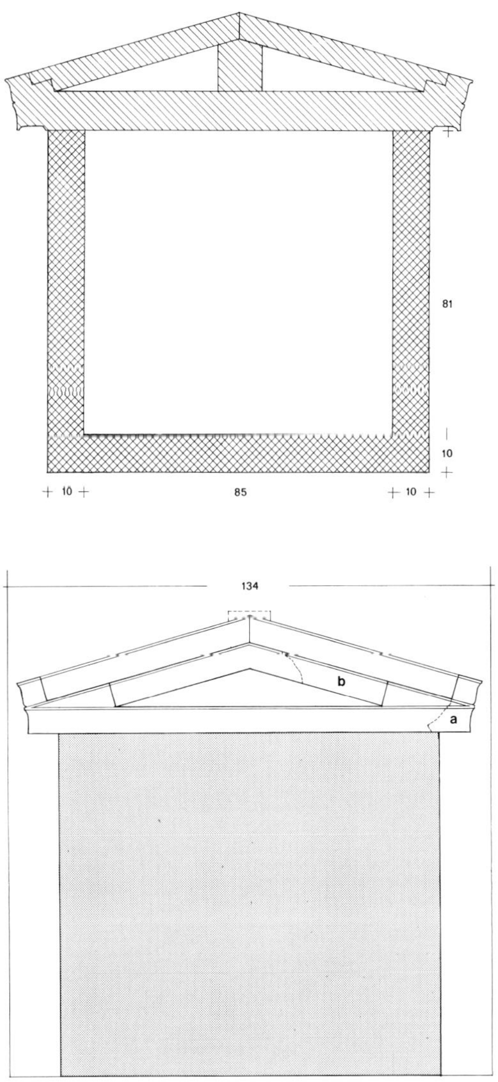

Fig. 19.2. Front elevation and cross sektion of the sarcophagus tentatively reconstructed from fragments and written evidence (cf. Appendix 3).

In his comparative evaluation of the samples from the marble door and the sarcophagus lid, Professor Herz is inclined to assume that all came from quarries at Ephesos, but that the two groups "were obtained from different parts of the quarries or were extracted at different times".[67]

The latter of the two possibilities can probably be dismissed, inasmuch as the provenance of the fragments from the mid-fourth century Maussolleion appear to be attested by their findspots within the Quadrangle (on the latter issue, see further below).

However, as the figure for the delta O plot of fragment a is strikingly low, Professor Herz doubts "very much that the differences in isotopic ratios [between this and the other fragments] can be explained by variation within the same block".[68]

As fragment a shows, individual sections of merely ornamental importance added up to

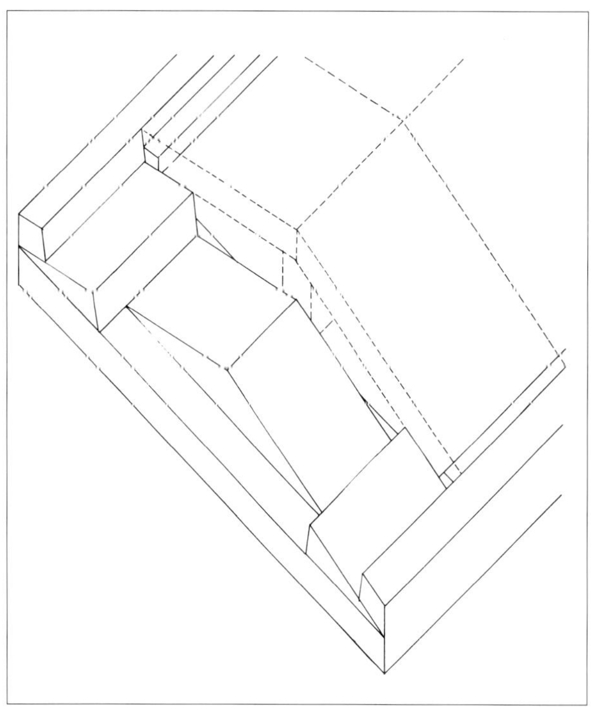

Fig. 19.3. Isometric projection of the gabled sarcophagus front. The pair of roof slabs in which the raking sima was carved and the separately worked sections of the raking geison have been removed, thus revealing the parts worked in the same slab as the lower lid: the tympanum, and the rebates for the raking geison and sima at the corners.

form the upper part of the roof-shaped lid. Judging from the rebate at the back of fragment c, the sloping sides of the roof were composed of slabs about 6 cm thick at the most. These must have rested in the rebate and on a support under the ridge of the roof – a construction that would have reduced the weight of the lid considerably.

As the geison fragment b was cut separately, and not in connection with the sima, it cannot have belonged to one of the longer sides of the lid. It might have come from the horizontal geison below the pediment, in which case, however, the 32 mm high letter A carefully carved on its upper surface and originally set off with red paint as well would have been patently visible to an observer standing in front of the sarcophagus.

The letter, it is true, might have been covered by some kind of pedimental ornament, floral or figural,[69] but considering the absence of any sculptural decoration whatsoever on the surviving fragments, it does not seem very likely that any was to be found in the recessed space of the pediments, which hardly exceeded 10 cm in height and some 70 cm in length and was rather too small to invite decoration.[70]

More likely, fragment b comes from the raking geison. Evidently, this was carved independently of the superincumbent sima, as indicated by the joint on fragment a. It remains to explain

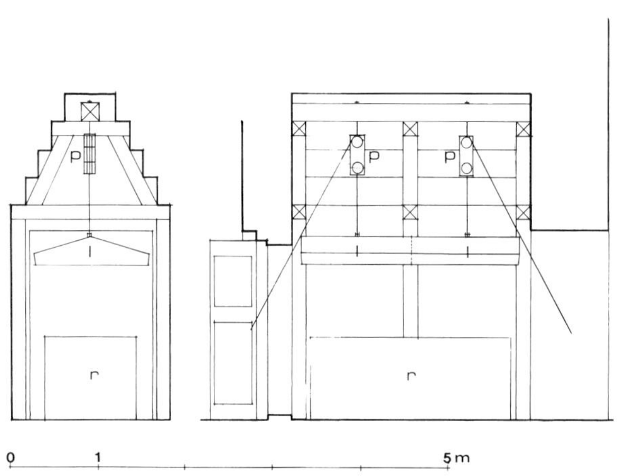

Fig. 19.4. Temporary scaffolding with two pulleys (p) put up in the tomb corridor to lift or lower the lid (l) of the sarcophagus (r) (or either half of the lid independently of the other half).

why so much care was bestowed on the beautiful alpha, if the letter was not intended to be permanently visible. Possibly the mason was an accomplished letter-carver who took a professional pride in the perfection of this part of his work, whereas the tiny A on fragment a was carved by a different artisan dealing primarily or exclusively with the lower part of the lid.

In all likelihood, as illustrated in figs. 19.3, the tympana were carved in one piece with the large slab forming the lower part of the lid, and the raking geisa added as separate pieces on top of the tympana, while the raking simas were moulded on the front of the roof slabs covering both ends of the lid.

Given the fact that four fragments survive, that all were found within the Quadrangle, and that they came from different parts of the lid, two (a and b) from the fronts, and two (c and d) from the longer sides, it may be reasonably assumed that these were not the only remains of the lid that ended up between the multitude of debris on the site of what was once the Maussolleion.

Possibly their dispersion issued from a point inside rather than outside the Quadrangle; in other words: the sarcophagus to which the lid belonged might well have stood somewhere inside the Maussolleion before its disintegration took place. As each of the fragments a, b, c consists of two parts, none of them exceeding c. 25 cm in length, they appear to have been hacked to pieces deliberately, presumably for the purpose of making lime of them (cf. de la Tourrette's report, Appendix 3).

The only sarcophagus virtually known to have stood in the Maussolleion – that is, if de la Tourette can be trusted – is the one which this eyewitness saw in the anteroom-like chamber adjoining the larger room in the foundations of the Maussolleion. Although grave-robbers had previously forced their way into these rooms (see below, chapter 21) and probably carried away most of their treasures, the sarcophagus was still largely intact, when it was discovered by the Knights; and it is not conceivable that it could have been placed in the tomb corridor after this was definitely closed with the colossal plug-block.

If, therefore, the fragments found in the

Quadrangle really came from this sarcophagus, they must be expected to display formal characteristics typical of the Hekatomnid epoch or at least not incompatible with a mid-fourth century date. As a comparison will make clear, the repertory of architectural details represented on the sarcophagus fragments from the Maussolleion is much more summary than the one displayed by the "Sarcophagus of the Mourning Women".

While the latter conforms very precisely to the composition of a late Classical temple of the Ionic order,[71] the fragments from the Quadrangle represent a somewhat simplified version of the eaves of a temple roof: the foot-moulding at the cavity underneath the soffit is just a plain fillet, and the front of the geison is not consistent with the traditional design of Doric or Ionic geisa, but has the form of a simple cavetto.

From the point of view of style and dating, the delicate, steep cyma recta profile of the sima is of particular importance, since it is closely paralleled by the sima on roof blocks from the South Propylaea at Labraunda, which probably date from around the middle of the 4th century BC.[72] One of these is a corner block, on which is indicated a spout in the form of a lion's head.[73] As this feature is missing on our fragment a, it seems justified to conclude that lion's head spouts were not at all represented on the sarcophagus lid; and similarly, if antefixes had existed, remains of them would probably have survived at least on one of the fragments a and c, or on fragment e from a similar sarcophagus lid found at Kos. It also seems unlikely that details on the raking sides of the roof such as pantiles and covertiles were represented in relief.

The date deducible from the profile of the sima is compatible with the shape of the letter A carved on fragment b. This has the form of a triangle with widely straddling vertical strokes connected by a horizontal stroke which is just slightly curved, and resembles very closely the alpha in the dedicatory inscription of the South Propylaea (see illustration appended to the description of fragment b in the catalogue).[74] The same letter type is exemplified in other dedicatory inscriptions from the Hekatomnid era in Labraunda.[75] In conclusion, to judge from the available evidence, there is nothing to suggest a date later than the 4th century BC, and a date around the middle of that century seems perfectly possible.

Considering the fact that so far not a single fragment of the receptacle underneath the lid has been identified, it is purely a matter of conjecture what the lower part of the sarcophagus may have looked like. The unconventional shape of the horizontal geison of the lid does not give the impression that it was supposed to rest on an elaborate entablature of traditional Doric or Ionic design. Quite possibly, its sides were plain and undecorated, and it is even conceivable that it was made of a less costly stone than the lid, for example of bluish limestone. The Knights might have found the latter material less attractive for lime-burning than marble, and if the receptacle had not been damaged by previous intruders (the composite lid might have yielded readily enough to their first approaches), it could have been removed and used for secular purposes, for example as a water tank, or as a trough for watering cattle.

The use of sarcophagi in the Halikarnassos area in late Classical times is confirmed by the sarcophagus of "the Carian Princess", which is a typical specimen.[76] Sarcophagi were usually cut of greenish tufa like that of which the foundation slabs in the Maussolleion were made, but sometimes bluish limestone was preferred. The receptacle was of a simple rectangular form, and the lid had sides like a roof sloping on both sides of a ridge. All sides were usually roughly tooled with the pointed chisel, but if made of limestone might be finely dressed.[77]

Judging from de la Tourrette's description (cf. Appendix 3, p. 141f), the burial he found in the antechamber-like room adjoining the larger room must have been a sarcophagus with a lid of white marble, while the context suggests the possibility that the receptacle was made of a different and less costly material.

It may be doubted, however, whether this sarcophagus could have stood in the anteroom proper that can be reconstructed on the basis of the archeological evidence (chapter 17). This room was so narrow that a sarcophagus placed in it would have had to be arranged with its longer sides in the transverse direction, and it could not possibly have been shifted into such a position from the corridor without getting stuck while being turned around. Presumably the marble door between the anteroom and the corridor had been opened or even smashed to pieces by previous intruders when the Hospitallers entered the anteroom, thus leaving the sarcophagus directly open to view.

On the other hand, it would have been comparatively easy to shift a sarcophagus from outside into the corridor by means of rollers, in particular if the corpse had already been placed inside the receptacle, with the lid in place. Alternatively, the complete sarcophagus, inclusive of the lid but without the corpse, might have been rolled into its final position in the corridor. The lid could then have been kept suspended by means of lifting gear, while the deceased was being laid to rest in the receptacle, and afterwards lowered again.(fig. 19.4) The corbelled vault of the corridor would have permitted a temporary framework of timber to be erected, from which two pulleys could be operated to lift the sarcophagus lid – and, in case this was composed of two halves, either half independently of the other – as high as required (fig. 19.4).

However, if the procedure had been started by placing the receptacle in the corridor empty and without its lid, the independent transport of the lid through the entrance would have been extremely difficult to accomplish, as the relatively low entrance (2.08 m high like the plug-block) would have impeded the continuous use of a tripod.

The corridor measured 182-184 cm in width and 265 cm in depth between the cross-wall with the marble door and the plug-block in its final position, while the lid of the sarcophagus as reconstructed may be estimated to have been about 250 cm long and 130 cm wide (figs. 19.1-2). This arrangement would have left a 30 cm wide passage on both sides of the sarcophagus lid, and 10 cm more at the level of the receptacle, i.e. just sufficient scope for the workmen to assist in the deposition of the sarcophagus.

A number of arguments and reasonings may be advanced in favour of the assumption that the deceased, who rested in the sarcophagus, could not have been any other than Maussollos' sister, wife, and queen, Artemisia:

Maussollos' body must have been cremated, and in all probability his ashes were deposited in the tomb chamber in an urn or a larnax of gold like the one discovered in the tomb attributed to Philip of Macedonia at Vergina.[78] No member of Maussollos' family, brother or sister, is reported to have died after Maussollos and before Artemisia,[79] and according to Strabo, the marriage of Maussollos and Artemisia was childless.[80] It is not reported in any ancient source where Artemisia was buried, but there is every reason to assume that she insisted on being laid to rest as close to Maussollos' tomb as possible, i.e. at any rate inside the Maussolleion enclosure, and perhaps even inside the monument.

When the plug-block had been shifted into position, it blocked the passage through the corridor, which therefore could be used to hold a sarcophagus, once the burial of Maussollos in the great chamber behind the corridor had taken place. The person who rested in the sarcophagus must have died after Maussollos, but before the entrance to the tomb was definitely closed. Possibly the final part of the sepulchral procedure was not accomplished immediately after Maussollos' burial, but postponed for some reason, presumably with the consent of his widow, and perhaps at her personal request.

According to Aulus Gellius, Artemisia "was said to have given many other proofs of the violence of her passion [than drinking her husband's ashes, cf. above note 78]; "for perpetuating the memory of her husband she also erected with enormous zeal and energy that highly celebrated tomb".[81] Moreover, it was said that she died of grief for her husband.[82] Under these circumstances she would hardly have permitted Maussollos' tomb to be permanently closed, while she was still alive and in a position to pay homage and perform sacrifices to the deceased in the very presence of his disembodied spirit in the tomb chamber.

When the corridor was planned and built, it was hardly envisaged that it might be used for any other purpose than that of giving access to the tomb chamber. If it had been set apart for the deposition of a sarcophagus for Artemisia, its dimensions would undoubtedly have been adjusted to satisfy such a requirement in more spacious surroundings. On the other hand, as the written sources testify, Artemisia's mental condition changed drastically in the course of her widowhood, and ultimately it may have been her most ardent wish to rest as closely to her husband as possible.

The "very low" doorway, which according to de la Tourette gave access to the anteroom adjoining the tomb chamber proper, might well have prevented the introduction of a sarcophagus for Artemisia into the tomb chamber. Besides, the tomb chamber should probably be seen as the strictly personal abode of the founder hero, for whom the monument had been erected, and not as an apartment for matrimonial use. However, the space of the corridor sufficed to contain a sarcophagus of modest dimensions, and it may be assumed that a sarcophagus of convenient size and reasonably good workmanship, though not ostentatiously luxurious in design and decoration, was immediately available on the market.

To judge from the fragment of a similar sarcophagus lid discovered at Kos (fragment e), this lid and the one from the Maussolleion may well have been manufactured in the same workshop. The find-spots suggest that this workshop was situated either at Halikarnassos or at Kos, and I am not aware of any other remains attesting its activities or whereabouts.

Unparalleled elsewhere, to my knowledge, is the type of sarcophagus lid not carved in one large slab of marble, but having a superstructure composed of separate pieces attached on top of the lower part of the lid. To the lower part must be attributed the fragments a and c which, however, differ so much in the composition of the marble they are made of (cf. the above-mentioned results of the stable isotopic ratio analyses of these fragments) that they cannot reasonably well have belonged to one and the same slab of marble. Either the fragments must have come from two different lids; or alternatively, the lower part of the lid to which they belonged was not monolithic, but subdivided into two halves each of individual geological composition.

The former possibility would imply that there were two sarcophagi in the Maussolleion, or that only fragments b, c, and d came from Artemisia's sarcophagus, while fragment a belonged to a sarcophagus standing somewhere outside the Maussolleion enclosure, from which position the fragment might have been thrown aside, eventually to end up in the NW corner of the Quadrangle where Newton found it.

However, it seems unlikely that a sarcophagus set up before the pre-Maussollan cemetery was decommissioned would have been permitted to remain in the area later incorporated in the enlarged city of Halikarnassos,[83] and even more improbable that any might have been placed in the neighbourhood of the Maussolleion enclosure, once this had been established.

If there were two sarcophagi inside the Maussolleion, one of them must have been intended for Maussollos. However, this inference is incompatible with the evidence, according to which his body was cremated. In all probability, as argued above (note 78), his bones were deposited in a larnax of gold, and while the type of sarcophagus of simple design that can be reconstructed from the fragments might well have sufficed to accommodate Artemisia's requirements, comparatively modest as they may have been, a lavishly decorated sarcophagus of much finer workmanship would undoubtedly have been needed to match the luxurious setting of Maussollos' tomb chamber.

Considering, however, the narrow dimensions of the corridor in which Artemisia's sarcophagus is assumed to have been placed (fig. 17.1), a composite lid would probably have been easier to handle than a monolithic one, as it could be assembled piecemeal, in particular if the lower part of the lid was composed of two sections.

In conclusion, to judge from the pros and cons advanced above, the surviving fragments are rather more likely to come from one and the same sarcophagus lid than from two different ones. At any rate, fragments b, c, and d are so closely compatible in terms of isotopic composition that they may well have belonged to the same sarcophagus, and possibly this was the one that was discovered in the anteroom by the Knights.

The available remains of sarcophagi surviving from the Classical epoch are too scanty to form a basis for generalizations as to what may have been habitual or exceptional in craftmanship in those days, but there is evidence from later periods that both receptacles and lids of sarcophagi were sometimes pieced together of several individual parts.[84] It is hard to imagine who else might have been buried in the corridor, if not Artemisia, and equally impossible to suggest another place at Halikarnassos where her grave should more likely be sought. The ancestral burial place of the Hekatomnid dynasty where she would have been entitled to rest was not at Halikarnassus, but at Mylasa. According to the literary evidence already quoted, it must have been her most ardent wish to lie as close to Maussollos as possible, and as she succeeded as satrap with absolute power at her spouse's death (after previously having shared the satrapal rule with him[85]), she was undoubtedly in a position to secure that her last wish was duly respected and duly carried into effect.

20. Catalogue of fragments of sarcophagus lids from Bodrum and Kos

All fragments are made of white marble of the composition described above in general terms. The veins run parallel, or approximately parallel, to the tooled surfaces.

a. *BM 1972.5-22.12*

Composed of two fragments. Found "within the north-west angle of the Mausoleum" (Newton, HD 114), i.e. in the immediate vicinity of the tomb chamber.

Angle piece of a sarcophagus lid, which had the form of a temple-like roof with a low pediment at either front. The lid was lined on all sides with a horizontal geison crowned by a sima, while members of the same size and profile were carried along the raking sides of the tympanum field.

At the corner, the raking sima terminates in a finely smoothed joint showing that most of it was added separately, whereas the raking geison underneath is broken and must have continued some way towards the centre of the pediment (cf. fragment b). The joint is preserved to a depth of c. 28 cm, reckoned inwards in a longitudinal direction from the upper edge of the raking sima, thus extending to a point considerably behind the projection of the horizontal geison below the pediment.

The overhanging soffit of the horizontal geison is 58 mm wide and is bordered by a drip (7.5 and 9 mm thick at the front and on the longer side, respectively) and a plain fillet at the rear, which is cut at an angle of about 60 degrees.

10-11 mm behind the fillet are incised setting lines indicating precisely where the lid should fit the outline of the receptacle underneath. As similar lines are not to be seen on the soffits of fragments c and d, which came from the longer sides of the lid, it must be assumed that setting lines on these sides were considered superfluous, once those at the corners were properly indicated.

The horizontal geison is moulded with a 61 mm high cavetto below and a plain, 6 mm high vertical fillet at the top. The horizontal sima is 66 mm high, measured at right-angles to the roof, and has the form of an elegant cyma recta, in which the curve at the lower extremity is somewhat more pronounced than the curve at the upper end.

On top of the sima on the longer side there remains half of a drilled 58 mm deep hole, 15 mm in diameter, which is placed only about 12 mm from the above-mentioned joint. Apparently the missing side of the hole broke away, when the object it contained was wrung or knocked out of it. However, there is no trace of the molten lead with which a clamp intended to fasten the adjoining part of the raking sima might have been fixed, and the position of the hole so close to the joint would not have been in keeping with such a purpose. Probably, therefore, the device had a different function.

Near the hole is a cut letter A, c. 9 mm high and 13 mm wide. This may indicate either one of the four corners of the lid, or one of its fronts, cf. the letter A incised on fragment b.

On the same surface remains a group of six small drilled holes – probably the deepest parts of holes, the upper parts of which were cut away when the piece received its final treatment – and an incised transverse line (at x) whose purpose is not apparent, cf. a similar line on fragment c.

The surface is dressed all over with the toothed chisel (teeth spaced 2-2.5 mm apart), but geison and sima on the fronts, and the sima on the longer sides are carefully polished. There is no trace suggesting that the lid was decorated with painted ornament, but this is not unlikely, considering the absence of any trace of sculptural decoration.

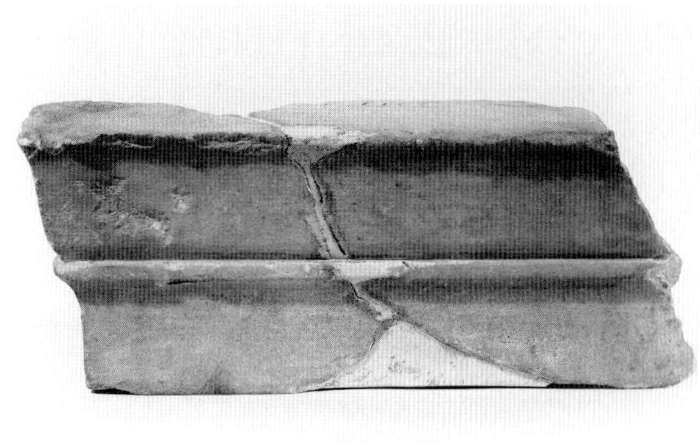

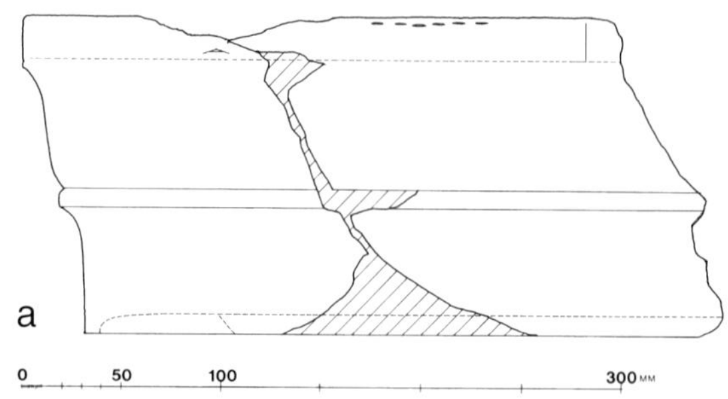

a

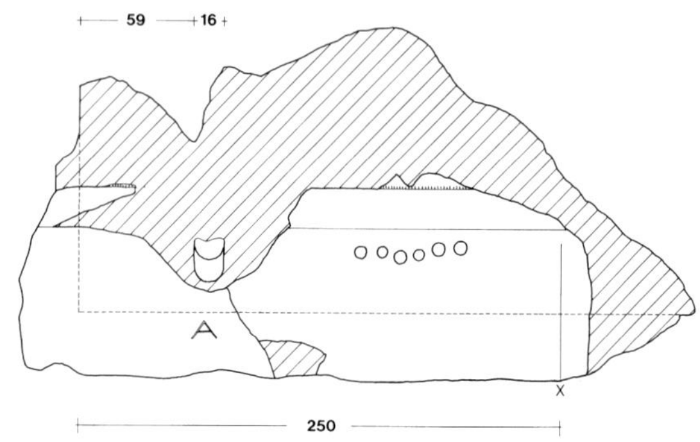

a

a

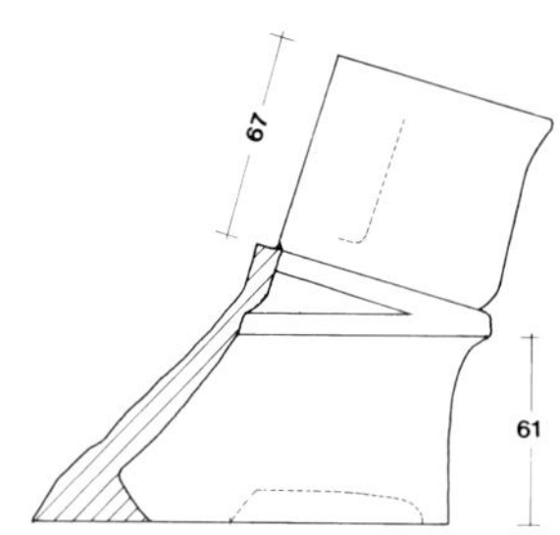

a

a

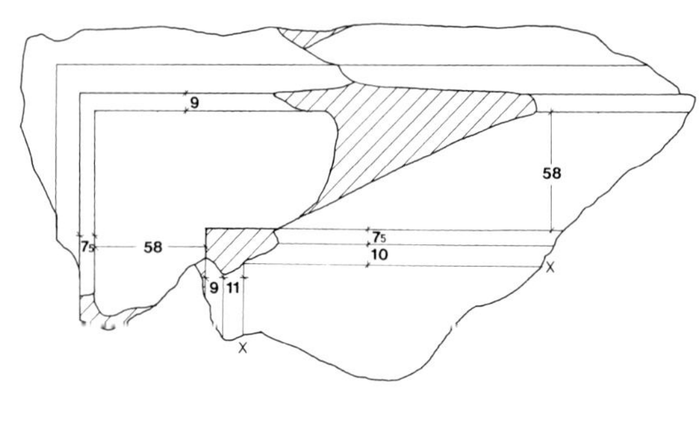

a

a

a

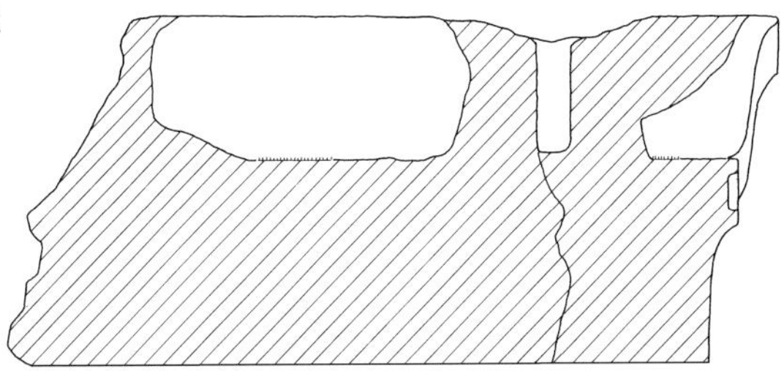

b. *Bodrum, Quadrangle*

Composed of two fragments. Find-spots not recorded. Identified by scrutiny of nondescript fragments.

The fragments comprise the anterior part of a geison exactly like the one preserved on fragment a. The concave overhang in its soffit is preserved to a distance of c. 65 mm from the front of the geison inclusive of the drip, i.e. very near the point where the fillet at the back of the cavity occurs on fragment a.

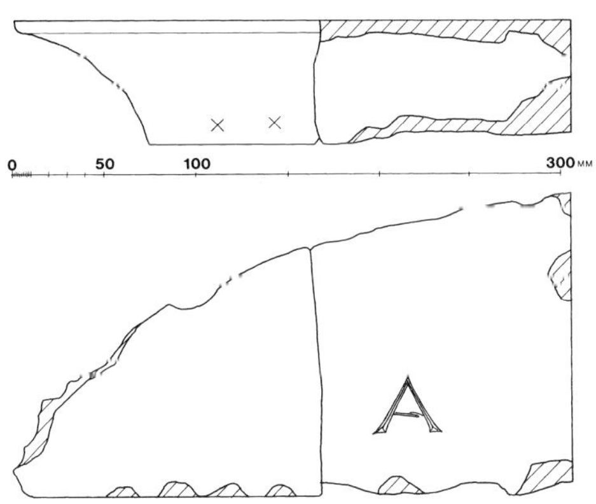

b

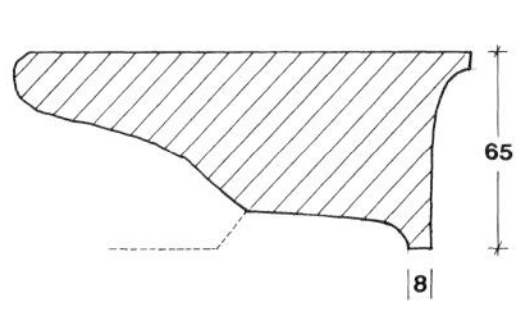

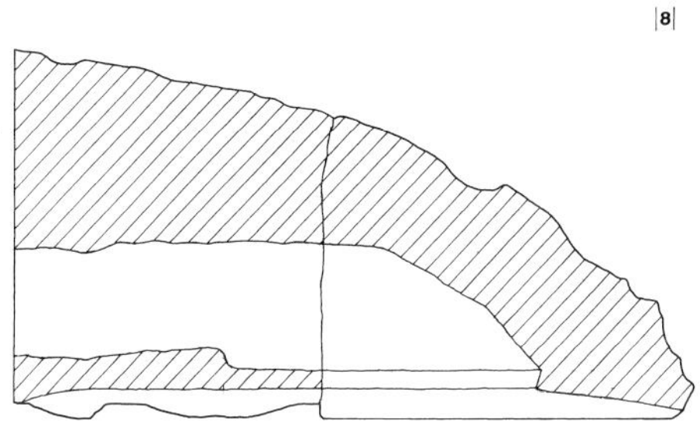

b

b

b

Fig. 20.1. Detail of Idrieus' dedication on architrave fragment K 81 from the South Propylaea at Labraunda (Jeppesen (1955) 26, fig. 18 and pl. X.7).

On the top surface, which is dressed with a fine claw chisel and polished along the front edge, is a beautifully carved capital letter A, c. 32 mm high. Its strokes, in which there remain traces of red paint, are angular in section and have serifs underneath, cf. the monumental type of letters used in the dedicatory inscriptions on the buildings erected at the time of the Hekatomnids in the sanctuary of Zeus at Labraunda.[86]

The scribe may well have been used to engraving letters of that type. At any rate, it was hardly the intention that the letter should remain visible when all the pieces of which the lid consisted had been put together. It is not likely, therefore, that the piece belonged to the part of the horizontal geison not covered by the sima, which was exposed to view in the pediments. In all probability, it was combined with a sima, but since the two members were cut in the same slab of marble on the longer sides of the lid (cf. fragment c), fragment b must come from the raking geison of one of the pediments. This conclusion agrees with the evidence of fragment a, on which the upper part of the raking sima was added separately on top of the raking geison.

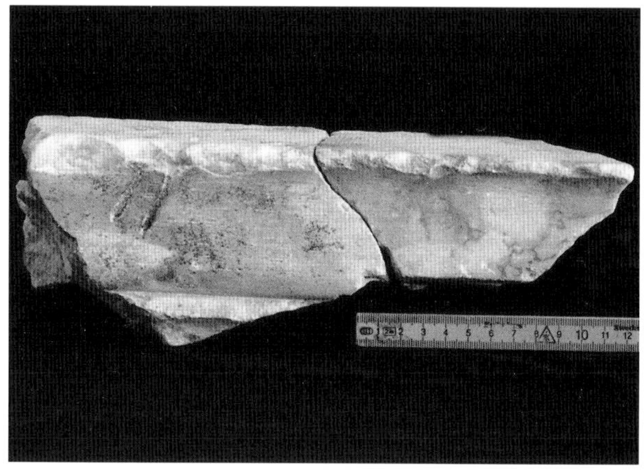

c

c

Faint traces of red paint are to be seen on the front of the geison (marked with crosses on the drawing).

c. *Bodrum, Quadrangle*

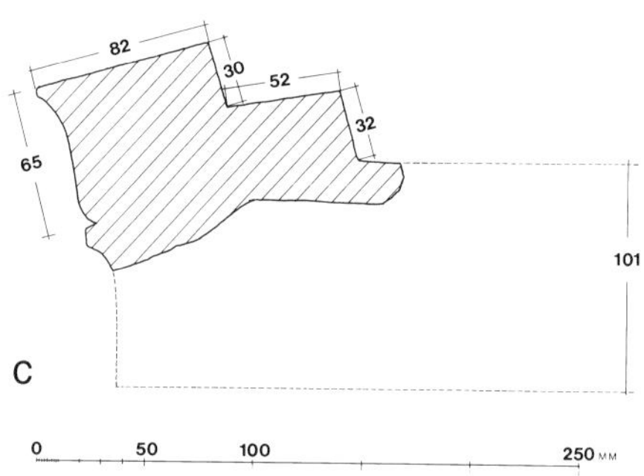

c

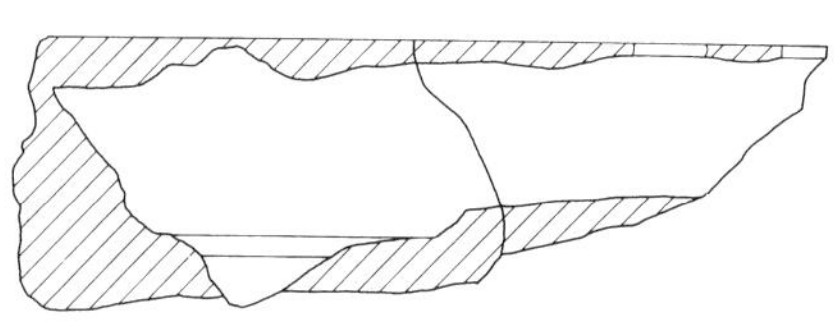

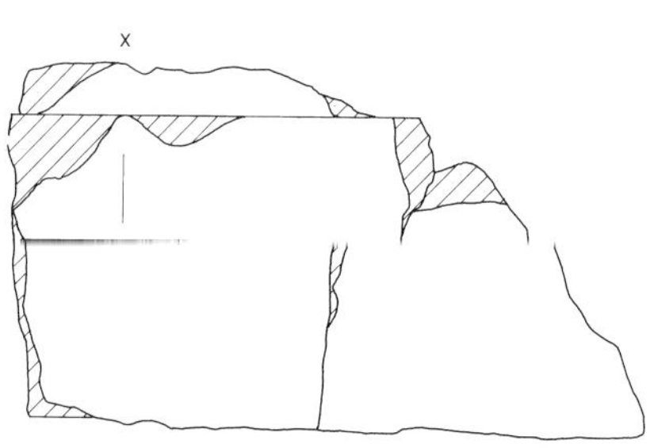

Composed of two fragments, one of which was found in square 9/5 south of the tomb chamber.

Fragment from one of the longer sides of a sarcophagus lid like that to which fragment a belonged, and possibly from one and the same lid. The lower part of the geison is missing, but the sima has the same height as the sima on fragment a, is decorated with an exactly similar moulding, and is polished in the same way.

Along the topmost edge of the sima, the slope of the roof is indicated by a 82 mm wide stripe dressed with a fine claw chisel. Behind this is a 30 mm deep and 52 mm wide rebate on which is incised a transverse line (at x), and 32 mm below the rebate is preserved part of the

c

d

horizontal interior top side of the big slab of marble, c. 10 cm thick inside the architectural framework on both sides, which constituted the lower part of the sarcophagus lid (101 mm thick on fragment e). This was undoubtedly monolithic from side to side, but possibly composed of two slabs in the longitudinal direction (cf. discussion above p. 103).

The rebates along its sides must have been intended to hold the topmost part of the lid representing the roof slope proper, which was probably composed of a number of sections laid athwart the ridge. The bottom of the rebate, and the interior top side of the lid have been smoothed with a claw chisel, while the vertical side of the rebate and the surface parallel to it below the rebate have been dressed with a flat chisel that was conducted at an oblique angle from above.

d. *Bodrum, Quadrangle*

XO 16. Find-spot not recorded. Identified by scrutiny of nondescript fragments.

Fragment comprising the lower part and soffit of a geison exactly like the one preserved on fragments a and b, except that an incised setting line like the one seen on the soffit of fragment a is missing. As the projection of the soffit, 59 mm, is almost exactly the same as on the lateral side of fragment a (58 mm), the piece can be plausibly ascribed to one of the longer sides of the lid. The soffit has been dressed with a fine claw chisel, its overhang smoothed, and the moulding polished.

d

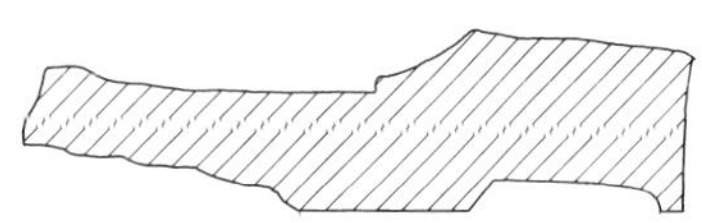

d

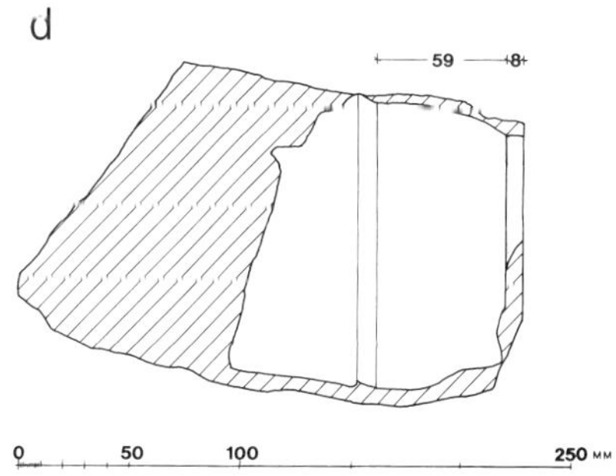

d

e. *Hospitallers' Castle, Kos.*

In 1986 the author found this fragment lying among other ancient fragments of sculpture and architecture in the Hospitallers' Castle at the harbour of Kos. It is now stored in the 'Mouseio architektonikon melon' inside the Castle. In the same museum I identified a fragment which, as proved by unmistakable characterisics, must have belonged to the bottom course of one of the coffers of the Maussolleion.[87] Presumably the latter piece happened to be discharged at Kos as ballast in a ship coming from Bodrum, and this might also have been the way in which the sarcophagus fragment ended up at Kos. It is, however, equally conceivable that it belonged to the lid of a sarcophagus which was used for a burial at Kos, and that this was manufactured in the same workshop as the sarcophagus from which the fragments found in the Maussolleion Quadrangle derived.

Fragment from one of the longer sides of the lower part of a sarcophagus lid of the same type as that to which the fragments a-d can be attributed. It is broken both in length and width, but the impressive dimensions that survive, c. 34 cm in width and 78 cm in length, suggest that it came from a slab of marble of considerable size. In section, it compares remarkably well to the fragments found in the Maussolleion Quadrangle except that the rebate in which the upper part of the lid rested is 14 mm wider than on fragment c. The two fragments, therefore, cannot be ascribed to the same lid, unless they are assumed to come from opposite sides. However, since the roof slope on fragment e is perceptibly lower than the one indicated on fragment a (see drawing fig. 20.2), the two fragments are most likely to come from two different sarcophagi.

In the middle of the rebate is a 24 mm deep hole 15 mm in diameter, and in the horizontal surface behind and below the rebate is a 47 mm deep cutting containing remains of molten lead.

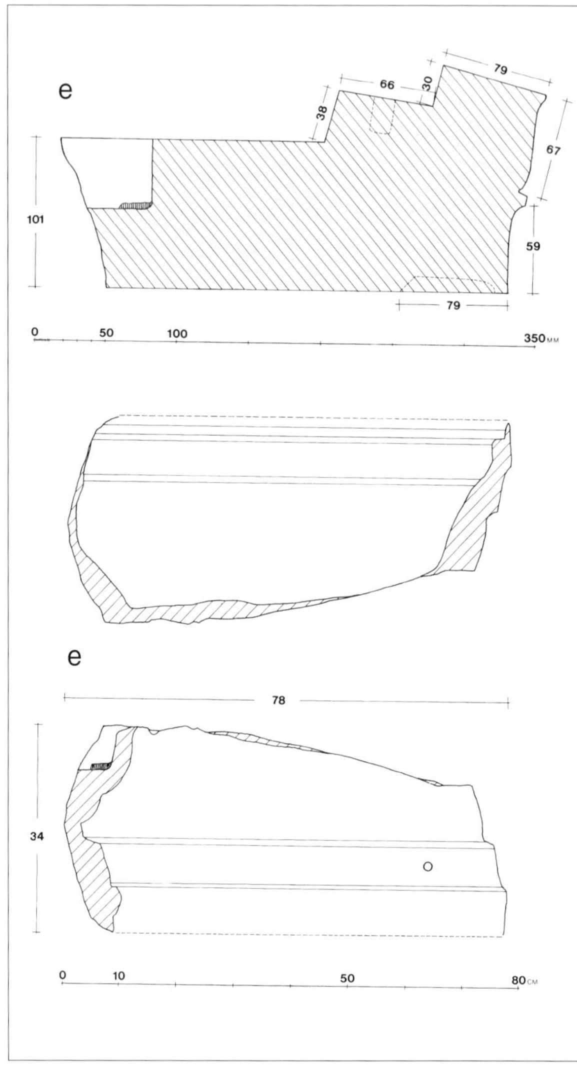

e

e

e

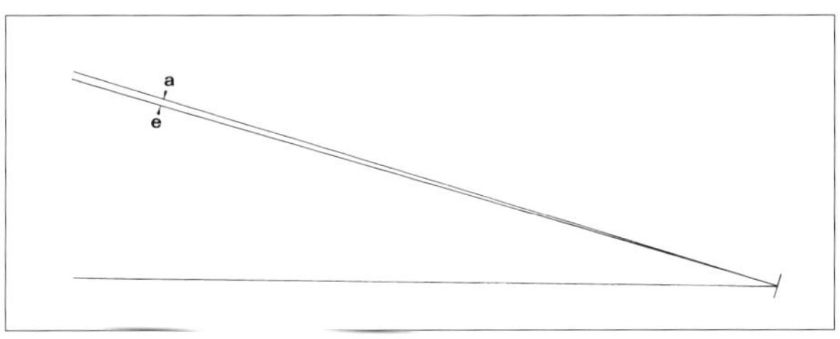

Fig. 20.2. Roof slopes at fragments a and e, respectively.

While still complete, the lid must have been exposed to the open air for a long period, for while the sloping surface in front of the rebate and the vertical side of the rebate itself are strongly corroded, the claw-chiselled surfaces further back retain their crisp character. The corrosion is characterized by small holes about half a millimetre in diameter. Such holes are not to be seen on the fragments from Bodrum, which show no conspicuous traces of weathering. Possibly the sarcophagus, to which the fragment from Kos belonged, stood in the open air for a long period, before its lid was smashed to pieces.

21. The tomb-robbers' subterranean mine

An irregularly cut passage in the bedrock which starts at the middle of the west side of the Quadrangle and follows a line along its longitudinal axis eastwards until it stops dead some seven metres past the centre of the Quadrangle was initially assumed by the Danish excavators to date from the time before the Maussolleion was built (figs. 1.18-19, 25, 28, 30-33; pls. E2, 7-9, 10, 11, marked T).

However, on closer examination of the available evidence it became clear that the passage must have been cut after the monument had been finished and at a time when it had not yet been fully demolished. For one thing, its bottom is rather irregularly cut and not at all as level as to provide a uniform basis for the courses of foundation slabs that would have been needed to fill up the cutting and to support the foundation courses above it.

Besides, the only entrance was from a vertical shaft cut in the bedrock immediately outside the west side of the foundations, which must have been cut after the foundations had been built, presumably for the purpose of tracing the position of the tomb chamber. And third, the passage must have been cut while the foundations above it were still in situ and daylight was not available, for holes for candles cut in the walls of the mine, in particular the innermost ones, prove that artificial light was needed.

In the westernmost part of the passage, its bed has a gentle slope towards the tomb chamber but is otherwise fairly even, and much the same is true of most of its eastward course beyond the tomb chamber. But where it passes along the tomb chamber, of whose south wall it happened to reveal the existence, it is strikingly irregular. Here the bed is not at all uniform, but cut down at various levels.

As the intruders came across the SW angle of the tomb chamber, they seem to have satisfied their curiosity by probing downwards until they reached the bottom level of the lowest wall course. Three metres further eastwards they made sure that the same course went on at the same level, then proceeded towards the SE angle of the tomb chamber, apparently without paying more attention to it for the time being and not at all suspecting that it might in any way be connected with the tomb chamber.

The logical inference is that the walls of the tomb chamber were built of foundation slabs of tufa and therefore thought at first sight to belong to foundations of the ordinary type of foundation masonry visible on the outside of the building. As demonstrated above (chapter 18), this assumption is supported by an examination of traces on the rock-cut sides of the tomb chamber, as well as by the technical argument that in order to support the corbelled vault properly, the upper courses of the walls facing the rock-cut sides (beginning with course C9 at level 678) must have been bonded with the courses of foundation slabs filling up the core of the building around the tomb chamber (p. 95).

The robbers therefore chose to continue some 8 m further eastwards until they reached the spot where the bedrock rises steeply (fig. 1.30, pls. E2, E8). The reason why they did not drive the mine any further in that direction was probably that they had already passed the centre of the ground plan of the building c. 19 m from its west side without making any discoveries rewarding their efforts: obviously the tomb chamber was not situated in the middle of the building, as they had probably anticipated, but must be sought elsewhere.

From the point that had been reached, a supplementary mine was driven southwards for some 6.5 m, and as this approach proved equally fruitless, extended some 4 m towards the west (figs. 1.30-32, pl. E11). At the last phase of prospecting, the height of the passage was gradually diminished to measure only 50-40 cm, thus forcing the workmen to crawl forward on their stomachs while using their tools (this difficult

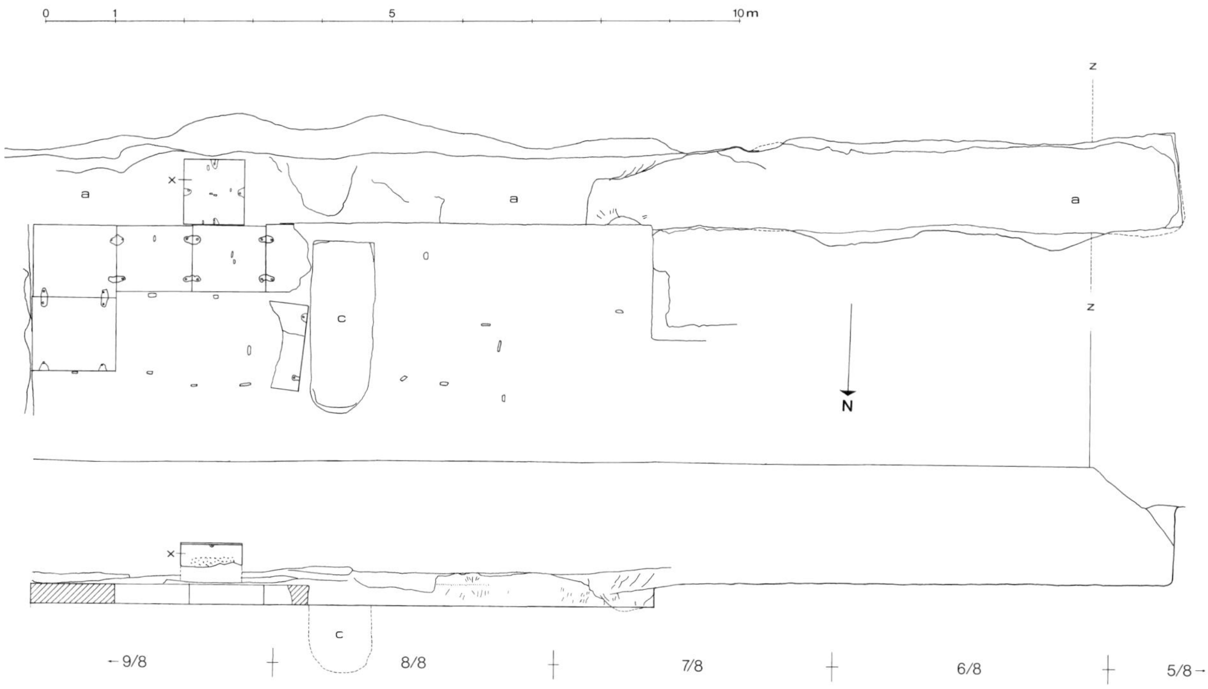

Fig. 21.1. Tomb-robbers' mine opposite and west of the tomb chamber in squares 8/8-5/8, plan (above) and elevation (below).
a-a Tomb-robbers' mine.
c Cavity in the rock-cut bottom of the tomb chamber (cf. chapter 22).
x Fallen foundation slab.
z-z W side of the Maussolleion foundations.

task may have been entrusted to boys), until eventually it was deemed useless to pursue investigations any further.

As the main passage was almost one metre wide, and its upper part was cut in a particularly soft layer of the bedrock not providing much support (cf. the rock-cut sides of the tomb chamber), the c. 90 cm wide foundation slabs of the course forming its roof (C9) were left hanging more or less in thin air, being fastened to the neighbouring ashlars exclusively by means of the clamps that connected them.

Inevitably some of these slabs would sooner or later fall down, as it happened to one that was found by the Danish excavators lying in the position exactly where it had fallen, perpendicularly underneath its original position (fig. 21.1 at X; pl. E7). This must have occurred a considerable time after the mine had been cut, for the slab was found resting on a c. 20 cm thick layer of earth that had accumulated above the rock-cut bottom of the passage.

When it fell, the courses of foundation slabs above the mine were evidently still in position, and the earth deposit could only have resulted from muddy rain torrents coming down from the mountains in winter and entering the passage through its entrance. While working in Bodrum, both Newton and his Danish successors had the opportunity to experience the violence of seasonal storms at Bodrum.[88] Presumably, however, the mine was not completely filled up with earth until after the Knights had completed their systematic demolition of the monument.

After the tomb chamber had been looted, the mine seems to have been used by local people as a kind of resort, possibly by shepherds for the purpose of securing their livestock. Based on earth fill about 15 cm above the rock-cut bottom of the passage, there remain in the innermost part of the mine a few fragments of tufa blocks constituting the lower part of a rubble wall (fig. 1.33, pls. E7-8 at q), and 3-4 m further eastwards (fig. 1.30, pls. E7-8 at p) pieces of the same material, perhaps the remains of a threshold.

Evidence confirming the assumption that

robbers eventually managed to find their way into the tomb chamber and stole its treasures was discovered in the mine between its entrance and the tomb chamber (diary 16.9-3.10.72), where gold ornaments were found similar to some of those excavated in a cavity in the rock-cut bottom of the tomb chamber (on this, see the following chapter, fig. 22.2).

Eleven gold items were found in the mine in square 8/8: rosettes, buttons, globular and half-globular beads, and lengths of exquisite gold thread. Only one gold item was unearthed outside the cavity, a solid ring lying at its western edge (cat.no. 41). It was pressed deep into the surface of the floor and only discovered when the floor was washed down with water.

Following a direction towards the entrance to the mine at its western end, the first items of gold in square 7/8 appeared some 70 cm west of the SW corner of the tomb chamber, where several gold threads and a rosette ornament were found lying on the bottom of the mine.

Digging westwards from this point, a layer immediately above the bottom of the mine, measuring 25 cm in height and consisting of earth and lumps of the soft yellowish rock, produced a triangular ornament, two semispherical beads, a button, and two long gold threads. Proceeding in the same direction a layer of earth mixed with lumps of yellowish rock produced one half-globular bead. Below this layer, in a layer of fine sand immediately above the bottom of the mine and in the middle of it, one metre from the SW corner of the tomb chamber, were found 19 gold objects, the most spectacular of which was the ornament of double gold plate cat.no. 52.

The layers of fine sand containing gold pieces which were observed in this place and further westwards in the mine (cf. below), may well have been deposited by seasonal rains, cf. Newton's information (HD 107) that "the soil in which they [the marbles found just outside the north wall of the Maussolleion enclosure] were lying was a fine sand, evidently deposited by the action of water".

From the part of the mine situated in square 6/8 only eleven gold objects and 14 gold threads were found, all in a fine layer of sand above the bottom of the mine.

However, the small area comprised in square 5/8 turned out to contain no less than 71 gold items, among these one cut in the shape of a dancing girl (cat.no. 67), twenty-seven gold threads and five beads of semi-precious stones. Most of them were lying in the NW corner of the mine, i.e. below its very exit, some in a layer of sand immediately above the bottom of the mine, some at levels as high as about 55 cm above the bottom (diary 16.9-3.10.72).

Evidently, much of this material must have been deposited very soon after the mine had been dug and before substantial layers of debris had accumulated in it. The likelihood is that it was inadvertently dropped by clandestine looters taking headlong flight for fear of being caught in their act.

It is remarkable that the finds were retrieved exclusively from square 8/8, approximately opposite the cavity in the tomb chamber, and from the squares west of it, 7/8-5/8, while none whatsoever were found in the innermost part of the mine east of square 8/8. Moreover, only precious objects were found, while fragments of alabaster vessels and sherds of 4th century pottery like those recovered from the cavity in the tomb chamber were not represented at all.

On the identity of those who dug the mine, see below p. 118. Evidence as to how and precisely where they managed to break into the tomb chamber will be dealt with in the following chapter.

22. The cavity cut in the rock-cut bottom of the tomb chamber, date and purpose

Unfortunately, the drawing of this cavity in plan and sections published in JdI 1992, Tf.22.2, was made on tracing paper and became inverted in copying. It is correctly reproduced in fig. 22.1 in the present volume.

In size and shape the cavity compares broadly to the inside of a modern bathtub. Its maximum length is 225 cm. In width it measures between 85 and 93 cm, in depth between 93 and 102 cm.[89] It has been roughly tooled all over with the pointed chisel, but while the east and south sides are approximately straight and perpendicular to a depth of some 50 or 60 cm, and are cut at right-angles to each other, the north and west sides are much less regular, both in plan and section.

In the lower part of the cavity, from c. 60-70 cm below its top, all its sides are rounded downwards, terminating not in a level bottom, but in an irregular depression which is almost 10 cm deeper in the northern than in the southern half of the cavity. In its lack of finish the cavity compares strikingly to the grave-robbers' mine, and if it was intended to hold a burial, it may be doubted that it was ever used for such a purpose. On the other hand, it is difficult to imagine any other function or functions of permanent applicability it might have been intended to serve.

If it had existed before the tomb chamber of the Maussolleion was built, it would undoubtedly have been filled up with slabs of tufa forming a solid basis for the pavement and its foundation course, and, in particular, for the south wall of the tomb chamber passing above it, through which much of the enormous weight of the superstructure would have had to be diverted.

In that case, the cavity would in all probability have been adjusted to fit the rectangular form of the foundation slabs, and its bottom would have been properly levelled in the same way as natural cavities and cavities evidently originating from pre-Maussollan activities such as the 'Green Stone Drain' and the 'Short Gallery'[90] were adapted to fit the requirements of the Maussolleion.

Besides, if the cutting had existed before the Maussolleion was built, it must have reached a level considerably above the floor of the tomb chamber (L478), perhaps even as high as that of the levelled bedrock around the tomb chamber (L678), for otherwise there could not have been access to it from the outside, and without access it could, of course, not even have existed. Moreover, if in actual fact it did exist, it must have had the form of a sort of perpendicular shaft leading nowhere and not to have been connected with any of the pre-Maussollan subterranean galleries, its bottom level at c. 376-385 being approximately 2 m lower than the bottom levels of the 'Short Gallery' and the 'Upper Gallery'.

Its longitudinal axis coincides precisely with the transverse axis of the big, rectangular cutting in the bedrock within which the tomb chamber was built, i.e. not including the walls facing the inside of the cutting, which were c. 30 cm thicker on the east than on the west side (fig. 17.2). This position suggests the possibility that the cavity was made after the Knights had demolished the walls and had stripped the tomb chamber of its marble pavement and of most of the foundation slabs underneath it, thereby laying bare its rock-cut bottom.

In that case, however, the cavity must have been cut at a time when the place was exposed to daylight, while there is evidence in the form of a small recess in its east side, of the type used to hold a candle found in several places in the tomb-robbers' mine (pls. E7-8), that in actual fact work on the cavity was accomplished by artificial light.

When excavated, the cavity was found to be filled with earth and disintegrated parts of the soft, yellowish rock of the site, scattered through which were tiny ornaments of gold plate, glass and agate beads, fragments of red-figured pot-

Fig. 22.1. Rock-cut cavity in the bottom of the tomb chamber completely emptied, looking S (1972). The same cavity in plan and sections.

C Line roughly delimiting the deepest part of the bottom.

D Lamp-hole.

E The spot where the gold ring no. 41 in the catalogue of gold finds was found.

tery, ribbed glass vessels, and alabaster vessels as well as objects of bone or ivory.[91]

As already mentioned (above, p. 114), gold ornaments similar to some of those found in the cavity were discovered in the robbers' mine between the tomb chamber and the entrance to the mine. However, in striking contrast to these finds, the only remnant of grave goods found on the bottom of the tomb chamber was the gold ring lying near the edge of the cavity (cat.no. 41).

Judging from datable evidence such as, in particular, the potsherds, it can hardly be doubted that both the deposit in the cavity and the pieces found in the mine came from Maussollos' tomb or from Artemisia's, or from both, and that the items in the mine were left by grave-robbers who had managed to force their way from the mine into the tomb chamber.

The evidence which will be discussed below suggests that they intruded exactly in the middle of the south wall of the tomb chamber, which must have been visible in its full extent on the side facing the mine (fig. 22.2). If so, they would have used the same procedure as the one applied when the mine was opened precisely in the middle of the west side of the Maussolleion foundations. The choice of the latter position was probably deliberate, for it implied the demolition of part of the south wall of the western staircase, where this abutted on the foundations (pls. E6, 12).

As there was no particular spot where an approach was easier or might be expected to prove more prolific than elsewhere, it might be argued, the middle of the wall seen in the mine might after all be the point most likely to reward a closer examination. Possibly the assumption initially held by the robbers (cf. above p. 112), that the masonry was just a particularly deep section of the massive foundations of the Maussolleion, might after all turn out to be true. Yet it might be worth the efforts involved to find out what lay behind the surface of the visible masonry, even if this was not Maussollos' tomb chamber, for if so this must be looked for elsewhere. Besides, the robbers might eventually have become aware of the plug-block and its possible implications.

To penetrate the c. 90 cm thick wall, they would have to hollow out gradually a recess widening downwards in depth to provide sufficient elbow room for the use of chisel and hammer (fig. 22.2). The inner side of the wall was probably sighted at the bottom of the recess, i.e. level with the rock-cut bottom of the tomb chamber, but at the time when this operation took place, the levelled surface of the bedrock inside the wall must still have been covered by a course of foundation slabs of greenish tufa and on top of

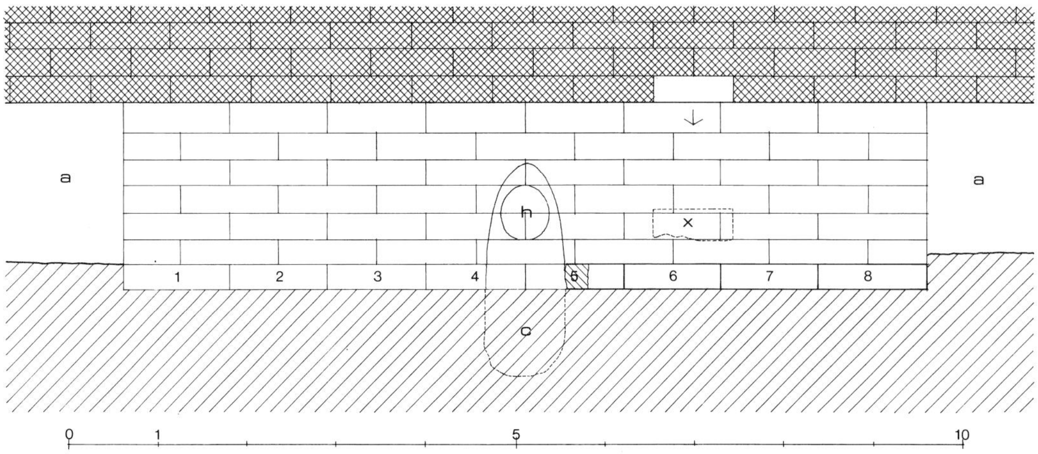

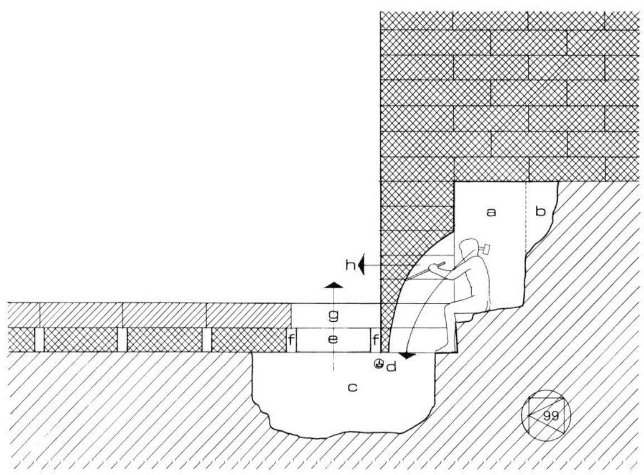

Fig. 22.2. Elevation and section of the S wall of the tomb chamber where the tomb-robbers appear to have intruded.

- a Tomb-robbers' mine
- b Soft layers of the bedrock which, when crashing, would have impaired support for the course of foundation slabs above the mine, one of which (x) was found to have fallen on the floor (cf. pl. E7).
- c Cavity in the rock-cut bottom of the tomb chamber (supplementary mine, cf. chapter 21).
- d Lamp-hole.
- e Foundation slab of greenish tufa.
- f Drain vents.
- g Pavement slab of white marble.
- h Point where the tomb-robbers may have entered, unless they preferred to break through from the cavity.

this a course of pavement slabs of white marble, altogether about 53 cm in height; and part of these slabs would have to be cleared away, if access to the tomb chamber was to be attempted from below.

Presumably in order to get a closer look at the obstacles lying ahead, and better scope for the work that would be needed to bring about the successful completion of the operation, it was decided to cut a supplementary mine extending underneath and northwards behind the wall. To make room for this, the western half of slab no. 5 of the foundation course for the wall (fig. 22.2) had to be cut away, while the other half of the slab remained embodied in the masonry and can still be seen in situ (fig. 21.1).

Slab no. 4, now completely lost, must have been curtailed to a similar extent for the same purpose. To provide sufficient space for the feet of the workman in charge, while he was seated in a convenient position on the bottom of the mine, the supplementary branch was begun along a line c. 30 cm inside the front of the wall.

The new trench must have permitted the observation that the foundation slabs covering the mine behind the wall (e) were separated by small intervals (the drains, at f), and that between them could be glimpsed the underside of the superincumbent pavement slabs of white marble (g). These indications must have convinced the intruders that they were on the right track, and that a complete break-through could be accomplished either by clearing away some of the foundation and pavement slabs above the trench, or by deepening and breaking through the recess in the wall (at h).

Then must have followed the pillage. After the robbers had taken possession of the most precious grave goods – among which was perhaps the golden casket in which Maussollos' bones may be assumed to have been contained – less costly items like tatters of gold-embroidered textiles were probably strewn all over the marble pavement.

From these positions some items may have been removed by subsequent robbers while others remained lying on the floor where they were later observed by the Knights from Rhodes supervising the complete demolition of the monument in 1522 (below, Appendix 3).

The latter items must have been cleared away when the tomb chamber was stripped of its pavement and course of foundation slabs, and just the contents of the cavity in the rock-cut bottom of the chamber remained untouched until it was discovered and emptied by the recent excavators.

The observations made during the excavation of the cavity can be summed up as follows (diary 24.6-9.7.72):

To a depth of about 15-20 cm the fill consisted of brownish earth intermixed with lumps of the yellowish rock. Further downwards, at a depth of c. 40 cm, it assumed the character of sterile yellowish clay. C. 85-90 cm below the top level of the cavity was observed, under the yellow earth, a layer of sand which was found to contain a large amount of gold ornaments, cf. similar deposits of sand intermixed with gold pieces discovered in the robbers' mine (above, p. 114).

In the fill were also gold items scattered in the upper layers, pot sherds, both of decorated pottery and of coarse ware, fragments of white marble and splinters of greenish tufa. That at least part of the finds fell into the cavity directly from the tomb chamber is suggested by the finds of a small knob and three bigger ones that came from the double-door in the corridor (cat.nos. O-R). Actually the door fragments F and G which both have holes for knobs were found inside the tomb chamber, in squares 9/9 and 7/9. The context suggests that the robbers entered through a hole in the floor of the tomb chamber through which remains of grave goods might subsequently have fallen into the cavity.

The fragments of marble and splinters of greenish tufa could have resulted from breaking through the pavement and foundation slabs of the floor, while the rock particles may have come from the soft upper layers of the sides of the principal mine, much of which was found to have crumbled away (fig. 22.2 at b).

Since the cavity was situated considerably below the level of the mine, the earth found in it is likely to have been deposited by floods entering the mine through the shaft at its entrance and bringing with it quantities of mud from the mountain slopes north of the Maussolleion. By this process, some of the gold items dropped in the mine may have ended up in the cavity, but as the earth fill grew, the mine ceased to be accessible and inhabitable. Eventually the entrance through the cavity and the recess cut in the wall must have been completely blocked up, and was hardly known to exist when the monument was completely demolished in 1522.

It must have taken a long time – weeks at the least, if not months – to cut the mine, and an achievement of such an extent could not have passed unnoticed by the neighbouring population. Presumably there was no local authority to prevent gangs of professional grave-robbers from trying their luck wherever a promising object to plunder could be found. Or, if such an authority existed, he might have been tempted to share the profit with the robbers.

23. Catalogue raisonné of finds from the cavity in the tomb chamber and the tomb-robbers' mine, part 1:

Gold ornaments and beads of semiprecious stones and glass.

Introductory note[92]

By far the larger part of the gold objects consists of dress ornaments: circular discs, rosettes of various size and decoration, half-globular beads of various sizes, and tiny buttons. A few ornaments are represented only by a single specimen, e.g. the figured appliqués, cat.nos. 14, 15, and 67, and the star-rosette cat.no. 74. The types of circular discs and rosettes are known from Asia Minor, from Macedonia and from the Pontic area, ranging in date from the 8th/7th century BC to the 1st/2nd century AD (parallels are referred to in the catalogue).

Appliqués with gorgoneia and lions' heads are well attested as types, but no exact parallels can be found. The appliqué in the shape of a girl dancing with her hands clasped above her head, cat.no. 67, possibly represents her performing the Persian OKLASMA, but her general appearance is Greek. Exact parallels are found only for the ornaments cat. nos. 52 and 24, both in Asia Minor. An ornament similar to cat. no. 52, only smaller, now in the British Museum, comes from the excavations at Ephesos. In the Kunst und Gewerbe Museum in Hamburg, ornaments like cat.no. 24 (cf. cat.nos. 53, 62, 80) can be seen. They allegedly come from a tomb in Smyrna, while some in the Brooklyn Museum and the Berry collection in Indiana are from 'Asia Minor'. The same type is represented by 174 appliqués found in the tomb of "the Carian princess" uncovered in 1989 in Bodrum.[93] This tomb contained a plain undecorated stone sarcophagus, which when opened revealed the undisturbed burial of a woman decked with spectacular jewellery and a great variety of dress ornaments. These finds are now on display in the Bodrum Museum of Underwater Archaeology.

The large amount of fine gold lamellae among the gold pieces from the Maussolleion is of particular interest. The lamellae are made from hammered gold foil cut into strips 0.02-0.1 mm wide, some even thinner, some as today's finest sewing thread. They are proof that a cloth or dress woven with gold was part of the burial. Such textiles have actually come to light in the excavations at Vergina and at Kertsch.[94] The purple and gold cloth found at Vergina includes gold lamellae similar to those from the Maussolleion, simple, tiny lamellae cut from hammered gold foil.[95] The lamellae from the Maussolleion burial (cat. nos. 40, 48, 61, 66, and 88) are preserved in lengths varying between 0.6 and 7.9 cm. They appear wrinkled, showing the imprint of the warp, presumably wool. The preserved maximum length, 7.9 cm, corresponds well with the statement by goldsmiths, reported by Dr. Jaro of the Textile Museum in Budapest, that only a palm sized piece of gold foil can be hammered uniformly into thin leaf.[96] The gold lamellae, however, give no clue whatsoever as to what type of cloth or what kind of design they belonged to.

The gold thread found at Kertsch is of another type, of circular section and easier to work with. It is mentioned in the report on the excavations at Kertsch in 1878-79: "... übrigens sind auch diese Gold-Fäden, wie alle übrigen, bisher im südlichen Russland gefundenen, fein gedreht und lassen daher keinen Zweifel daran übrig, dass sie ursprünglich in Verbindung mit einem zweiten Faden von einem leichter vergänglichen Stoff zusammen gesponnen waren".[97]

These gold threads, "fein gedreht", presumably originally had a core of linen or silk, which had disintegrated at the time of excavation. This type of gold thread, wound z- or s-wise around a core, is known also from the tomb of a Sarmatian 'priestess' at Sokolova Mogila from the 1st century AD. The reconstruction of her dress gives an idea of what such a gold-woven and gold-decorated garment looked like.[98]

Apart from the finds from the early excavations at Kertsch, the only find from a Greek locality which attest the technique of creating the twisted gold thread is a fragment of a linen cloth recovered from a bronze vessel allegedly found at Koropi near Athens.[99] Its present whereabouts are not known, but the cloth is kept at the Victoria and Albert Museum in London. The linen is embroidered with a design of pacing lions in Achaemenid style made of true gold and silver thread, i.e. lamellae wound around a linen or silk core, each lion being placed in the centre of a lozenge.

The Achaemenid style of the embroidery may indicate that the cloth was made in the East where the art of making gold thread was known in the 5th century BC.[100]

Other Greek sites have so far yielded only gold lamellae isolated or incorporated in weavings. The earliest find derives from the vaulted tombs at Mesara in southern Crete of Early Minoan date. Among the pottery and bronze objects from tholos A at Platanos is "a tangled mass of flat wire". The "wires" are flat, about 1 mm wide, and wrinkled like the Maussolleion lamellae.[101]

Some of the gold items from the Maussolleion are jewellery or pieces of jewellery, for instance the tear-shaped earring, cat. no. 16, the solid cast ring, cat.no. 41, and the globular and oblong beads. The double rosette, cat.no. 12, with the protruding tube at the back, could be an earring, and the flat rings, cat.no. 1, may belong to earrings, although they show no traces of attachment at the back. The palmette, cat. no. 13b, is broken from a larger ornament, in which it may have been inlaid. A palmette of similar shape is seen inlaid on the hilt of an iron sword from Vergina.[102]

The jewellery pieces may be viewed together with the beads of semiprecious stones and glass found scattered in the cavity and in the robbers' mine. Comparative material will be referred to in connection with the cat.nos. 89-105. In the British Museum are a gold sheet and two beads, one of glass and one of sardonyx, which are reported to originate from Newton's excavations of the Maussolleion. The gold sheet and the sardonyx piece were found in the outskirts of the Quadrangle, while the other bead was recovered from "the soil of the platform"[103]

None of these items are paralleled among the recent finds from the Maussolleion, but the glass bead resembles one of the gold items from the "Tomb of the Carian Princess" (HalStud 1 (1994), 92, fig. 11), and though it is much larger, the sardonyx piece is typologically comparable to our cat.no. 89.

Gold is natural to the East Greek area, and gold jewellery was produced in the East Greek cities in the 8th century BC, especially in Ephesus, and on Rhodes. In the 6th, and especially in the 5th century BC, the production was on a much lower scale, but the 4th century shows a marked increase in the output of gold jewellery coinciding with the growing wealth of the East Greek cities of Lydia and Caria. At the excavations at Sardis in the 1960s, a series of furnaces for refining gold were unearthed.[104] The Maussolleion gold is thus most probably the work of local craftsmen.

As mentioned above, some objects find their exact parallels within the same area and others show influence from the East, as might well be expected. The gold ornaments include several simple types which seem to have been produced through several centuries and do not offer any safe ground for dating. The appliqués for the burial dress and the other grave gifts may represent a mixture of old and new material, heirlooms as well as ornaments made for the occasion.

Pending preparations for the publication of the second part of the catalogue, a few words of introduction should be said about the objects that will be dealt with in a supplementary issue:

In the cavity a couple of hundred fragments of glass were found ranging from mere splinters to fragments of rims and walls of vessels, plain or decorated. As the fragments are all fairly small, it is hardly possible to determine the shapes represented with any certainty. In all instances the glass is transparent, often with bubbles, a shiny yellowish or sometimes greenish patina and eroded surface. The vessels were probably made by placing ground cullet in a mould which was then slowly heated for the glass to fuse. After removal from the mould, the decoration was cut and the vessel polished. The decoration mainly consists of horizontal parallel grooves, vertical flutes, and little nicks.

Also in the cavity was found a considerable number of fragments of ivory or bone (an osteological analysis of the material will determine the proper designation). Most of them are small and plain, but some have carved decoration suggesting that they should be seen as remains of inlays or veneerings for wooden furniture.

Among the gold ornaments, fragments of ivory or bone, and sherds of glass vessels excavated in the cavity were also fragments of alabaster vessels and sherds of red-figured pottery. The pottery fragments clearly date from the first half of the 4th century BC, showing heads of kalathiskos dancers, an arm of a Scythian, drapery in relief lines, egg-and-dart borders, and a chequered maeander. It seems safe to assume, therefore, that both the pottery and the other objects found in the cavity came from the Maussolleion, and arguments will be produced below in support of the assumption that the finds from the cavity and from the robbers' mine derive from one and the same source, primarily from Maussollos' tomb chamber, but probably also from Artemisia's burial in the corridor adjoining the tomb chamber. Together with the fragments from objects of other materials, the Maussolleion gold bears witness to a lavish burial containing many different grave gifts.

From the gold ornaments alone there is evidence of jewellery, objects inlaid with gold ornaments, textiles decorated with gold appliqués, and gold-woven cloth possibly carrying some elaborate design. Since Maussollos' corpse was cremated (above, note 78), his bones and ashes could well have been wrapped in a gold-woven cloth like the one enclosing the burnt bones of a woman deposited in a gold larnax which was found in the antechamber of the tomb attributed to Philip of Macedonia.[105] If it was Artemisia who rested in the sarcophagus seen by the Knights to which fragments of a lid found in the Quadrangle can be attributed (chapters 19-20), it seems likely that remains from both burials would have been mixed with one another. It may be reasonably expected, therefore, that the finds are fairly representative in both respects. On this issue, more will be said below. The gold ornaments and beads of semiprecious stones and glass are both in the Bodrum Museum of Underwater Archeology, carrying the reg. nos. 6356-6443 and 6444-6450, respectively. In the following list comprising altogether 105 items or groups of items, the finds are classified according to materials and find spots:

Gold finds from the cavity comparing with similar items from the robbers' mine, as shown in the lists below, indicate that the finds may well be contemporary and come from one and the same context:

GOLD			
Square 8/8	Cat.nos.	1-40	From the cavity
–		41	Found at the edge of the cavity
–		42-48	From the robbers' mine
Square 7/8		49-61	– –
Square 6/8		62-66	– –
Square 5/8		67-88	– –
BEADS OF SEMIPRECIOUS STONES AND GLASS			
Square 8/8	Cat.nos.	89-98	From the cavity
Square 7/8		99	From the robbers' mine
Square 5/8		100-105	– –

A

Gold items cat.nos. 1-40 from the cavity as compared to cat. nos. 42-88 from the robbers' mine:

1	–
2	50, 70
3	69
4	55, 71
5	–
6	53, 62, 80
7	49, 68
8a	–
8b	42b, 51
8c	42a, 73
9	72
10	–
11	–
12	–
13a	–
13b	–
14	–
15	–
16	–
17	–
18	–
19	43
20	77
21	58, 78
22	44, 59, 79
23	(no ill.)
24	53, 62, 80
25	60, 81-82
26	81-82
27	84
28	46
29	–
30	83
31	–
32	–
33	56, 63
34	–
35	–
36	–
37	–
38	–
39	–
40	48, 61, 66 (no ill.), 88.

B

Gold items cat. nos. 42-88 from the robbers' mine as compared to cat. nos. 1-40 from the cavity. In brackets are given the number of specimens of each well-defined type found in the robbers' mine (first figure) and in the cavity (second figure).

42a	8c (3-3, incl. no. 73)
42b	8b (3-6, incl. no. 51)
43	19 (1-4)
44	22 (18-39, incl. nos. 59, 64, 79)
45	25-26 (26-104, incl. nos. 60, 65, 81, 82)
46	28 (1-3)
47	–
48	40
49	7 (4-4, incl. no. 68)
50	2 (2-4, incl. no. 70)
51	8b (cf. no. 42b)
52	–
53	24 (cf. no. 62)
54	21 (22-21, incl. no. 78)
55	4 (2-7, incl. no. 71)
56	33 (6-9, incl. nos. 63a, 86)
57	37b (1-1)
58	21 (3-21)
59	22 (cf. no. 44)
60	25-26 (cf. no. 45)
61	40, 48, 88
62	24 (9-18, incl. nos. 53, 80)
63a	33 (cf. no. 56)
64	22 (cf. no. 44)
65	25-26 (cf. no. 45)
66	40 (cf. no. 61)
67	–
68	7 (cf. no. 49)
69	3 (1-2)
70	2 (cf. no. 50)
71	4 (cf. no. 55)
72	9 (1-2)
73	8c (cf. no. 42a)
74	–
75	–
76	–
77	20 (3-5)
78	21 (cf. no. 54)
79	22 (cf. no. 44)
80	24 (cf. no. 62)
81	25-26 (cf. no. 45)
82	25-26 (cf. no. 45)
83	30 (1-7)
84	27 (1-4)
85	–
86	33 (cf. no. 56)
87	34 (1-3)
88	40 (cf. nos. 48, 61, 66)

It should be noted that due to the dispersion of the finds in the robbers' tunnel, samples of the same type were collected individually in different places, thus:

Nos. 42a, 73 in squares 8/8, 5/8
- 42b, 51 in squares 8/8, 7/8
- 44, 59, 64, 79 in squares 8/8 - 5/8
- 45, 60, 65, 81, 82 in squares 8/8 - 5/8
- 49, 68 in squares 7/8, 5/8
- 54, 78 in squares 7/8, 5/8
- 56, 63a, 86 in squares 7/8 - 5/8
- 62, 53, 80 in squares 7/8 - 5/8

By juxtaposition of the two columns A and B, it will be seen that 22 items from the cavity are not paralleled by any found in the robbers' mine, while only 7 of those found in the mine are not comparable with any coming from the cavity.

Of most of the types common to both places only a few specimens come from the mine, while many more were found in the cavity.

Statistics cannot well be based on the small number of beads of semiprecious stones and glass that were found in the cavity and in the mine, 10 and 7, respectively. It seems possible, though, that no. 96 from the cavity and no. 102 from the mine belonged to one and the same necklace.

As argued above, there is ample evidence in support of the conclusion that the finds from the cavity and the mine came from Maussollos' tomb chamber, and it may well be assumed that they were mixed to some extent with funerary furnishings from Artemisia's sarcophagus. If so, it might be possible in theory, at least, to distinguish gold appliqués particularly typical of female dresses from those more often used for the garments of men.

Most of the repertory of appliqués represented in the 'Tomb of the Carian Princess' is entirely different from the material found in the Maussolleion, however, with one obvious exception: between knee and ankle were found a total of 174 appliqués of exactly the same type as the one represented by 27 pieces excavated in the Maussolleion (cat. nos. 24, 53, 62, 80). Possibly, therefore, the latter pieces came from a garment wrapped around Artemisia's legs in her sarcophagus. Admittedly, these ornaments are so slovenly made that they would hardly have been accepted for any royal burial of conventional standards, and least of all for that of Maussollos whose funeral was known to have been planned in every detail by his widow. Only pieces of first-rate craftmanship like the rosettes cat. nos. 10-12 and the figural appliqués cat.nos. 14-15 might have matched the requirements of the luxurious setting she reportedly wanted to establish for the after-life of her husband.[106]

Nothing is positively known of the circumstances under which her own burial took place. Unless death overcame her unexpectedly, she could have made due preparations for the sepulchral ceremony in all details, and even have ensured that her intentions were carried duly into effect. At her death, the new satrap Idrieus and his sister and co-ruler Ada must have taken over immediately. Whatever was their personal attitude towards the deceased, they may have found it convenient to entrust the practical management of the burial to officials usually in charge of such operations, perhaps leaving it to these to carry out their functions at their own discretion and at a reasonably modest rate of expenditure. If such an arrangement is assumed, it may account both for the mediocre quality of the sarcophagus, in which she is supposed to have been laid (above, chapter 19), and for the second-rate execution of some of the appliqués most likely to have decorated her grave-clothes. Very few of the surviving pieces of jewelry seem to be definitely female in character. Possibly, however, the tiny bobbin-like object cat. no. 17 should be understood to hint at female occupations.

Catalogue of gold ornaments and beads of semiprecious stones and glass.[107]

The references to comparative gold items are due to Mrs. Bundgaard Rasmussen who also took the photos. As the exact dimensions of the details of each individual piece can be deduced from the scale shown on the photos, the maximum measurements of the gold items recorded are only approximations to integral numbers of millimetres. However, as regards the objects of polished, semiprecious stones nos. 89-91, 95-97, 99-104, indications of greater precision were deemed appropriate and achieved by using an electronic measuring instrument (tolerance 0.03 mm).
Note that photos of cat. nos. 23 and 66 were not available, and that the photos of cat. nos. 1, 21, 22, 25-26, 60, 78, and 80-81 show only selections of the groups of items to which they refer.

(1) Gold items found in the cavity in square 8/8:

1. Three flat rings, each embossed with twelve dots. Around the inner and outer edge raised rim. Composed of two sheets of gold, the lower one not having the raised rim. The rings show no traces of attachment. Diam. c. 11 mm. Mus. no. 6356.
Cf. Greifenhagen I, Tf. 23.6 (ex Merle de Massoneau, 1st-2nd cent. AD); Rudolph (1995) no. 22 K-M.

2. Four circular discs with convex centre and a groove around the edge. One is pierced at the edge at two opposite points. The rest are pierced at three irregularly placed points, some in the grooves, some within the centre. The discs are cut rather roughly from gold sheet. One is damaged. Diam. between 11 and 12 mm. Mus. no. 6357.
Cf. MonPiot 26 (1923) 115, fig. 10 (Kertsch, 2nd-3rd cent. AD).

3. Two circular discs with convex centre and corrugated border. Pierced at three points along the margin for attachment. Diam. c. 12 mm. Mus. no. 6358.

4. Seven circular discs with convex centre and raised edge. Pierced at opposite points for attachment. One piece is damaged. Diam. c. 6 mm. Mus. no. 6359.

5. Circular disc with convex centre. Twenty raised dots around the outer edge. Pierced at opposite points for attachment. Diam. c. 7 mm. Mus. no. 6360.
Cf. Greifenhagen I (1970) pl. 28.8 (southern Russia, 2nd-3rd century AD; BMCJ (1911) no. 1190, pl. 12 (from Kameiros, Rhodes, 7th century BC); Louvre (1924) 6, no. 66-67, pl. 1 (from Kertsch); Brooklyn (1984) no. 32 (with 14 raised dots, 4th century BC).

6. Ovoid-shaped ornament. At the top two rows of raised dots. Groove around the edge. Max. dimensions c. 11 x 8 mm. Mus. no. 6361.

7. Four ornaments in the form of equilateral triangles. On the reverse a loop at each corner. Side length c. 7 mm. Mus. no. 6362.

8a. Two rosettes with eight concave petals around central knob. Petals bordered by raised edge. Pierced at four points. Diam. c. 7 mm. Mus. no. 6363.

8b. Six rosettes with seven concave petals around central knob. Petals bordered by raised edge. Pierced at four points. Diam. c. 6 mm. Mus. no. 6363.

8c. Three rosettes with six convex petals around central knob. Petals bordered by raised edge. Pierced at three points. Diam. c. 6 mm. Mus. no. 6363.

9. Two plain rosettes with six convex petals. Irregularly cut. Pierced between petals at three points around central knob. Diam. c. 8 mm. Mus. no. 6364.

10. Rosette with eight convex petals bordered by raised edge around raised centre. Pierced at three points between the petals. Diam. c. 11 mm. Mus. no. 6365.
Cf. Breitenstein (1941) no. 582, pl. 71 (two gilded terracotta rosettes from grave at Tanagra, found lying at the breast of the deceased. Hellenistic).

11. Five rosettes with six convex petals around central knob. Petals borded by beaded wire. Every second petal pierced for attachment. Diam. c. 10 mm, 9 mm, and 5 mm, respectively. Mus. no. 6366.
Cf. Greifenhagen I (1970) Tf. 4,8 (from grave at Corinth, 8th century BC); BMCJ (1911) no. 1952, pl. 35 (necklace from Tarentum, 4th century BC); ibid. nos. 1653-4, pl. 30 (earrings from Eretria, c. 420 BC).

12. Double rosette. The larger rosette has six petals, the smaller five petals around central knob. Each petal is bordered by thin gold wire. A cylindrical tube pro-

jects at the back. Diam. c. 12 mm. Height c. 5 mm. Mus. no. 6367.
Cf. Greifenhagen I (1970) Tf. 28,19 (from southern Russia. Has been inlaid with reddish paste. Ring loop at the back. 3rd century BC); Thrakische Kunst (1973) fig. 196 (double rosettes as parts of earrings. From Vraca, 400-350 BC); BMCJ (1911) no. 1952 (necklace from Tarentum with triple rosettes, 4th century BC).

13a. Palmette. Cast with hook at the back. Height c. 8 mm. Mus. no. 6368.

13b. Palmette of the brush-like type. No loop or hook at the back. Possibly broken from some larger ornament. Mus. no. 6368.
Cf. Carapanos (1878) pl. 47,11 (handle ornament from bronze vase, palmette between two volutes); Vergina (1984) figs. 99-100 (brush palmette of gold inlaid on the hilt of a sword from the tomb attributed to Philip).

14. Die-formed appliqué in the shape of a lion's head. The mane is rendered in horizontal waves, the ear triangular, and the forehead bulging. The edge is raised around the open mouth. Pierced at four points. Length and width c. 11 mm. Mus. no. 6369.
Cf. for the type, Amandry (1958) 9, pl. 7,1; Greifenhagen II (1975) Tf. 12,4 (lion's head in necklace, southern Russia, 3rd century BC); ABC (1854) pl. 8,3; Artamonov (1969) pl. 263 (Kul Oba).

15. Die-formed appliqué in the shape of a gorgoneion bordered by a corrugated edge. Wavy hair above the forehead, flat nose and prominent cheeks. The mouth is wide open, the tongue protruding, and the eyes large and bulging. Four holes for attachment. Diam. c. 12 mm. Mus. no. 6370.
Cf. From the Land of the Scythians (1973/74) 104 (Greek bronze handle, 6th century BC); Providence (1976) cat. no. 20 (Disc with head of Medusa, provenance unknown, 4th century BC); Thrakische Kunst (1973) fig. 226 (cuirass plate, Duvanli, mid-fifth century BC); Artamonov (1969) no. 104.

16. Tear-shaped earring or pendant from a necklace. Crushed at the back. Length c. 14 mm. Mus. no. 6371.
Cf. Artamonov (1969) pl. 98 (boat-shaped earring).

17. Bobbin, solid cast. Length c. 17 mm. Mus. no. 6372.
Cf. Carapanos (1878) 115, pl. L,20.

18. Triangular ornament. Round wire attached down the middle and along the edges, curled up in spirals around granules at the corners. At the top one spiral and its gradule are missing, At the back a flattened tube. Length c. 12 mm. Mus. no. 6373.
Cf. Brooklyn (1984), Funerary Jewelry from Asia Minor no. 15 (two end pieces from a necklace, 4th century BC).

19. Four perforated globular beads. Diameters c. 6, 4 and 3 mm, respectively. Mus. no. 6374.

20. Five half-globular beads pierced at opposite sides for attachment. Diam. c. 7 mm. Mus. no. 6375.

21. Tventy-one half-globular beads pierced at opposite sides for attachment. Diam. between 3 and 4 mm. Mus. no. 6376.

22. Thirty-nine half-globular beads pierced at opposite sides for attachment. Diam. between 2 and 3 mm. Mus. no. 6377.
Cf. Greifenhagen II (1975) Tf. 72.3 (pierced at four points); Rudolph (1995) no. 22 S-T.

23. (photo missing). Twenty-four half-globular beads pierced at opposite sides for attachment. Diam. c. 2 mm. Mus. no. 6378.
Cf., for cat. nos. 20-23, Greifenhagen I (1970) Tf. 37,4-5 (possibly from Maikop, southern Russia).

24. Eighteen egg-shaped ornaments with plain, raised border. At the top corrugated tube. Below this, row of raised dots. Pierced at the pointed end for attachment. C. 5 mm high and 4 mm wide. Mus. no. 6379.
Cf. JbKuGewHamb 13 (1968) 217 (from Smyrna, 3rd century BC); Brooklyn (1984) no. 16 (seven pieces 'from a necklace or a fringe' found together in tomb in Asia Minor. End of 4th century BC); Rudolph (1995) no. 22 V: HalStud I (1994) 96, fig. 19 ('Tomb of the Carian Princess').

25. Forty-seven buttons with hook of wire for attachment. Diameters varying between c. 1 and c. 4 mm. Mus. no. 6380.

26. Fifty-seven buttons with hook of flat band. Diam. c. 2 mm. Mus. no. 6381.

27. Four tear-shaped ornaments with two loops for attachment at the back. Length c. 5 mm. Mus. no. 6382.

28. Three square buttons bordered by raised dots. The two larger ones measure c. 4 mm in side length and have two loops at the back, while the third measures c. 2 mm in side length and has only one loop at the back. Mus. no. 6383.

29. Two thorn-like pieces broken from their original setting. Length c. 5 mm. Mus. no. 6400.

30. Seven ring beads. Diameters between one and two mm. Mus. no. 6401.

31. Ornament composed of three triangles arranged on a common base decorated with a row of convex dots between raised lines. Length c. 12 mm. Mus. no. 6384.

32. Spade-shaped ornament pierced at top and bottom. Part of one side is broken off. Length c. 7 mm. Mus. no. 6385.

33. Nine oblong beads, plain or corrugated. Diameters vary between c. one and two mm, lengths between c. two and twelve mm. Mus. no. 6386.

34. Three perforated beads c. 2 mm square and rectangular in section. Mus. no. 6387.

35. Curved ornament with two hooks at the back. Length c. 3 mm. Mus. no. 6402.

36. Flat ring, c. 1 mm wide and 5 mm in diam., bent double. Mus. no. 6403.

37. (a) Flattened bead decorated with parallel grooves, length c. 5 mm, estimated diam. c. 4 mm. (b) Contorted piece of similar type, max. dim. c. 3 mm. Mus. no. 6404.

38. Piece of gold band curled at one end around a solid bead. Max. dim. c. 5 mm. Mus. no. 6405.

39. Two pieces of gold wire bent as if originally incorporated in a woven or crocheted fabric. Max. length c. 8 mm. Mus. no. 6406.

40. Gold lamellae from textiles. Mus. no. 6407.

(2) Gold item found at the edge of the cavity in square 8/8:

41. Solid-cast ring. Traces of the join at the casting gate. Circular in cross section, but of uneven thickness. Diam. c. 19 mm. Mus. no. 6388.
Cf. Taranto (1984) no. 247; Providence (1976) no. 2 (Etruscan ring, between c. 530 and 490 BC); Hill (1904) XX-XXI; Breglia (1966); for classification: RendAccNapoli (1959) 56-57, 87-88; SINDOS (1985) no. 438.

(3) Gold items found in the robbers' mine in square 8/8:

42a. Rosette with six convex petals bordered by raised edge around central knob. Pierced at three points. Diam. c. 6 mm. Mus. no. 6388.
Cf. cat. no. 8c.

42b. Two rosettes with seven concave petals bordered by raised edge around central knob. Pierced at four points. Diam. between 5 and 6 mm. Mus. no. 6389.
Cf. cat. no. 8b.

43. Globular perforated bead. Diam. c. 3 mm. Mus. no. 6408.
Cf. cat. no. 19.

44. Two half-globular beads pierced at opposite points. Diam. c. 3 mm. Mus. no. 6409.
Cf. cat. no. 22.

45. Two half-globular buttons with hook of wire at the back. Diam. 1-2 mm. Mus. no. 6410.
Cf. cat. no. 25.

46. Square button with raised dots along the edge and two loops at the back. Side length c. 3 mm. Mus. no. 6411.
Cf. cat. no. 28.

47. Curled gold band. Max. dim. c. 3 mm. Mus. no. 6412.

48. Gold lamellae from textiles. Mus. no. 6413.
Cf. cat. no. 40.

(4) Gold items found in the robbers' mine in square 7/8:

49. Ornament in the form of an equilateral triangle. Side length c. 7 mm. Mus. no. 6414.
Cf. cat. no. 7.

50. Circular disc with convex centre and a groove around the edge. Originally pierced at three points along the edge, now damaged at the place where the third perforation was. Diam. c. 12 mm. Mus. no. 6390.
Cf. cat. no. 2.

51. Rosette with seven concave petals bordered by raised edge around central knob. Pierced at three points. Diam. c. 6 mm. Mus. no. 6415.
Cf. cat. nos. 8b and 42b.

52. Ornament of double gold foil. At the top corrugated tube with two parallel channels. Below this, herringbone pattern bordered by v-shaped indentations. Width c. 10 mm. Mus. no. 6391.
Cf. BMCJ (1911) 984, pl. 9 (= Hogarth (1908) pl. 9,27).

53. Two egg-shaped ornaments with plain, raised border. Corrugated tube at the top, below which a row of raised dots. Pierced at the pointed end for attachment. Height 5-6 mm, width c. 4 mm. Mus. no. 6416.
Cf. cat. nos. 24, 62, 80.

54. Half-globular bead pierced at opposite sides. Diam. c. 4 mm. Mus. no. 6417.
Cf. cat. no. 21.

55. Battered and distorted circular disc with convex centre and raised edge. Pierced at opposite sides. Diam. c. 6 mm. Mus. no. 6418.
Cf. cat. no. 4.

56. Plain tubiform bead. Diam. c. 2 mm, length c. 9 mm. Mus. no. 6419.
Cf. cat. no. 33 (the piece at the left in the middle row on the photo).

57. Bead decorated with parallel grooves. Length c. 2 mm. Mus. no. 6420.
Cf. cat. no. 37b.

58. Three half-globular beads pierced at opposite sides. Diam. c. 3 mm. Mus. no. 6421.
Cf. cat. no. 21

59. Five half-globular beads pierced at opposite sides. Diam. c. 2 mm. Mus. no. 6422.
Cf. cat. no. 22.

60. Six buttons with hooks of flat band at the back. Diam. between 1 and 2 mm. Mus. no. 6423.
Cf. cat. nos. 25-26.

61. Gold lamellae from textiles. Mus. no. 6424.
Cf. cat. nos. 40, 48, 88.

(5) Gold items found in the robbers' mine in square 6/8:

62. Battered egg-shaped ornament with plain raised border and corrugated tube at the top, below which a row of raised dots. Pierced at the pointed end. Height c. 6 mm, width c. 4 mm. Mus. no. 6425.
Cf. cat. nos. 24, 53, 80.

Note that like the 18 pieces of this type found in the cavity (no. 24), the 9 pieces excavated in the mine (nos. 53, 62, 80) differ strikingly from one another, both in details of the shape and dimensions, some being markedly irregular and pointed rather than ovoid in form.

63. (a) Plain tubiform bead. Length c. 4 mm. (b) Ring bead c. 1 mm in diameter. Mus. no. 6426.
Cf. cat. nos. 33 (the piece at the right in the middle row on the photo) and 30.

64. Three half-globular beads pierced at opposite sides. Diam. c. 3 mm and less. Mus. no. 6427.
Cf. cat. no. 22.

65. Six buttons with loops at the back. Diam. 1-3 mm. Mus. no. 6428.
Cf. cat. nos. 25-26.

66. (no photo). Gold lamellae from textiles. Mus. no. 6429.
Cf. cat. nos. 40, 61, 66, 88.

(6) Gold items found in the robbers' mine in square 5/8:

67. Die-formed appliqué in the shape of a dancing girl dressed in a long chiton, possibly doing the Persian OKLASMA. Bending her knees, she is represented with her hands raised and clasped above her head and her face turned frontal. The edges of the piece are irregularly cut. Max. dim. c. 12 mm. Mus. no. 6392.
Cf. BMCJ (1911) 2076 pl. 39 (three types: winged Victory alighting [13 specimens]; Maenad dancing with head thrown back [8 specimens]; woman dancing [2 specimens], 5th-3rd century BC); From the Land of the Scythians (1973/74) no. 65 (= Artamonov pls. 266-267), Great Bliznitsa, 4th century BC, Hermitage BB 50-52; Greek Gold (1994) no. 108 (gold ring with blue glass bezel onto which gold motifs are fused, on one side two dancing girls, on the other ketos and dolphins. From Pavlovsky Kurgan, c. 350 BC).

68. Three ornaments in the form of equilateral triangles. On the reverse a loop at each corner. Side length c. 7 mm. Mus. no. 6430.
Cf. cat. nos. 7 and 49.

69. Circular disc with convex centre and corrugated border. Diam. c. 12 mm. Mus. no. 6393.
Cf. cat. no. 3.

70. Circular disc with convex centre and groove around the edge. Pierced at the edge at two opposite points. Diam. c. 11 mm, Mus. no. 6394.
Cf. cat. nos. 2, 50.

71. Circular disc with convex centre and raised edge. Pierced at opposite points for attachment. Diam. c. 6 mm. Mus. no. 6431.
Cf. cat. nos. 4, 55.

72. Rosette with six convex petals around central knob. Pierced between petals at three points. Diam. c. 8 mm. Mus. no. 6432.
Cf. cat. no. 9.

73. Two rosettes with six petals bordered by raised edge. One has convex petals and is pierced at three points, the other has concave petals and is pierced at two opposite points. Diam. between 5 and 6 mm. Mus. no. 6433.
Cf. cat. no. 8c.

74. Star-rosette. Four lancet-shaped petals alternate with four rosette tripartite petals around raised centre, the rosette petals being pierced. Diam. of rosette c. 12 mm, diam. of star c. 16 mm. Mus. no. 6395.

75. Ring decorated with sixteen bead-like indentations. Max. dim. c. 7 mm. Mus. no. 6396.

76. Spade-shaped ornament pierced at the middle of the curved end and at the corners of the opposite end. Length c. 8 mm. Mus. no. 6397.
Cf. cat. no. 32.

77. Three half-globular beads pierced at opposite sides. Diam. between 6 and 7 mm. Mus. no. 6398.
Cf. cat. no. 20.

78. Twenty-one half-globular beads, pierced at opposite sides. Diam. c. 3 mm. Mus. no. 6399.
Cf. cat. no. 21.

79. Eight half-globular beads, pierced at opposite sides. Diam. between 2 and 3 mm. Mus. no. 6434.
Cf. cat. no. 22.

80. Six egg-shaped ornaments with raised border. Corrugated tube at the top. Below this, row of raised dots. C. 6 mm high, and c. 4 mm wide. Mus. no. 6435.
Cf. cat. no. 24, 53, 62.

81. Seven buttons with hooks at the back. Diam. between 1 and 2 mm. Mus. no. 6436.
Cf. cat. no. 25.

82. Five buttons with hooks of flat band at the back. Diam. between 1 and 3 mm. Mus. no. 6437.
Cf. cat. nos. 25-26.

83. Ring bead. Diam c. 2 mm. Mus. no. 6438.
Cf. cat. no. 30.

84. Tear-shaped ornament with two loops at the back. Length between 4 and 5 mm. Mus. no. 6439.
Cf. cat. no. 27.

85. Plain bead with double perforation, round in section and cut at right-angles at both ends. Length between 3 and 4 mm, diam. c. 3 mm. Mus. no. 6440.

86. Four tubiform beads, varying in length between 13 and 2 mm, in width between 2 and 1 mm. Mus. no. 6441.
Cf. cat. nos. 33, 63a.

87. Bead of rectangular form. Length c. 2 mm. Mus. no. 6442.
Cf. cat. no. 34.

88. Gold lamellae from textiles. Mus. no. 6443.
Cf. cat. nos. 40, 48, 61, 66.

(7) Beads of semiprecious stones and glass found in the cavity in square 8/8:

89. Circular bead, c. 10 mm in diameter, slightly convex on both sides. Thickness along the edge 2.84 mm, in the middle 3.50 mm. Perforated along the diameter. Of red, translucent cornelian. Mus.no. 6444.

90. Perforated globular bead, 4.58 mm in diameter. Of red, translucent cornelian. Mus.no. 6444.

91. Fragment of perforated globular bead, 6.27 mm in diameter, broken along the perforation. Of red, translucent cornelian. Mus.no. 6444.

92. Biconical bead, 14.56 mm long, perforated across the middle, where it measures 6.27 mm in thickness. Of blue glass. Mus.no. 6445.

93. Perforated globular bead, 5.14 mm in diameter. Of blue glass. Mus.no. 6445.

94. Perforated globular bead, 4.75 mm in diameter. Of blue glass. Mus.no. 6445.

95. Bead of barrel-like shape, 7.49 mm long and between 5.35 and 6.74 mm in diameter, perforated lengthwise. Of brownish-black onyx with whitish transverse vein. Mus.no. 6446.

96. Bead of barrel-like (not perfectly symmetrical) shape, 6.98 mm long and 3.61 mm in max. diameter, perforated lengthwise. Of brownish-black onyx with whitish transverse veins bordering at one end on a lighter brownish shade. Mus.no. 6446.

97. Half-globular bead with flat bottom, 5.86 mm in diameter and 2.98 mm in height. Of brownish-black onyx with whitish vein which like the perforation runs parallel to the bottom. Mus.no. 6446.

98. Three fragments, A, B, and C, of beads of the same barrel-like type, the first of which is shown on the photo. Of bluish glass of ultramarine colour. Both the original surfaces and the breaks are covered by a yellowish incrustation.
Dimensions as preserved:
A: Length 16.82 mm, diameter between 9.00 and 12.35 mm.
B: Length 16.71 mm, max. width 11.80 mm.
C: Smaller fragment similar in cross section to A and B, length 15.11 mm, max. width 8.76 mm.

The diameter of the perforation is nearly 9 mm on A, but slightly smaller on B and C. The fragments must therefore come from at least two different beads. Mus. no. 6449.

(8) Bead of cornelian found in the robbers' mine in square 7/8:

99. Perforated, globular bead, 3.39 mm in diameter. Of red, translucent cornelian. Mus.no. 6447.

Beads of semiprecious stones and glass found in the robbers' mine in square 5/8:

100. Bead of triangular, slightly convex shape with beveled edges on all the sides, perforated lengthwise. Length 16.35 mm, height in the middle 6.63 mm, at the ends c. 3.5 mm, thickness 3.11 mm in the middle, 2.22 - 2.28 mm at the ends. Of cornelian changing in colour from red to brownish. Mus. no. 6450.

101. Bead of barrel-like (not perfectly symmetrical) shape, perforated lengthwise. Length 11.10 mm, diameter 4.22 mm at the middle, c. 3 mm at the ends. Of brownish agate with 17 closely spaced transverse veins of lighter colour and varying thickness. Mus.no. 6450.

102. Bead of barrel-like shape, perforated lengthwise. Length 7.21 mm, diameter at the middle 3.30 mm, at the ends c. 2.5 mm. Of brownish-black onyx with three transverse veins of whitish colour. Mus.no. 6448.

103. Pendant of prismatic shape, hexagonal in section, terminating at one end in a pointed pyramid, at the other end in a truncated cone which is perforated. Length 8.40 mm, max. thickness (= the spacing of opposite sides) c. 3.6 mm. Of brownish-black onyx with three whitish veins. Mus.no. 6448.

104. Bead of barrel-like (not perfectly symmetrical) shape, perforated lengthwise. Length 6.43 mm, diameter at the middle 4.60 mm, at the ends 2.76 and 3.31 mm, respectively. Of brownish-black onyx with a whitish transverse vein. Mus. no. 6448.

105. Fragment of fluted bead broken at one end, perforated lengthwise. Length as preserved 16.92 mm, max. width 7.03 mm. Estimated diameter of the perforation c. 4.3 mm. Judging from the surviving indications, the complete bead may have had some eight or nine flutes. Of blue glass of ultramarine colour. Both the original and the broken surfaces are covered by a whitish incrustation. Mus.no. 6449.

Judging from the finds, not a few jewels in the original treasure were partly – some perhaps entirely – composed of beads of semiprecious stone. Five are made of red, translucent cornelian (nos. 89-91, 99, 100), while seven are of brownish-black banded onyx (95-97, 101-104). In comparison, the only semiprecious stones found in the tomb of "the Carian princess" were two seal stones, one of chalcedony and one of agate, the rest of the ornamented pieces consisting entirely of gold plate.

The forms of the barrel-shaped beads nos. 95-96, 101-102, 104, and the flat-bottomed half-spherical 'eye bead' no. 97, all of banded onyx, are exemplified in a tomb excavated on the Acropolis of Susa in 1901. The find consisted of 65 pieces of banded onyx, possibly from a necklace. Among these were found two Aradus coins dating between 350 and 332 BC which seem to indicate that the burial took place at the end of the Achaemenid period.[108]

A treasure found at the bottom of a water jar in Pasargadai and datable in the period c. 450-350 contained 25 beads, among these one barrel-shaped and five 'eye beads'.[109] The banded pendant no. 103 possibly derived from a context of somewhat similar date.

The above-mentioned forms appear to have been imitated in Iran in the Hellenistic period, cf. History of Beads (1987), ill. 42 (p. 52, left row); Bead Chart, 333a-c, in which nos. 323-325 seem to derive from a prototype like our no. 100. On the other hand, 'eye agates' (believed to be evil-averting) "are to be found in the Near East as early as 2000 BC down to those from Persepolis" (Williams, cf. the note below).

Though much smaller, our cat.no. 89 of red cornelian is typologically comparable with the onyx disc c. 4.8 cm in diameter and perforated through the diameter which Newton found "in a branch of the Upper Gallery in the Vakuf field, some yards to the west of the Quadrangle". A similar disc that formed the centrepiece of a bracelet comes from finds from the Ikiztepe tumuli in Lydia.[110]

The globular forms of the beads of cornelian (nos. 89-91, 99-100) are of little direct use as regards the question of their provenance and date, and I am not aware of any datable parallels to those of bluish glass (nos. 92-94, 98, 105).

It seems obvious, though, that part of the material came from Persia or imitated prototypes of Persian origin, and that this may well be assumed to date from a period prior to the middle of the 4th century BC.

So far, I am not aware of any indication supporting the assumption that the surviving beads were mixed up with remnants from other parts of the Quadrangle. At any rate, this is not very likely to have happened to the pieces excavated in the cavity in the tomb chamber, while those recovered from the robbers' tunnel were found in close context with gold ornaments representing much the same types as the items from the cavity.

1

1

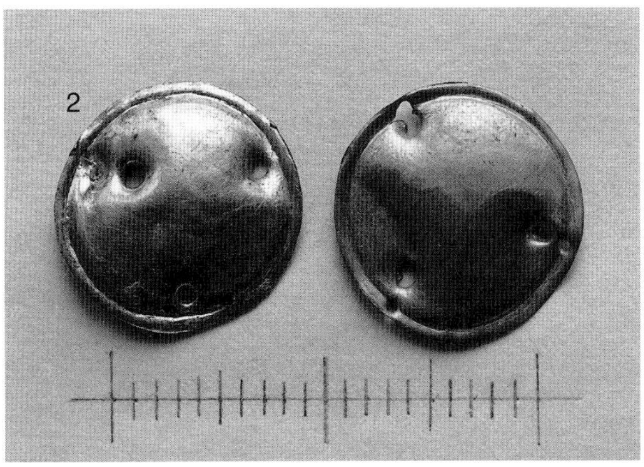
2

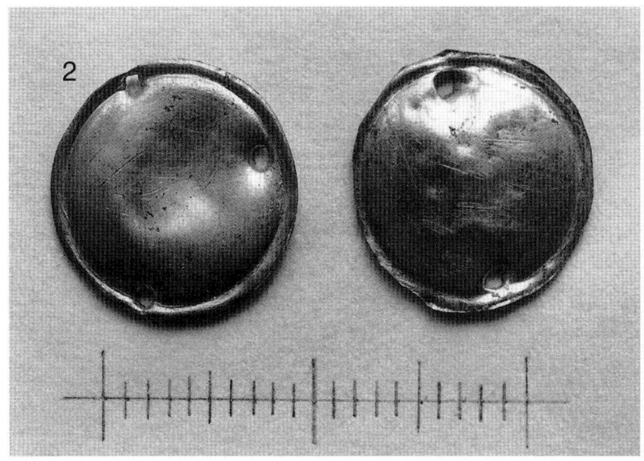
2

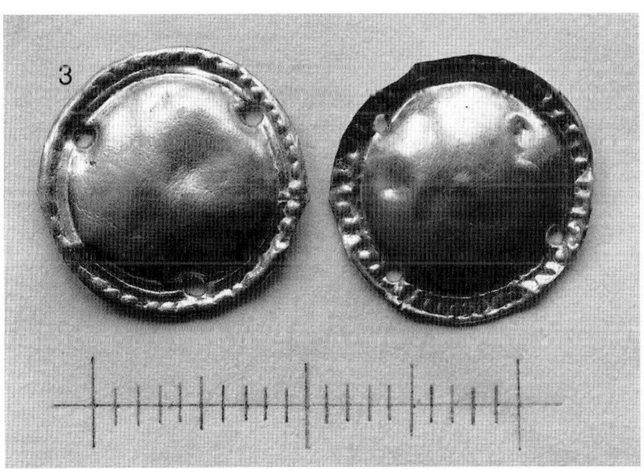
3

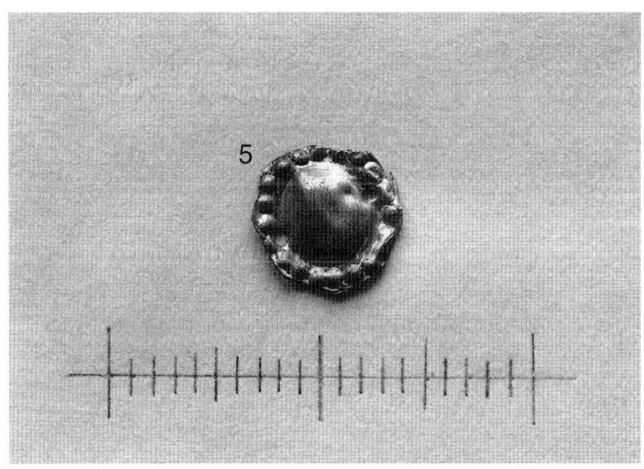
5

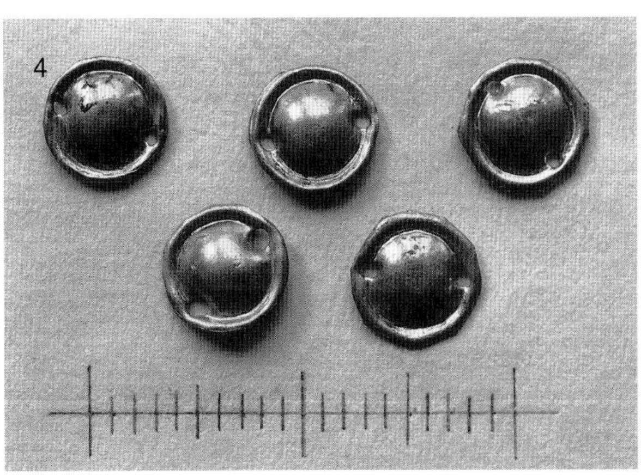
4

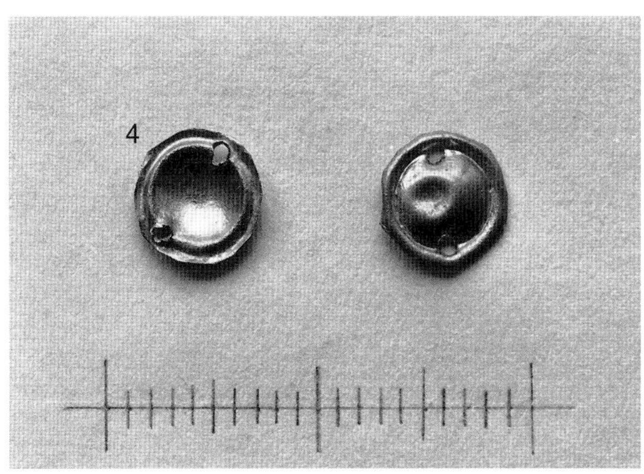
4

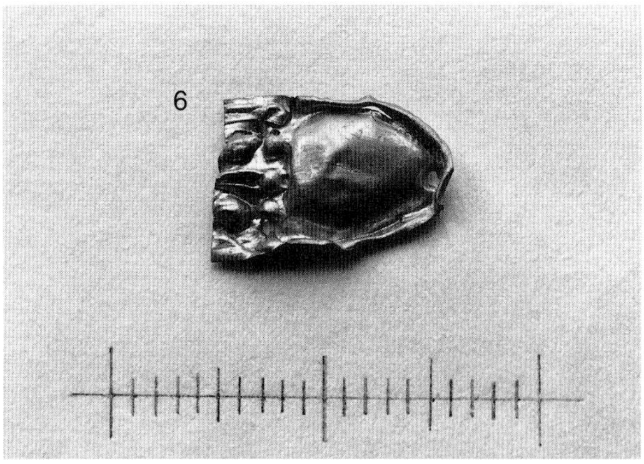
6

7

8a
8a
8b
8b
8b

8b
8b
8b
8c
8c
8c

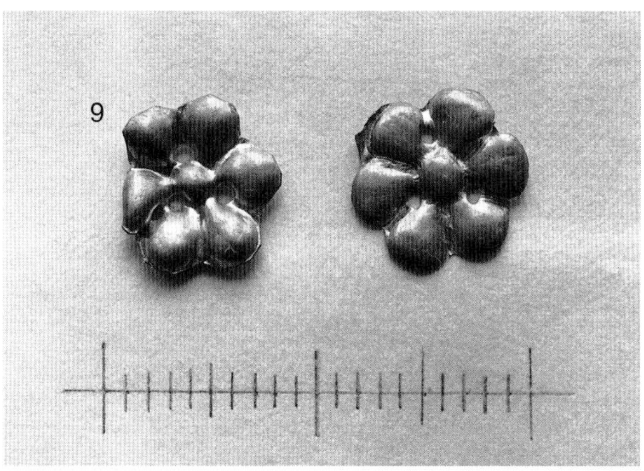
9

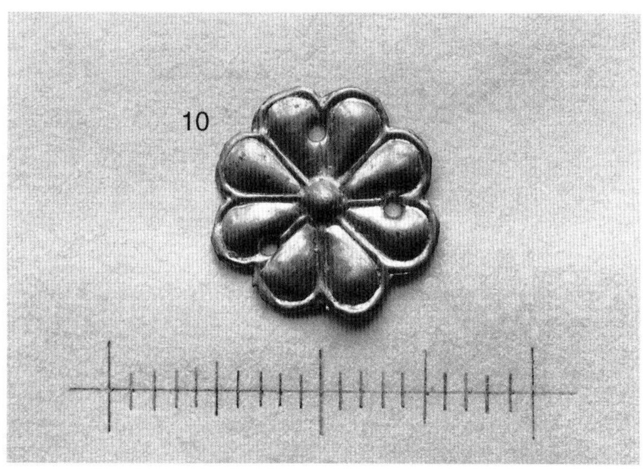
10

11

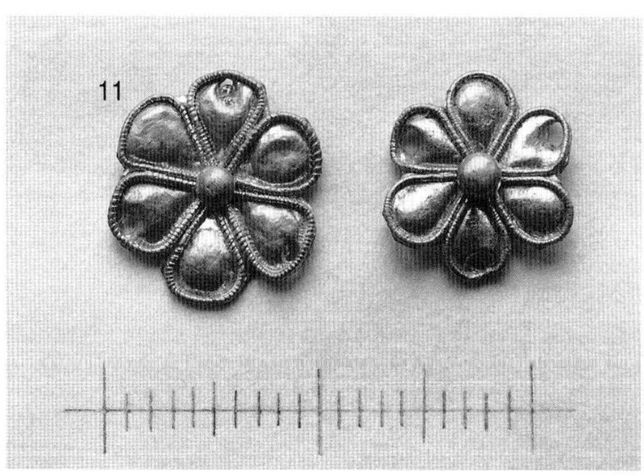
11

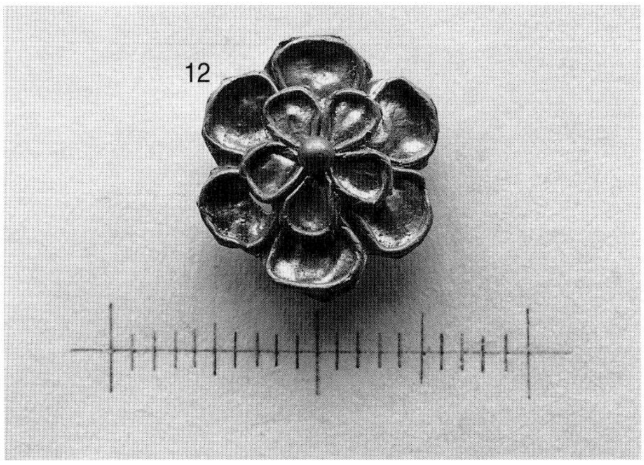
12

13b
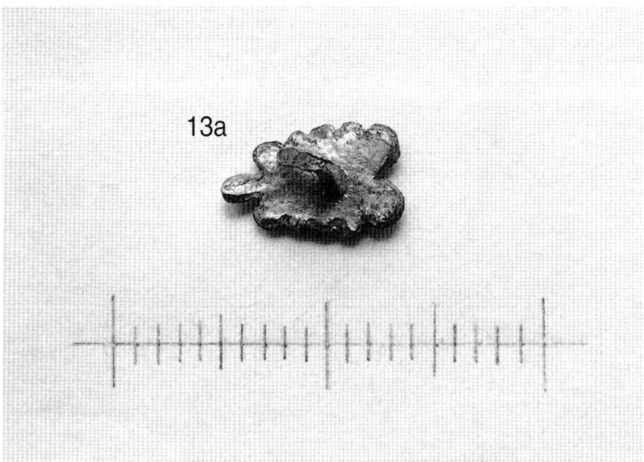
13a

13a
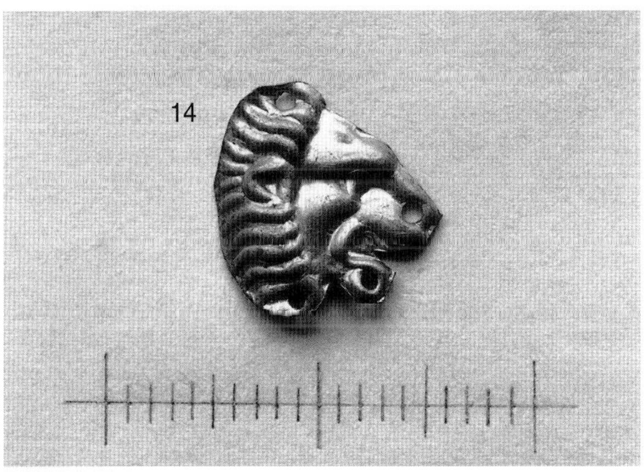
14

15
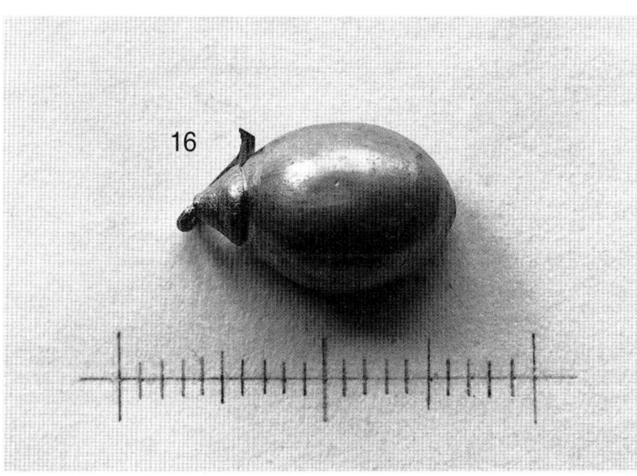
16
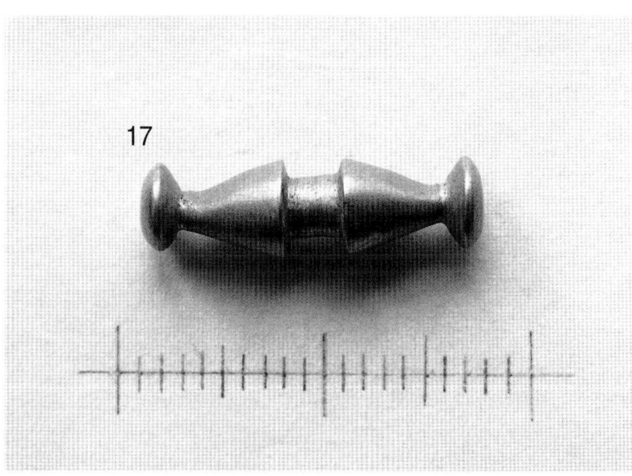
17

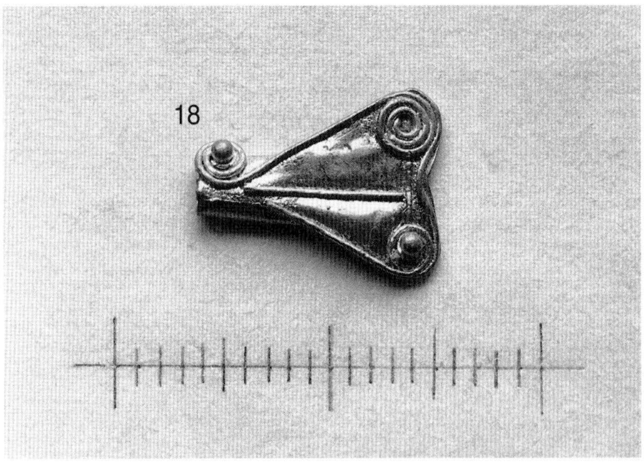
18

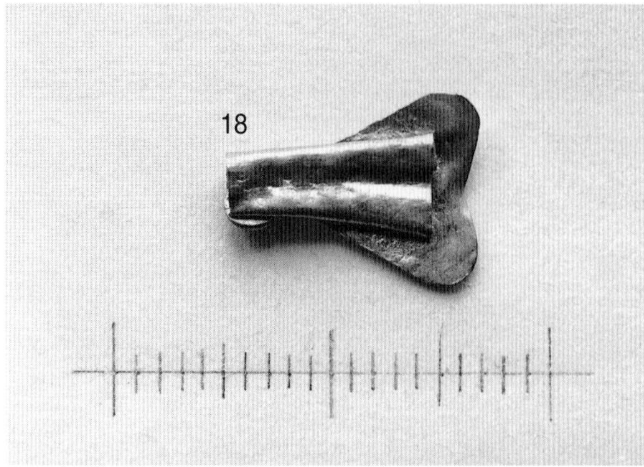
18

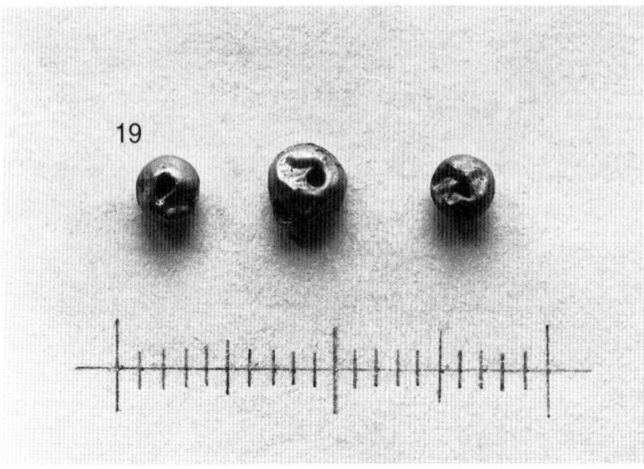
19

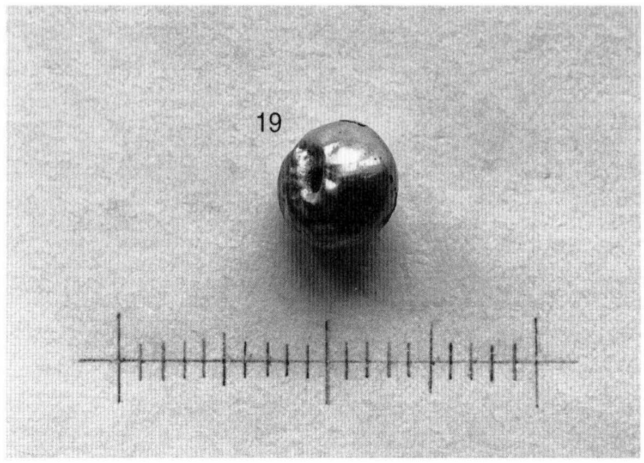
19

20

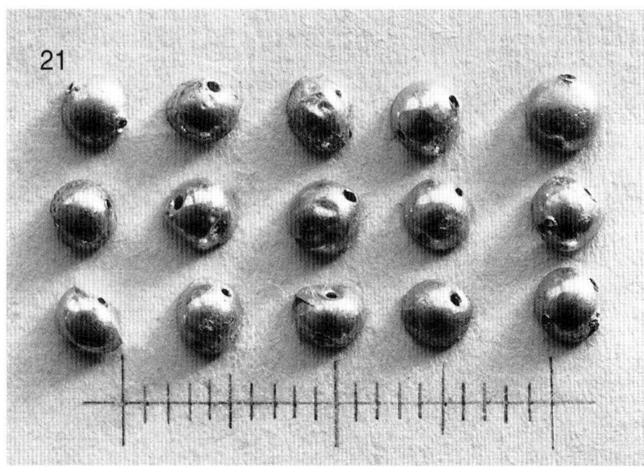
21

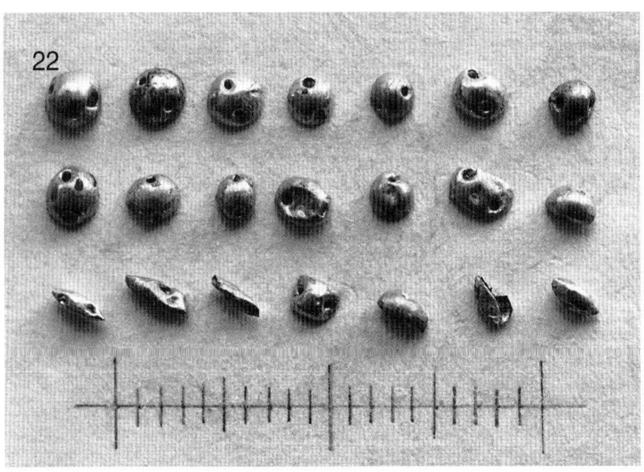
22

24

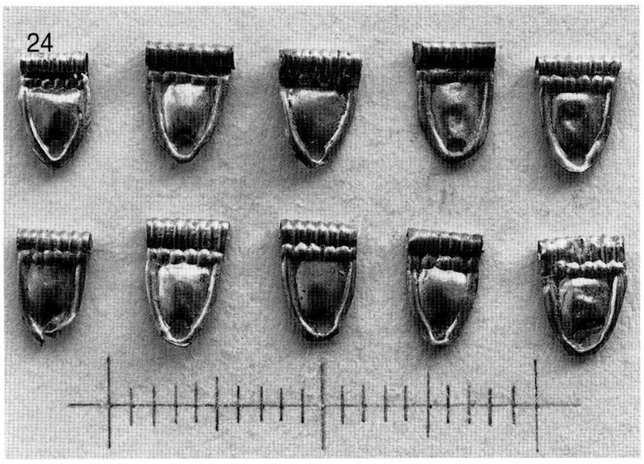
24
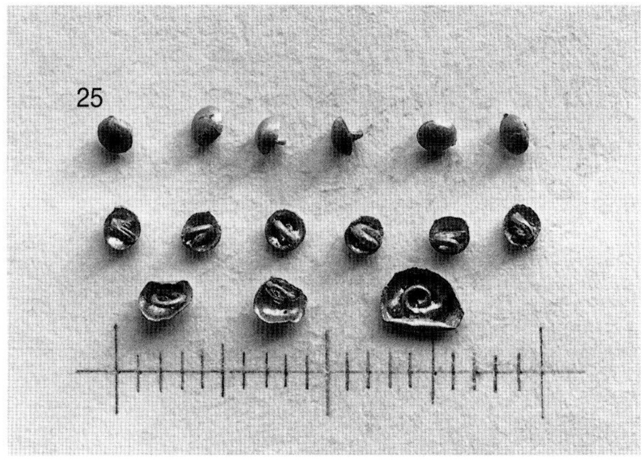
25
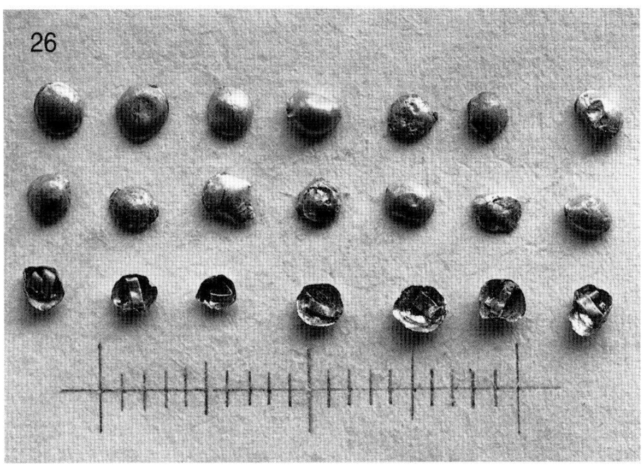
26
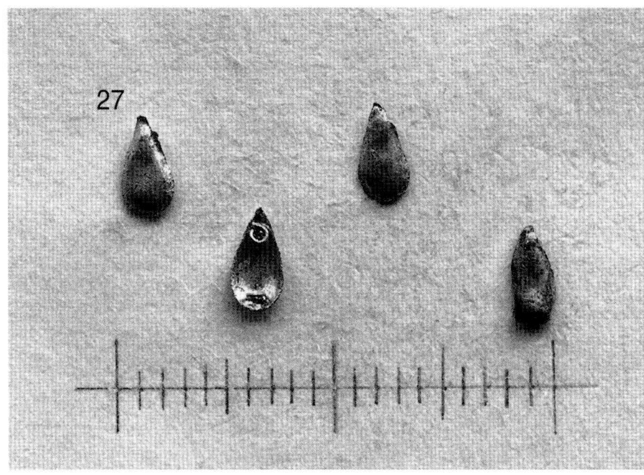
27
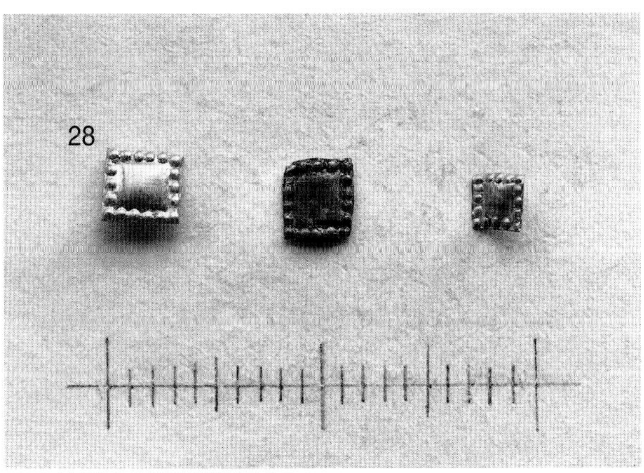
28
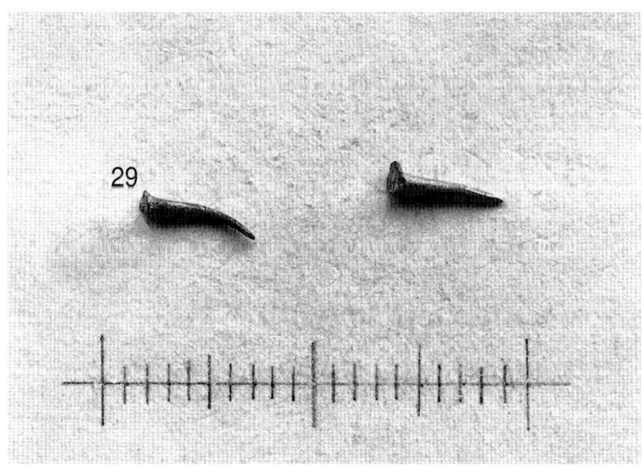
29
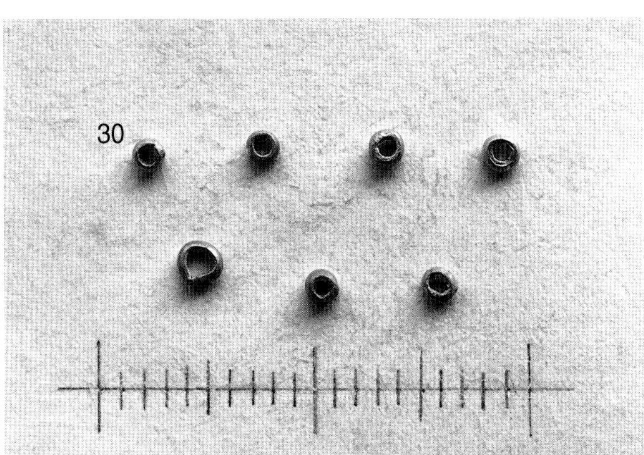
30
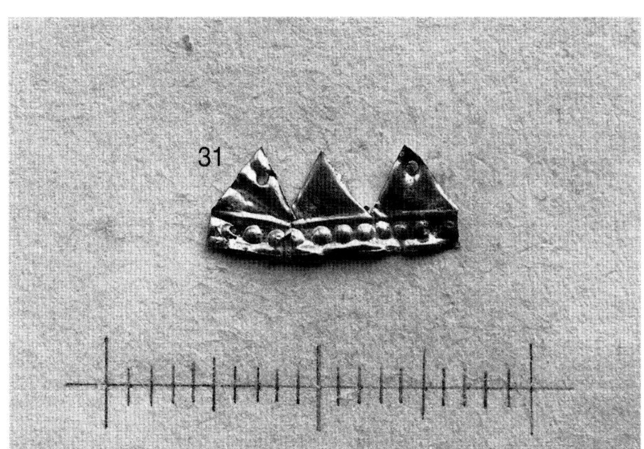
31

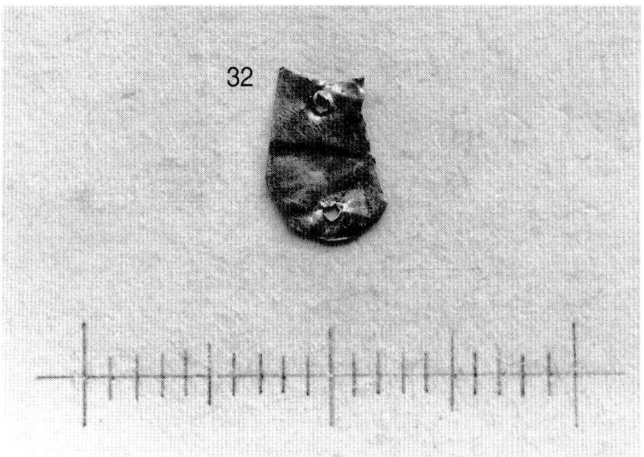
32
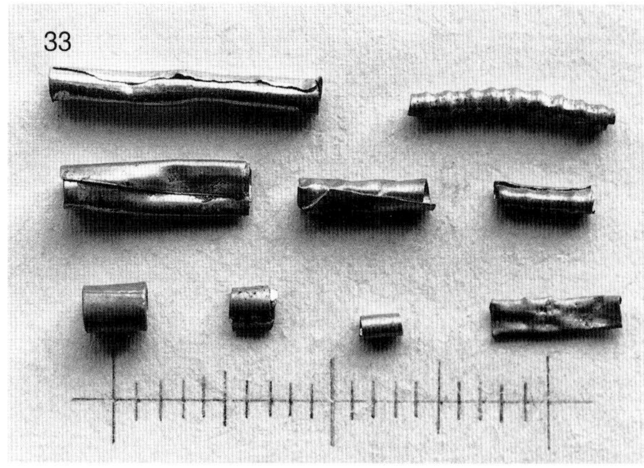
33
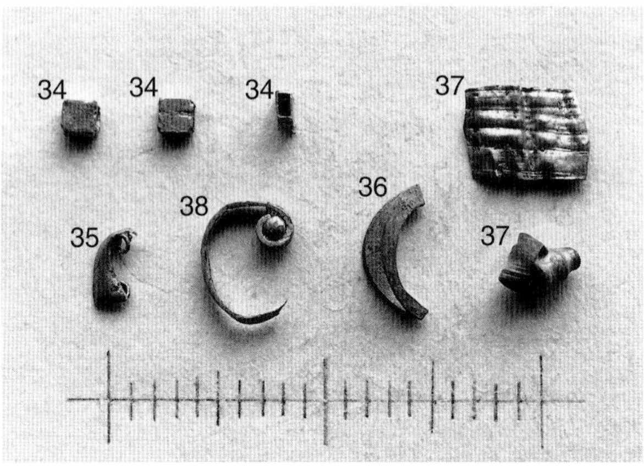
34
34
34
37
38
36
35
37
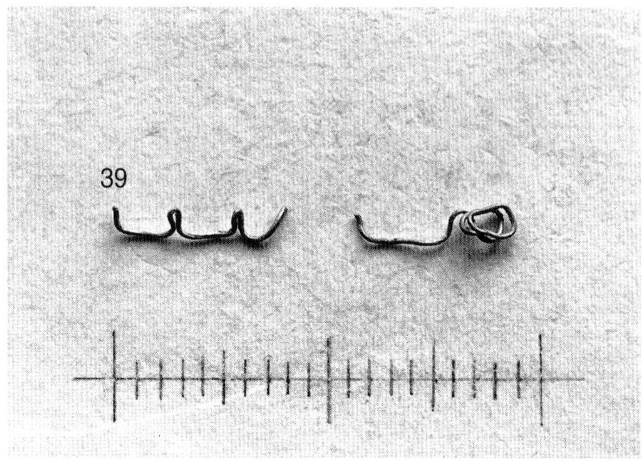
39
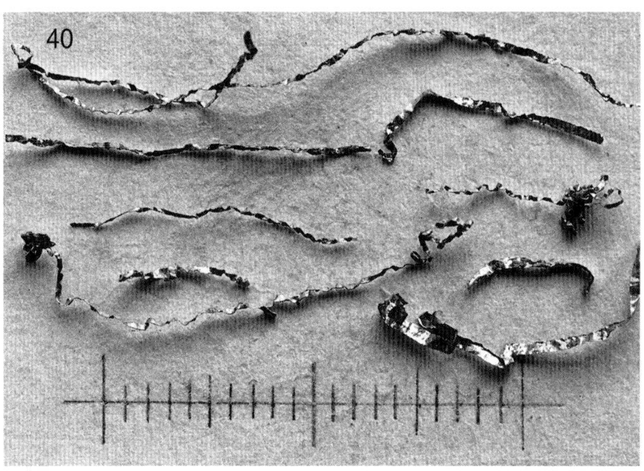
40

41

42b
42b
42a
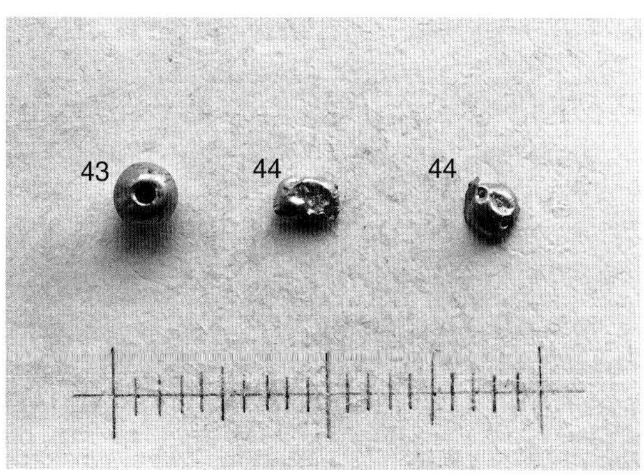
43
44
44

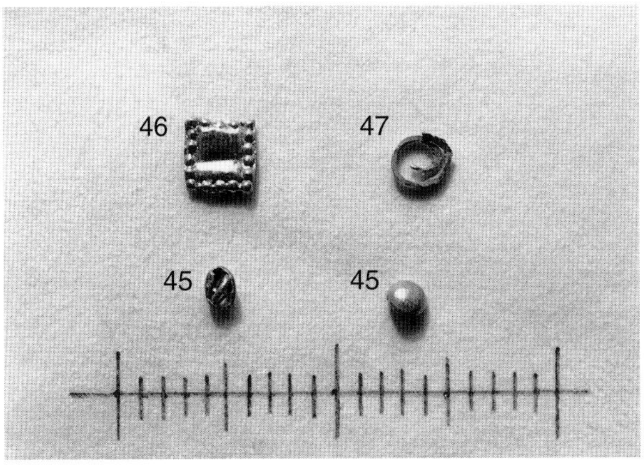
46
47
45
45
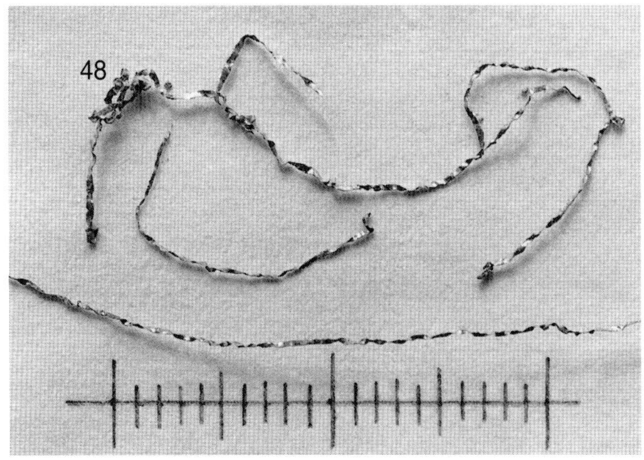
48
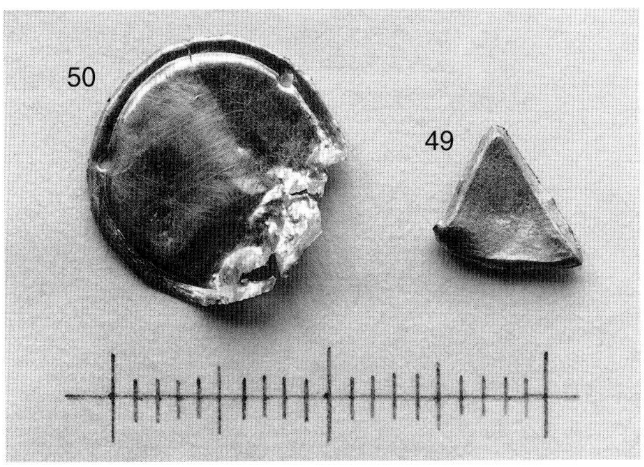
50
49
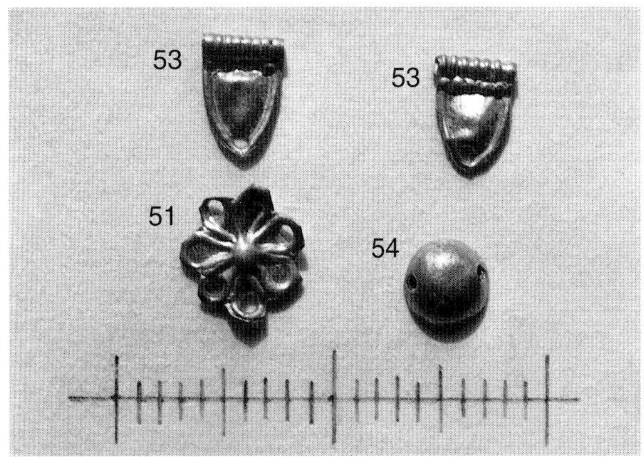
53
53
51
54
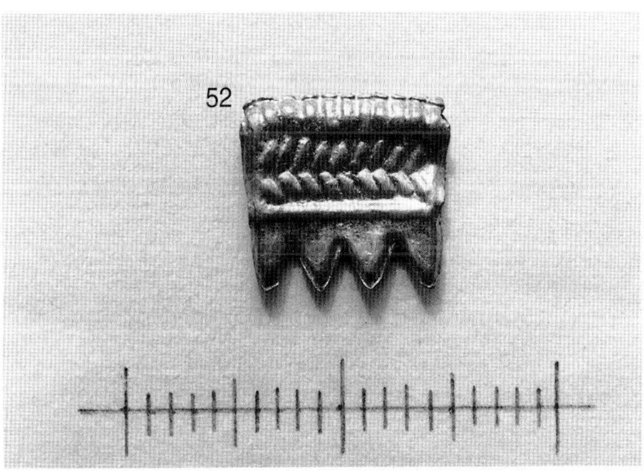
52
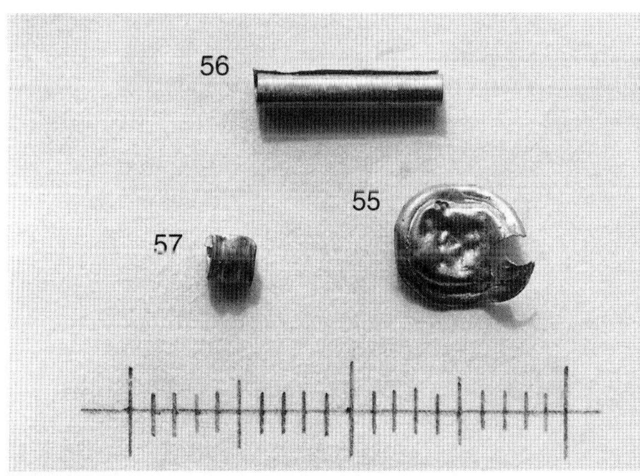
56
55
57
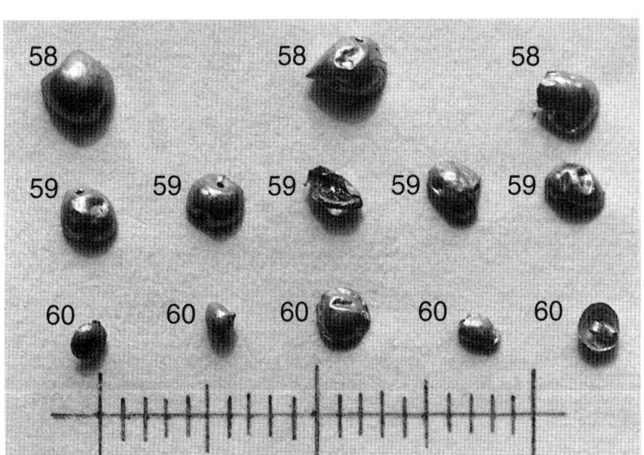
58
58
58
59
59
59
59
59
60
60
60
60
60
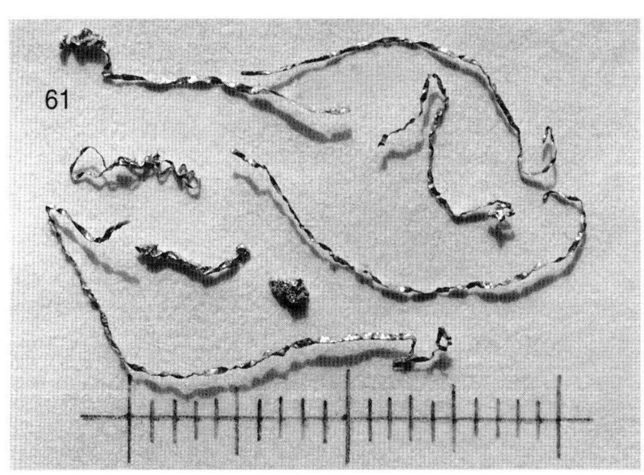
61

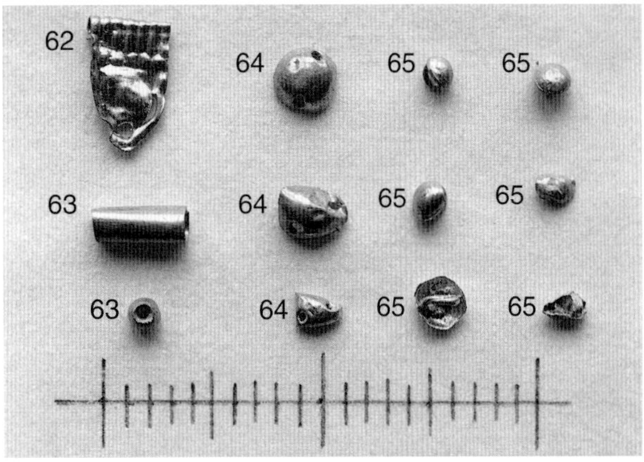
62
64
65
65
63
64
65
65
63
64
65
65

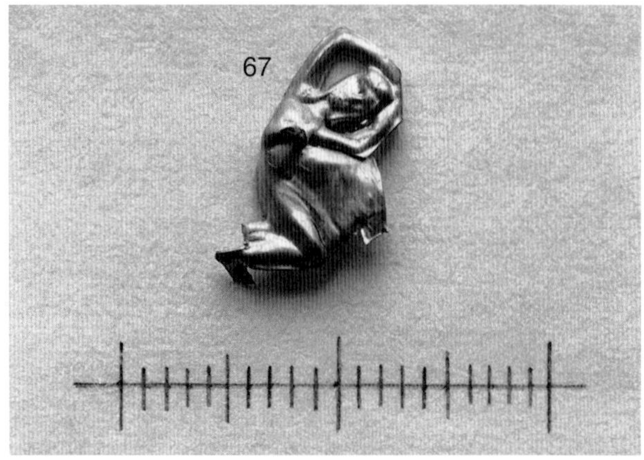
67

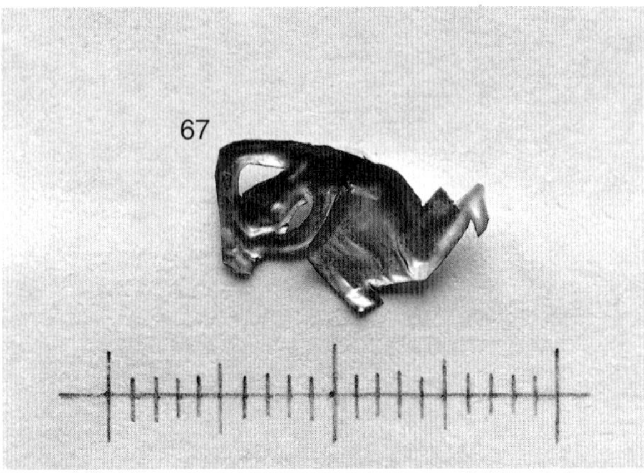
67

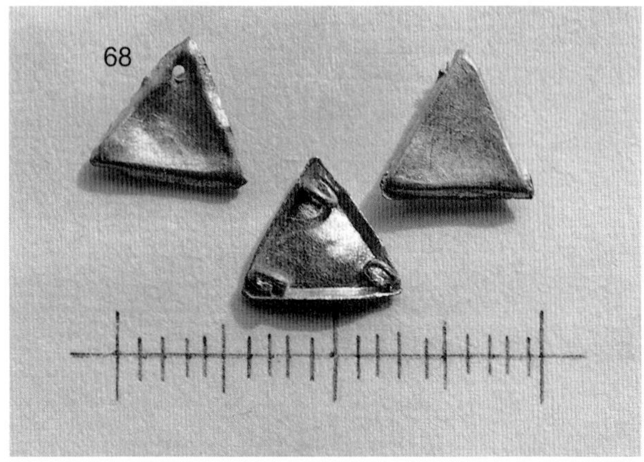
68

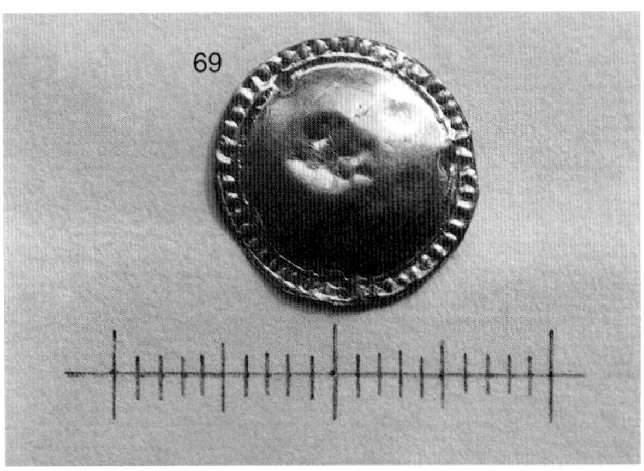
69

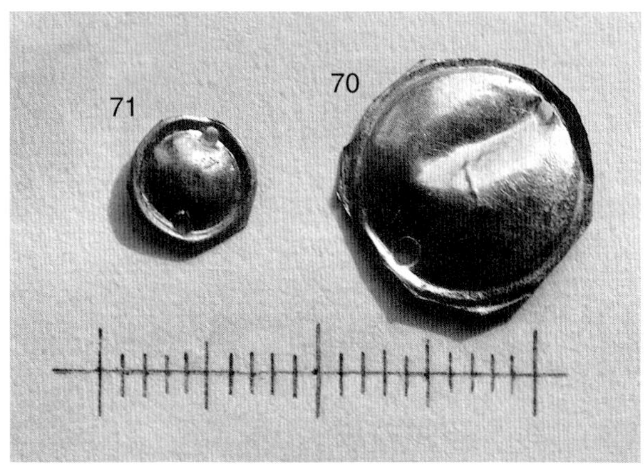
71
70

72
73
73

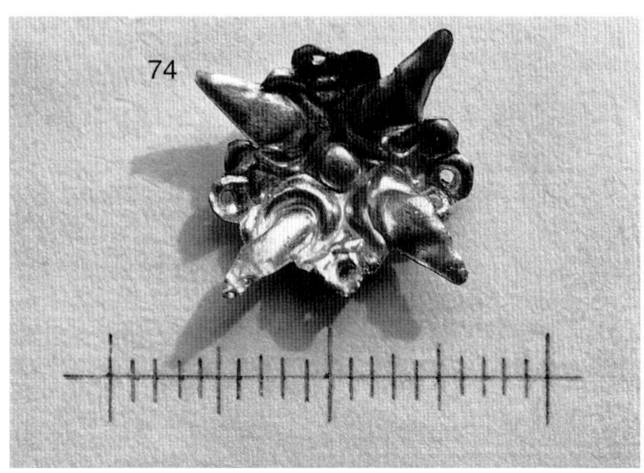
74

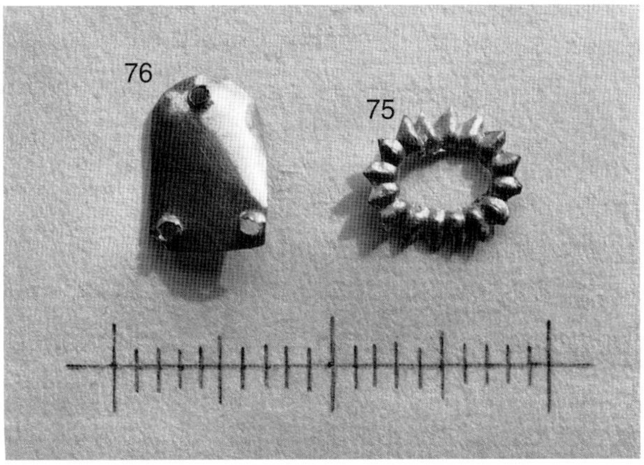
76
75
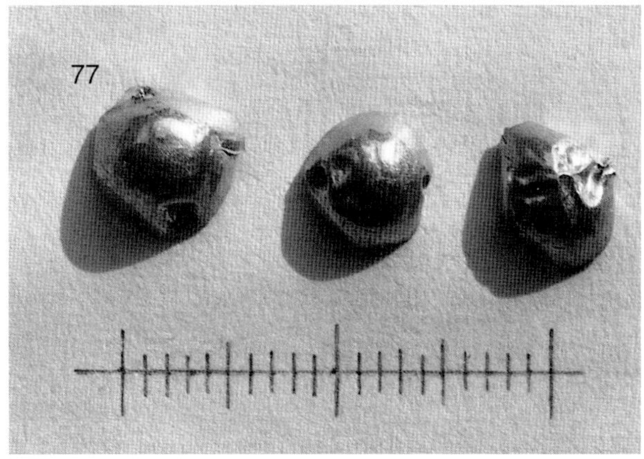
77
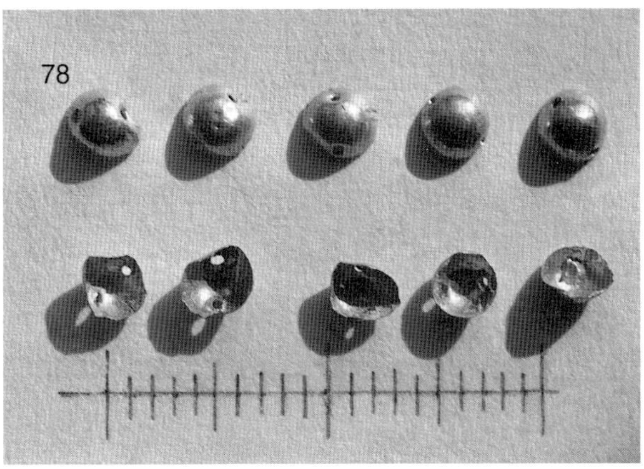
78
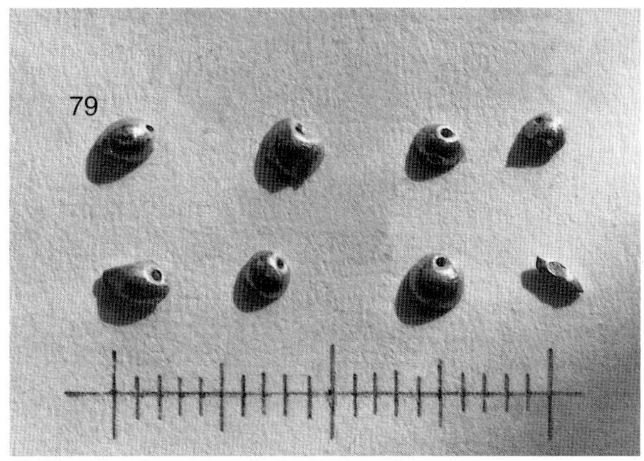
79
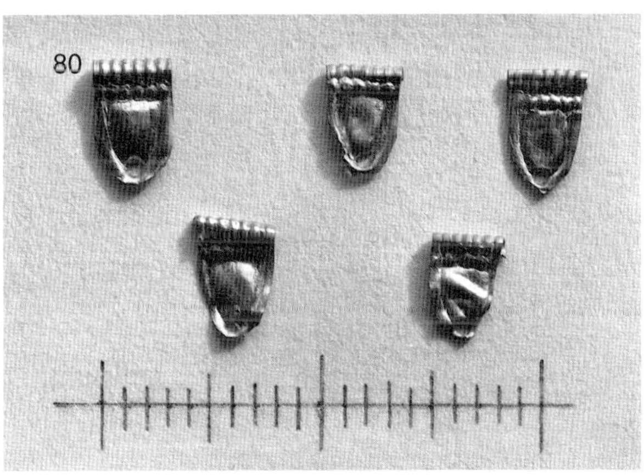
80
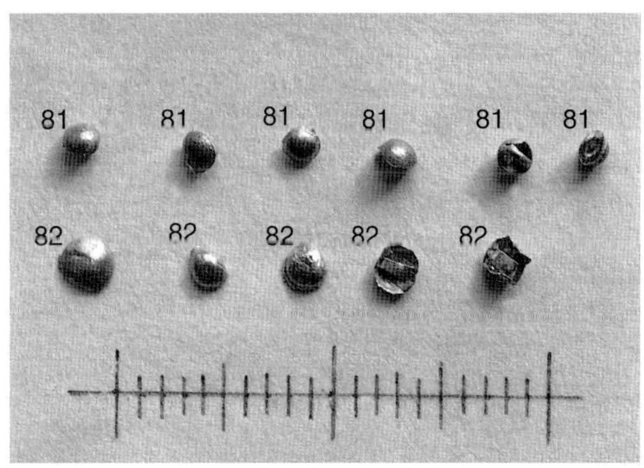
81
81
81
81
81
81
82
82
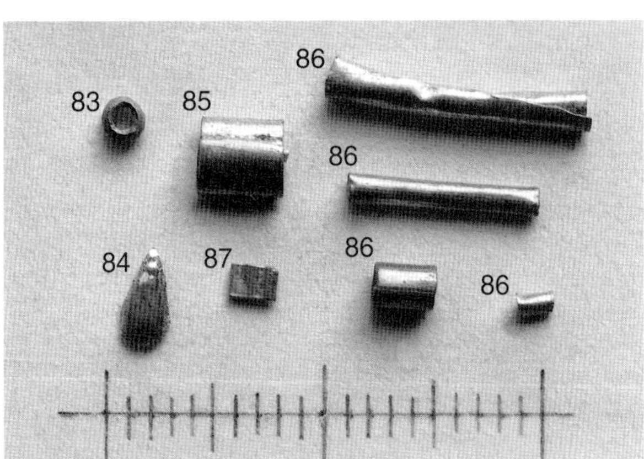
83
85
86
86
84
87
86
86
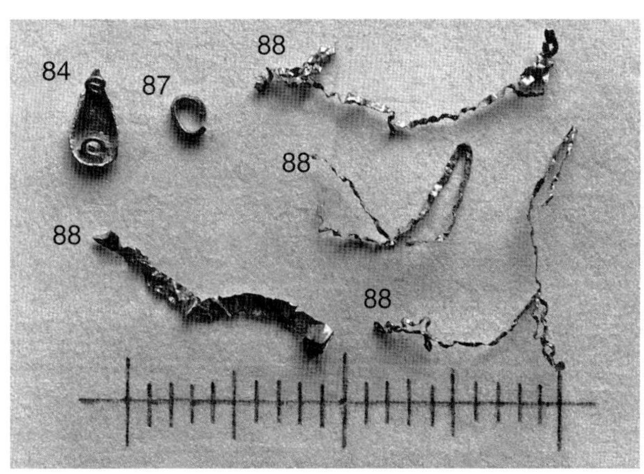
84
87
88
88
88
88

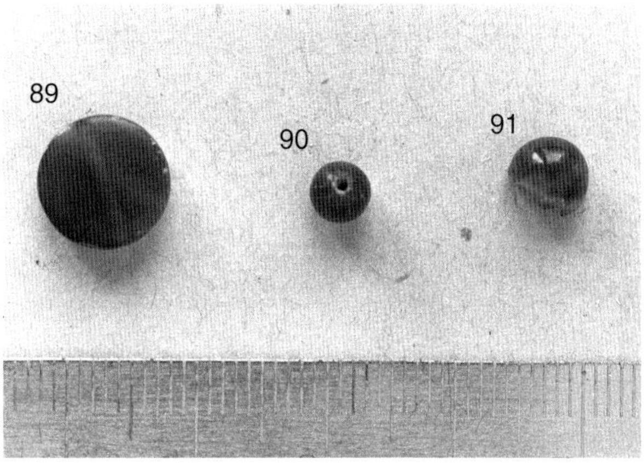
89
90
91

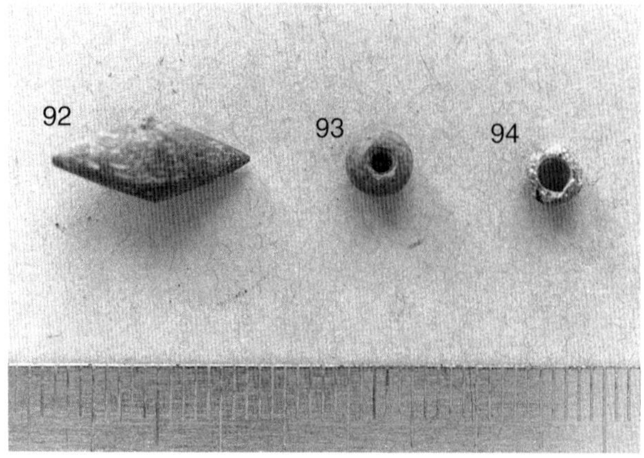
92
93
94

95
96
97

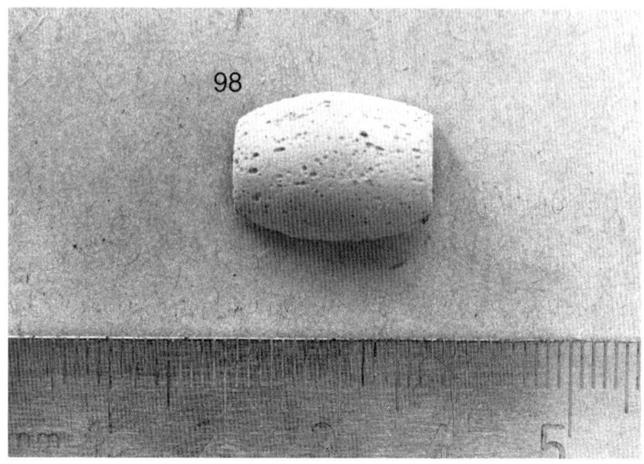
98

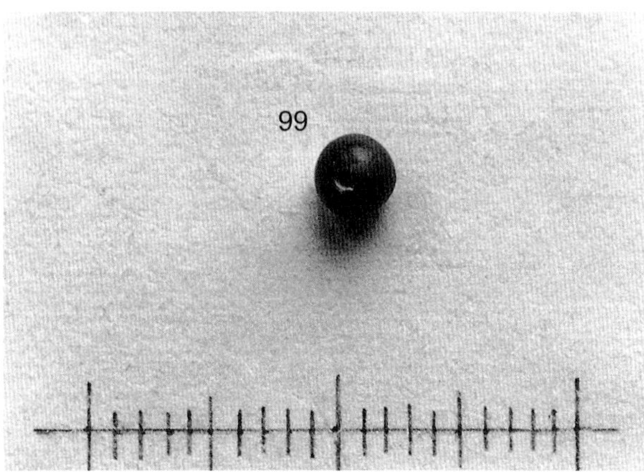
99

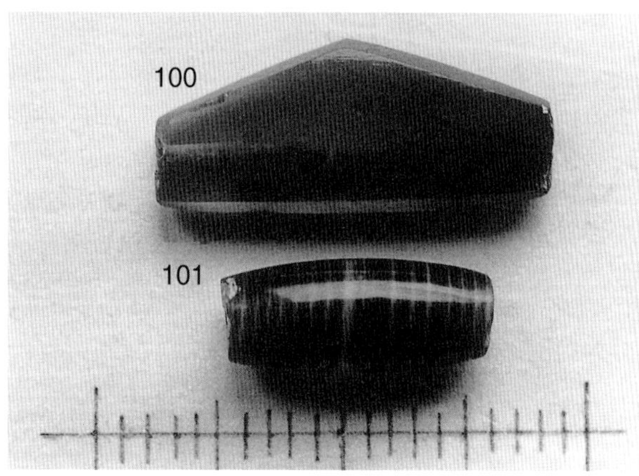
100
101

102
104
103

105

24. Provisional report of recent investigations into Pre-Maussollan remains underneath and south of the Maussolleion

It was hoped that Jan Zahle and Kjeld Kjeldsen could finish their investigations on the material related to pre-Maussollan activities underneath and south of the Maussolleion and publish their results in the present volume, but unfortunately the printing has had to be postponed, and the study is expected to appear in a forthcoming volume of the Maussolleion Publication.

During the recent excavations, Zahle took upon himself the demanding task of clarifying, in collaboration with Kjeld Kjeldsen, what the Maussolleion site might have looked like before the monument was built, and their studies have produced important results, which certainly deserve to be published.

Provisionally, reference must be made to the report given by A. M. Carstens in her recently published Ph.D. dissertation on "Funerary Architecture on the Halikarnassos Peninsula" (Copenhagen 1999), 107-113, which, as appears from her note 421, refers to oral information from Zahle communicated in April 1999. The report is accompanied by drawings by Kjeld Kjeldsen (figs. 147-148) and by a sketch fig. 149 drawn by Carstens herself, but referring to Zahle's instructions. Based on the same evidence, the drawing fig. 24.1 in the present publication explains a few more details.

Judging from the position of its rear wall, the tomb chamber of grave *a* must have been rather small, containing at the most three couches; and the irregular outline of tomb *c* is copied from Newton's pl. XIII. As the sketch shows, a branch of the Upper Gallery which joined the Short Gallery must have been conducted around the tomb chamber.

Newton observed that the line of the Upper Gallery was continued east of the landing at the foot of the southern staircase, where it gave access to two subterranean chambers, *b* and *c*, at all appearances both sepulchral. It seems likely, therefore, that the site was used for burials already before the Maussolleion was built, at which time Halikarnassos and Salmakis had not yet been united (it appears from an important inscription found at Halikarnassos[111] that around the middle of the fifth century or even later, Halikarnassos and Salmakis were still administered as separate communities), and the area separating them could well have been used as a cemetery.

Carstens p. 112 seems inclined to believe that the pre-Maussollan tombs belonged to a local dynasty preceding the Hekatomnid epoch, and suggests that the first Artemisia may have been buried in tomb chamber *a*. If so, however, it is hard to understand why the tomb of such a renowned predecessor of Maussollos was entirely eradicated instead of being reverently restored and incorporated in the foundations of the Maussolleion.

The fact that Newton found chambers *b* and *c* further east almost completely empty of grave goods and funerary equipment also suggests that remains of previous graves on the site were systematically removed, perhaps as an act of purification,[112] before the Maussolleion was erected.

This assumption is corroborated by Newton's observation that "the soil with which the chamber [of tomb *b*] was filled was the friable white soil which everywhere formed the lower stratum of the artificial platform".[113] Presumably the contents of the graves were relocated outside the walls of the newly enlarged city of Halikarnassos. Rather than being chosen with reference to dynastic predecessors – Maussollos' father Hekatomnos and the earlier ancestors were citizens of Mylasa and must have been buried there – the position of the Maussolleion was dictated by the proximity of the market square.[114]

The complicated context around the southern staircase and its connection with the Upper Gallery and the Short Gallery poses a number of problems of which a thorough account is ex-

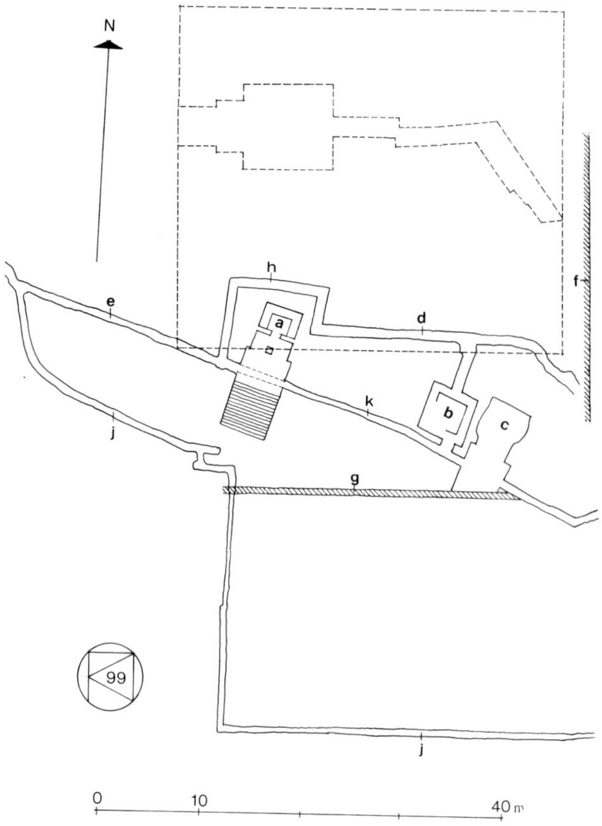

Fig. 24.1. Reconstructed plan of the pre-Maussollan necropolis on the site of the later Maussolleion according to Jan Zahle's and Kjeld Kjeldsen's investigations and hypotheses:

- a Tomb chamber behind the lower landing of the S stairway.
- b-c Two decommissioned tomb chambers accessible from a tunnel continuing the line of the Upper Gallery towards the east (k).
- d Short Gallery.
- e Upper Gallery.
- f-g S and E retaining walls of bedrock ashlars.
- h Branch connecting Short Gallery with Upper Gallery.
- j S branch of Upper Gallery.

pected to appear in Zahle's and Kjeldsen's final publication. Judging from the evidence available to the present writer, the history of the site should probably be summarized more or less in the following terms:

As the SW corner of the Maussolleion foundations partly encroached on the eastward course of the Upper Gallery (without, however, blocking it entirely), this must have been cut before the Maussolleion was erected, and so were undoubtedly the southern staircase, its landing, the chamber behind it, the detour of the Upper Gallery around the chamber where it joined the Short Gallery, and the tunnel giving access to the tomb chambers further east.

At the building of the Maussolleion foundations, the Short Gallery was filled with foundation blocks indicating that it had ceased to be in use, and so had evidently the branch connecting the Short Gallery with the Upper Gallery, whose crooked plan can be deduced from the pattern of the irregularly laid foundation slabs preserved at level L9.

In consequence of these changes, it must have been the intention to fill up with earth the open space remaining south of the foundations, in particular the staircase and its landing, however, without obstructing the course of the water that might come from the Upper Gallery west of the Maussolleion. The easiest way of achieving this was to construct a covered passage across the landing like the one which was actually built, thus permitting water from the Upper Gallery to pass into the tunnel beginning on the opposite side of the landing. In its previous capacity this tunnel had given access to the tomb chambers aligned with it, but when the burials in these rooms were relocated elsewhere, it could well have been used as a spillway in continuation of the Upper Gallery.

This attempt to reconstruct some basic facts of the evolution in the area before the Maussolleion was built seems compatible with the observations and conclusions drawn in Zahle's and Jeppesen's preliminary report AJA 79 (1975), 74. According to this, the pottery found in the BOTHROS below the south wall of the covered passage (corridor) "consists mainly of coarse ware mixed up with a few sherds of Attic black stamped ware with rouletting. The latter type of pottery was not manufactured until ca. 390-375 BC, and the corridor, therefore, must have been built shortly before or at the same time as the Mausoleum was erected."[115]

Zahle's hypothesis has the advantage of motivating the building of the covered passage across the landing, which would otherwise be hard to explain. In the acute angle between the foundations of the Maussolleion and the vertical side of the adjoining bedrock was placed one of the pillars built along the southern margin of the monument (P15), and rubble walls abutting on this seem to have been part of a structure roofing the course of the Upper Gallery between the covered passage and the opening at the SW corner of the foundations, from which water might be expected to emerge.

For further information, Zahle's and Kjeldsen's prospective description and interpretation of all details relevant to the abovementioned issues may bring about important additions to or corrections of the provisional observations advanced by the present writer (cf. the discussion above, chapter 7).

Appendix 1

Geological Aspects of the Construction of the Mausoleum at Halicarnassus[116]

Professor John A. Gifford
Rosenstiel School of Marine and Atmospheric Science
Miami, Florida, USA

The location of the Mausoleum site at the southern base of the hill presently called Göktepe was certainly dictated by considerations other than geological, as the rock types and ground water conditions there are notably unsuited for bearing a heavy building foundation. A detailed discussion of these two aspects of the site forms the substance of this article.

The regional geology of the southwestern coast of Turkey is well described by Bremmer (1971). The Bodrum Peninsula is recognized to be composed primarily of an Upper Jurassic-Cretaceous cherty limestone sequence in its central and eastern portions, and andesite lava flows in the west. In the immediate vicinity of Bodrum are exposed undifferentiated strata of Upper Cretaceous-Eocene flysch, and the most recent deposits in that area are Neogene tuffs and volcanic conglomerates. Göktepe was evidently a small volcanic vent and the local source for tuff in the Bodrum area.

A more detailed Neogene stratigraphy for southwestern Turkey, based on lithological, palynological and paleontological studies, is summarized by Alpan and Lüttig (1971). They recognize four major transgressive sedimentary cycles in the Neogene, with the most recent (Upper Pliocene-Lower Pleistocene) resulting in the deposition of the lacustrine sediments of the Millet Member of the Tortonian. Postorogenic (Pleistocene) uplift ended major sedimentation in the area. It may reasonably be assumed that the rock units exposed at the Mausoleum site are correlatable with the Millet Member as defined by Alpan and Lüttig.

The general lithological sequence at the Mausoleum site comprises claystones overlain by tuffaceous sedimentary rocks (volcanic sandstones). Table 1 presents the detailed stratigraphy.

An interpretation of the original depositional environment of these units suggests that the claystones represent shallow lake sediments, with variation in source area responsible for the different textures of Units 1, 2a and 2b. Continuous but small-scale volcanic activity occurred during the deposition of these units, as evidenced by the included tuff fragments. An increase in the number and size of tuff fragments at the top of unit 2b indicates increased volcanic activity, culminating in a major and prolonged eruption of andesitic pyroclasts (Unit 3) which seems to have taken the form of numerous, discrete ash falls, judging from the multiple, thin, graded bedding of this unit. Through infilling by tuffaceous sediment (and possible local uplift) the area of the Mausoleum site became shallower and finally rose above the lake level. Discontinuous fluvial sandstone and gravel beds were deposited in the area, were partially lithified and covered by renewed outbreaks of pyroclastic deposition (producing Unit 4). This volcanic activity and subaerial sedimentation continued sporadically until the regional uplift that marked the end of Neogene lacustrine deposition in the Bodrum area. Quaternary sea level oscillations and subaerial weathering combined to erode much of Unit 4 from the Mausoleum site, so that pre-Mausoleum constructions were cut primarily into the homogeneous mass of Unit 3.

The five major units exposed at the Mausoleum site are disconformable, low-angled and unfolded, but the stratigraphy is somewhat complicated by extensive faulting and jointing. One major fault system strikes northwest-southeast and consists of almost-vertical normal fault sets that have dropped the southwest and northeast corners of the Quadrangle area one to one and one-half meters relative to the central sector. Traces of these fault sets are clearly exposed in the horizontal and vertical cuttings of the Quadrangle.

A second joint system is best exposed in the subsurface Upper and Lower Galleries. It too consists of almost-vertical normal faults, but striking more east-west than the major system. Amount of vertical displacement along the second system of faults varies from a few decimeters to one meter.

The claystone units (1, 2a and 2b) are extensively fractured on a scale of centimeters to decimeters, while the overlying tuffaceous sandstone units (3 and 4) are relatively homogeneous and free of such fractures. Units 3 and 4 are therefore much more desirable as a foundation surface than Unit 2b.

Those persons charged with the construction of the Mausoleum must have made the utmost use of preexisting galleries and chambers to map out the faulted contact between Units 2a and 3 before excavation of the Quadrangle. They seem to have compromised between the utilization of Units 3 and 4 as the bearing surfaces for the foundation blocks, and the necessity of removing large masses of these units in order to reduce to a common level the various pre-existing structures within the Quadrangle area. This compromise is illustrated in the minimal amount of downcutting done in the northeast sector of the Quadrangle, where no pre-existing structures had to be cut away; consequently, the bedrock of Units 3 and 4 was planed to a level almost two meters higher than in the central and western portions of the area.

Similar considerations affected the depth of foundation cutting in the central and western portions of the Quadrangle. As noted above, northwest-southeast trending fault systems lowered the southwest and northeast corners of the Quadrangle, resulting in a greater thickness of Units 3 and 4 in these sectors relative to the remaining area. In addition, extensive pre-Mausoleum quarrying in the north-central and northwest corner of the Quadrangle had resulted in the removal of most or all of Unit 3 down to the claystone of Unit 2b. Similarly, portions of pre-Mausoleum chamber tombs and galleries in the center and southwest of the Quadrangle area had been cut below Unit 3, into Unit 2b.

These factors dictated what must have been an unsatisfactory course of action for the Mausoleum builders: the removal of all remaining vestiges of Unit 3 down to the top of Unit 2b in the central and western sections of the Quadrangle. It must also have been decided that, in contrast to the northeast sector, the mass of Unit 3 exposed in the downthrown side of the southwest fault system was not extensive enough to serve as a solid foundation surface at a higher level than the central portion of the excavation, and therefore this mass of Unit 3 was also cut down to a common level with the top of Unit 2b, approximately seven meters above modern sea level.

The removal of various other pre-Mausoleum cuttings and galleries in the south-central area of the Quadrangle produced a number of shallow step-like terraces differing in height by the thickness of the andesite foundation blocks (c. 30 cm.).

All remaining open cavities cut below the common bedrock foundation level of the Quadrangle were then filled with stone blocks of average dimensions (c. 30 × 90 × 90 cms), which were quarried from coastal sites just north of ancient Myndus, at the west end of the Bodrum Peninsula. This foundation stone is a porphyritic hornblende andesite, greyish-yellow green (5GY 7/2) on a fresh surface, and composed of phenocrysts of hornblende, biotite, magnetite and angular lithic fragments in a groundmass of andesine feldspar. Geologically, it belongs to the "Neogene volcanic extrusive rocks" of the Bodrum Peninsula (Bremmer, 1971). With a uniaxial compressive strength probably in the region of $12\text{-}15 \times 10^6$ kg/m^2, it is an excellent foundation stone.

In sharp contrast, a reasonable estimate of the compressive strength of the bedrock foundation of the Mausoleum (tuffaceous, friable sandstone and a highly fractured claystone) would lie between .1 and 1×10^6 kg/m^2, or one to two orders of magnitude less than the value for the andesite foundation blocks. This disparity, in combination with the differential loading of the bedrock with foundation blocks in the eastern versus the western half of the Quadrangle, could have produced severe settling problems in the Mausoleum structure.

As a final (and major) complicating factor, groundwater conditions in the vicinity of the Mausoleum are far from ideal. The hydrogeological map of the Bodrum Peninsula (T.C. Department of Hydrology, 1974) shows the groundwater level in the vicinity of the Mausoleum at 2 m above modern sea level, but it slopes steeply over a distance of only 500 m from 4 m to the north of the site to .5 m to the south, at the harbor's edge. Spot measurements made in August of 1974 (dry season) showed a standing water level of +3.28 m in an unused well immediately north of the Quadrangle, and +2.11 m in a well approximately 10 m west of the southwest corner of the Quadrangle (identified as "Ismail's Well" in Newton's plan of the Mausoleum site). Slope runoff from Göktepe during the winter rains might be expected to raise the ground water level by one or two meters for several months.

Although the question of the magnitude of eustatic sea level variation in the Mediterranean over the past few thousand years is not yet completely answered, survey work on archaeological sites along the southwest Turkish coast (Flemming et al., 1973), indicates that the Bodrum Peninsula has sunk approximately 1 m since the 4th century B.C. By itself, this fact suggests that the position of ground water level at the time of the Mausoleum's construction was some fraction of a meter lower than at present (relative to the foundation levels), and would therefore have constituted *less* of a problem to the builders. Working in opposition to this lowering, however, was a general increase in precipitation due to climatic changes. It is thought that a rainy, cooler period began in the Mediterranean c. 500 B.C., reaching a maximum rainfall peak about the beginning of the 4th century B.C. (Lamb, 1968, p.6). Thus, even if ground water level in the 4th century B.C. was (on the average) at or below the modern position, its seasonal oscillation with an amplitude greater than at present could have produced even worse problems for the builders.

Only one part of the Mausoleum structure, the tomb chamber itself, could reasonably be considered close enough to ground water level to have suffered occasional flooding. However undesirable this might have been from a religious or aesthetic standpoint, it would not in itself affect the stability of the entire structure. Rather, major problems arise from the indirect effects of ground water oscillations on the bedrock underlying the Mausoleum.

This bedrock is primarily a highly fractured claystone (Units 1, 2a, and 2b). Although indurated, this material is not far removed from a consolidated clay sediment, or "soil" in civil engineering terminology. Two properties of the claystone would be affected through alternating saturation and drainage caused by a rising and falling ground water level. First, the shearing resistance of the claystone in an undrained versus a drained state would vary considerably due to changes in the neutral stress of the sediment (Terzaghi and Peck, 1967, art. 18). Second, changes in seepage pressure in the claystone below the Mausoleum would be transmitted to the foundation in the form of local settling (Terzaghi and Peck, 1967, art. 59).

In order to stabilize the permeable bedrock below the Mausoleum, the builders evidently utilized a (presently) well-known civil engineering technique (Terzaghi and Peck, 1967, art. 21): surrounding the area to be excavated with a subterranean drainage system ("Lower Gallery") located below the lowest level of the foundation, and providing the means of removing the ground water collected in the system. Because of the tremendous hydraulic pressure differential between the water-saturated claystone and the open drainage galleries, ground water was forced into the galleries and drained away to the southeast of the Quadrangle area by gravity flow. The Lower Gallery system prevented ground water from rising above a level 4-4.5 m above modern sea level, thus stabilizing the mechanical properties of the bedrock between this depth and the Mausoleum foundation itself and lessening the possibility of major settling of the structure. It is rather unlikely that the builders appreciated all the finer points of soil mechanics, but they evidently realized for some reason, that before the Mausoleum could be constructed, the ground water had to be drained away from the area.

With the advent of sump pumps in the Middle Ages, and more recent and efficient wellpoint drainage systems, subterranean galleries long ago ceased to be an important drainage technique in foundation construction. For the Mausoleum builders, however, time and manpower were not major considerations, and the relative ease with which the claystone can be excavated with only picks made tunneling an eminently suitable approach. The early sequence of events in the construction of the Mausoleum may have been as follows:-

1. Investigation of subsurface conditions by means of pre-Mausoleum chambers and galleries; surveying of the margin of the Quadrangle.
2. Sinking of the Lower Gallery shafts and driving horizontal tunnels toward each other from adjacent shafts. Only one major offset occurred during this operation, when the tunnel driven southward from Shaft Ll drifted too far to the east and almost intersected the future west wall of the Quadrangle. Minor offsets occurred in the tunnels between Shafts L6 and L7, and L7 and L8. Almost the entire system is cut through Units 2a and 2b, with only the tunnels in the vicinity of Shaft L6 intersecting the top of Unit 1. Drainage of the system was effected through a tunnel leading southeastward from Shaft L10 [cf. the plan Zahle/Jeppesen (1975), Ill. 1].
3. Open-pit excavation of the Quadrangle, involving differential removal of Unit 3 in the light of pre-Mausoleum structures within the area. A portion of the Lower Gallery between Shafts Ll and L6 was removed during the cutting of the west staircase landing; the remaining part of the tunnel was roofed over with rough-finished foundation blocks and the "marble drain" from the Mausoleum tomb chamber was led into it. The cutting of the west staircase landing also exposed a part of the abandonded Lower Gallery tunnel from Shaft Ll; this breach was probably walled off with andesite blocks.
4. Pre-Mausoleum cuttings below the common bedrock level of the Mausoleum foundation were infilled with andesite blocks. This most notably includes the "short gallery", the chamber associated with the south stairway, and the gallery, angular in plan, trending east and southeast from the Mausoleum tomb chamber. Surface shaft entrances to the Lower Gallery system were evidently covered over with andesite blocks prior to their burial, but the system remained accessible for inspection and sediment removal through the Upper Gallery and Shafts L8 and L9.
5. Construction of the podium with andesite foundation blocks.

Over the months, as thousands upon thousands of foundation blocks were laid to form the solid core of the podium, the Mausoleum builders must have closely watched the water level in the Lower Gallery and the alignment of the foundation itself for indications of differential settling. Whether their innovative engineering technique was entirely successful is unknowable, but it is not an entirely improbable speculation that the adverse geological and ground water conditions at the site may have contributed in some way to the Mausoleum's eventual collapse.

References

Alpan, Sadrettin, and Gerhard Lüttig, 1971. "The German-Turkish lignite exploration in Turkey of the years 1965 to 1969." *Newsletters on Stratigraphy*, 1 (3), pp. 11-18.

Bremmer, Heinrich, 1971. "Geology of the coastal regions of Southwest Turkey" *in: Geology and History of Turkey*. Petroleum Exploration Society of Libya Annual Field Conference, no. 13, pp. 257-274.

Flemming, N.C., Czartoryska, N.M.G., and P.M. Hunter, 1973. "Archaeological evidence for eustatic and tectonic components of relative sea level change in the Southern Aegean." *in: Marine Archaeology*, Colston Papers, *23*, London: Butterworth. pp. 1-66.

Lamb, H.H., 1968. *The Changing Climate*. London: Methuen & Co.

Terzaghi, Karl, and R.B. Peck, 1967. *Soil Mechanics in Engineering Practice*, 2nd ed., Wiley & Sons: New York.

Table 1. Stratigraphic Section, Mausoleum Site.

Unit	*Description*	Thickness
	Top of section	
4	Siltstone, friable, pinkish-grey (5YR 8/1) thin (.1-1cm) parting laminae, interbedded with light grey (N7) fine sandstone beds as shallow, discontinuous lenses 1-10 cm in thickness. Sandstone lenses show crossbedding and occasionally grade into gravel comprising well-rounded rock fragments 3-4 mm average diameter. Upward in section siltstone and sandstone are interbedded with pure tuffaceous sandstone (Unit 3). Unit 4 is exposed in the natural bedrock surface surrounding the Mausoleum Quadrangle, and in the northeast corner of the Quadrangle cutting.	(Upper contact not observed) 2 m+
3	Tuffaceous sandstone, very light grey (N8), friable, comprising coarse sand-sized rounded fragments of andesite crystal ash and mica fragments in a matrix of finely-comminuted crystal ash. Sequence comprises thin (.1-1 cm) laminae distinguished by graded bedding. The crystal ash which is the primary component of this unit and which occurs as scattered included grains throughout Units 1, 2a and 2b, is composed of phenocrysts of hornblende laths (.1-1 mm long) plus crystalline masses of quartz in a matrix of broken plagioclase (bytownite?) crystals. Small fragments of the pure ash exhibit surficial alteration zones .5-1 mm thick where the matrix has been altered to clay. A trace of calcium carbonate is present in the unaltered ash, possibly from reaction of magma with limestone walls of volcanic vents. Unit 3 is exposed in the extreme southwest corner and along the east side of the Mausoleum Quadrangle.	4 m
2b	Claystone, greyish-orange on fresh surface (10 YR 7/4), dense, unstratified, blocky, conchoidal fracture, contains inclusions of siltsized quartz and mica flakes, and crystal ash fragments (Unit 3). Extensive fracturing and jointing in surface and subsurface exposures. This unit is exposed in the Quadrangle in the central and western portions of the excavation excluding the extreme southwest corner.	1-1.5 m
2a	Claystone, lying disconformably below 2b, is characterized by 2 component grain sizes: clay identical in texture and composition with Unit 2b, plus intercalated laminae and lenses of fine sand-sized grains of quartz and rock fragments. Scattered evenly through both clay and fine sand laminae are rounded fragments of crystal tuff (Unit 3) having a median diameter of app. 3 mm. This unit is exposed in the walls of the Mausoleum tomb chamber and in parts of the south section of the Lower Gallery between Shafts L7 and L8.	app 1 m

Unit	Description	Thickness
1	Claystone, moderate yellow-brown (10YR 5/3), massive, unstratified, resting disconformably below Unit 2a. Blocky, angular fracture, well-indurated. Contains occasional sand-sized, well-rounded acidic rock fragments, a very small percentage of angular, silt-sized quartz crystals, and andesite crystal ash fragments with a median diameter of 1 mm. Hematite coatings and pyrolusite dendrites are commonly segregated along microjoints in the rock. This unit was only observed in subsurface exposures in the southwest corner of the Lower Gallery around Shaft L6.	1 m+ (Lower contact not observed)
	Bottom of section	

Appendix 2

Excerpts from C.T. NEWTON, A HISTORY OF DISCOVERIES

pp. 91-93; 96-99; 101-102; 138-145

HD 91-93:

...To the west of the spot where I had discovered the group of the Persian horseman, finding that the earth was very deep, and sufficiently solid to admit of mines being driven without wooden frames to support them, I opened two parallel galleries, working westward from the line of excavation. After advancing a few feet, we came to a staircase cut out of the solid rock, which we ascended step by step, driving the galleries upwards till we came to the surface of the field. I then succeeded in obtaining possession of the ground, and cleared the staircase. It was twenty-nine feet wide, and consisted of twelve steps. The mass of earth accumulated over the lowest step was twenty feet in depth. This soil was of a white and friable nature, containing much decomposed native rock, and little or no vegetable matter. On the north, as will be seen by the cut, this staircase is flanked by a wall of good isodomous masonry, built of large blocks of native rock. A few feet to the east of the stair we discovered some alabaster jars of remarkable size and beauty, such as were used by the ancients for precious ointments, and are called, from their material, *alabastra.*

On one of these jars I discovered, to my great surprise, two inscriptions, one in hieroglyphics, the other in the cuneiform character. The inscription in hieroglyphics contained a royal cartouche, which led me at the time of the discovery to think that the name was that of Mausolus. I was not then aware that the vase which I had discovered was identical with one now in the Bibliothèque Impériale at Paris, and that the inscription, according to the best authorities, contains the name of Xerxes written in four languages. A view of this vase, with a facsimile of the inscriptions on it, is given Plate V-II., and a dissertation on this and similar *alabastra* will form one of the Appendices to this work.

Several fragments of small terra-cotta figures were found on the same spot, one of which, a female head, is of exquisite beauty; also some bones of oxen. Immediately to the east of the spot where I discovered these remains, was a block of green stone, 7' high, by 4½' square, weighing probably about ten tons. (See Plate VIII.).

This stone was in its original position, resting on a marble pavement; and, as I shall presently show, there is every reason for believing that it closed the entrance into the tomb through which the body of Mausolus was conveyed.

HD 96-99:

At what level the sepulchral chambers in the basement were situated, cannot now be ascertained.

It is worthy of note that the great stone east of the staircase rested on two slabs of white marble, to which it had been carefully adjusted in the following manner: – In the great stone, bronze dowels were fixed, corresponding with bronze sockets let into the marble slabs. The accompanying cut shows one of these dowels within a bronze collar, which was fixed in the great stone with lead. Doubtless it was intended by the architect that, on lowering this stone, the dowels should drop out of their collars into the sockets below; but, whether through accident or *fraud*, they appear to have remained in the collars instead of descending into the holes to which they had been fitted. This may be seen on examining the ends of these dowels, which are united all round the edge to the collars by a strong patina. Perhaps the workmen employed on this operation purposely contrived that it should be thus incomplete, with the same motive as actuated the builder of the treasury of the Egyptian king Rhampsinitus.[117] On the west or outer side, the marble slabs were flush with the green stone, which was continued as a pavement till within 16' of the stair,[118] where it ceased flush with the native rock. It may be inferred that on the inner or east side of the great stone, the marble pavement was continued eastward at the same level; for, as will be seen by Plate VIII., the ends of the slabs under the great stone projected over a lower course of green stone, below which was the native rock. This marble pavement covered a drain which runs east and west from the interior of the basement into a gallery to be presently described. Between the great stone[119] and the gallery, this drain is cut in the native rock: within the Quadrangle, it runs between courses of green stone. It is to be observed that these slabs were the only marbles belonging to the edifice which were found in position; and it is to be presumed that they would not have escaped the spoilers of the Mausoleum, had it not been for the difficulty of displacing the immense stone placed upon them, – a difficulty which we only overcame by the application of two screw-jacks.

The position of this remnant of marble pavement leads me to infer that a passage paved with marble led from the great stone into the royal sepulchral chamber, which may have been nearly in the centre of the basement, where the cutting is deepest, and to which part the drain already mentioned, and a similar drain running eastward, both lead.

HD 101-102:

It will be seen, by reference to the Plan, that the line of cutting on the north side of the Quadrangle is not continuous, but that, at a few feet from the north-west angle, a break occurs, extending for 59', after which the line of cutting is resumed. In this interval were three square piers, and a fourth pier occurred in the space between the staircase wall and the north-west corner of the Quadrangle. These piers were all built of squared blocks of native rock. Their courses were not properly bonded, and from the want of solidity in the masonry, it is evident that these piers formed no part of the structure of the Mausoleum. The three piers on the north had their southern faces flush with the north side of the *peribolus*. All the four were carried to the same height, and this level, as will be seen by the sections, is nearly uniform with the native rock at the foot of the north wall of the *peribolus,* at the head of the stair, and all round the west, south, and east sides, where no break occurred in cutting the lines of the Quadrangle.

This level must have nearly corresponded with that of the original surface of the platform, which, for reasons which I shall presently state, must, I think, have been raised a little above the rock.

The irregular excavation in which the north piers were placed, was filled up with the same white soil which we found over the stair on the west. Behind the piers were several drums of circular columns, roughly hewn out of the native rock, which were rudely piled up, as if in a quarry. These drums exceeded 3' in diameter.

HD 138-145:

I have already stated that at the distance of 18' to the north of the south-east corner the west line of the Quadrangle fails, being interrupted by a wide opening, leading to the staircase already noticed.

At the distance of 26½' to the east of the foot of this staircase was a great stone, originally designed, as I have shown, to be solidly bolted into bronze sockets in a marble pavement. The space between this stone and the native rock on its south side had been filled up with slabs of green stone, with which it had been wedged in. On the opposite side, as will be seen by Plate VIII., a rebate, or groove, passes down the stone, which must have served to hold in their place the slabs wedged in on this side. From the solidity of its insertion, and its great size, I am led to the conclusion that the great stone was used to close the entrance to the sepulchral chamber in which the body of Mausolus was deposited, and that it was dropped into its place like a portcullis.[120] This is further proved by the finding of *alabastra,* terra-cotta figures, and bones of oxen, between this stone and the foot of the staircase;

for such objects would remain at the entrance to the tomb, after the performance of certain periodical rites, *enagismata*.[121]

I am further of opinion that the stair was cut for the express purpose of conveying the body of Mausolus into the tomb, and that it was covered over with soil immediately afterwards, there having been no further occasion for it.

I have been led to adopt this opinion from the following observations:-

1. The steps of the stair are cut out of the native rock, which, being friable and easily wrought, would necessarily have been much worn, had the stair been subjected to weather and thoroughfare for any length of time. The edges of the steps, however, were sharp, exhibiting no sign of wear or weather, as may be seen by the woodcut, (*ante*, p. 92).
2. On the north side the stair is flanked by a wall of isodomous masonry, built of blocks of the native rock. (See the cut already referred to.) On the south side the boundary of the stair is a cutting in the rock, which, as will be seen by the Plan (Plate III.), turns below the stair at a right angle to the south, and, after making two more returns, falls in with the west side of the Quadrangle.

   If this stair had been designed to form a visible feature in so sumptuous an edifice as the Mausoleum, it would not have been finished in so rough a manner, having only a wall of coarse material on one flank, and an irregular and unsightly cutting on the other. It would more probably have been faced with marble or the green stone of the basement. In that case the holes for the insertion of metal clamps would still be visible on the steps and flanks. No such marks, however, were discernible, though the surface of the rock and wall was carefully examined.
3. The earth with which this stair was covered was a white soil, full of crumbling fragments of the native rock. This white soil is, as I have already stated, the substratum throughout the Mausoleum platform, below the black superficial *humus*. No fragments of the architecture or sculpture of the building itself were ever found in the lower soil; moreover, it exhibited no trace of vegetable matter, either in a decomposed or growing state. I am, therefore, of opinion that this ground had never been disturbed since the platform was originally formed round the Mausoleum.
4. By reference to Plate VIII., it will be seen that the side of the large stone facing the stair was left rough, while its inner or eastern face was wrought to a smooth surface.

   If it had been intended that this stone should be seen from the outside, its western or external face would have been tooled in the same manner as its opposite or inner face.

About two feet to the east of the lowest step was a wall running from flank to flank, and in a direction nearly parallel to the width of the stair. It was built of massive blocks of native rock, exhibiting a great contrast to the neat work of the isodomous flanking wall, the blocks being squared but not bonded.[122]

This wall was rather more than a yard broad. Its width, and the style of the masonry, lead me to think that it must have been built for the purpose of consolidating the soil of the platform when this cutting was filled in.

If we suppose that the stair was cut to admit the sepulchral procession into the tomb, and immediately afterwards covered with earth, we may thus account for the preservation of the alabaster vases which were discovered at the foot of the rough wall.

Two of these were unbroken, and their surface generally was remarkably fresh. If, according to Greek custom, they had been placed at the door of the sepulchre on some occasion when the tomb was visited by mourners, and if they had remained in their original position for any length of time, exposed to weather and accident, as would have been the case had the stair been left open, they would hardly have been preserved in so perfect a condition to the present day.

Supposing the stair to have been filled in flush with the level of the rock behind it, the entrance to the tomb would have been concealed under a depth of nine feet of soil, and this superincumbent mass of earth would, of course, have added greatly to the security of the sepulchre.

It may be observed, in reference to the western side of the Quadrangle, that the large stone which closed the entrance to the tomb, ranges with the pier in which the flank wall of the stair terminates, as shown in the Plan. If, then, we suppose the large stone to have been inserted in the masonry of the basement, the western line of the foundation would include the stair pier.

On examining the Plan and Sections of the Mausoleum, it will be seen that the native rock of the platform is pierced by subterraneous galleries at two different levels. These passages are consequently distinguished in this work as the Upper and Lower Galleries.

It will be perceived, on reference to the Plan, that the Lower Gallery runs all round the Quadrangle of the Mausoleum, having no outlet except on the eastern side, near the south-eastern angle. There can hardly be a doubt that this gallery served for the drainage of the building. On the eastern side, a drain issuing from under the paved area of the Quadrangle at the point marked ε in the plan, flows into the eastern gallery, and on the western side, another drain passed out of the building, at β as has been already stated. This drain, found in position, flowed under the great stone, emptying itself into the gallery through a bronze grating inserted in the covering slab of pavement. (See the cut.)

Ten shafts occur in this series of galleries – one at each of the four corners of the Quadrangle; and on the north, east, and south sides, respectively, two intermediate between the angle shafts.

On referring to the Plan, it will be seen that this lower gallery, though it surrounds the Quadrangle, does not run parallel to its lines, making many deflections, especially in its southern branch, which makes a bend inward within the line of the Quadrangle. If we suppose that this gallery was cut by the builders of the Mausoleum, and formed part of its plan, it is difficult to account for such deflections where parallelism might have been expected.

It is possible that parts of this gallery were cut at a previous period for the drainage of the deeper excavations in the quarry, and that the architects of the Mausoleum adapted these earlier passages to the plan of their building, connecting them together so as to form one duct. If this was not the case, we can only account for the deflections by supposing that they were made to avoid faults in the rock. The sides of the cutting, however, exhibited no sign of any such flaws.

The lower gallery is cut throughout in the solid rock, to a height ranging from 6' to 8', except in the part on the west side, where it passes the front of the stair.

Here it is a trench only 2' 10'' in depth, and covered over with slabs of green stone.

If we suppose this branch of the gallery to have been a work anterior to the Mausoleum, its upper portion would have been cut away in the course of the excavation for the stair.

It will be seen by reference to the Plan, that the centre pier on the north overhangs the corner of a shaft below it; from which it may be inferred that the pier was built after the shaft.

The external drainage of the building was probably conducted into the shafts. No sign of such drains was observable on the rocky margin of the shafts; but the external drainage may have been conducted through soil laid, as I have suggested, to produce an artificial level, or all the channels may have converged in that branch of the eastern lower gallery, which, entering the eastern side of the Quadrangle, receives the contribution of a small internal drain already noticed at ε in the Plan.

The shaft, where this branch from the Quadrangle enters the eastern gallery, may be considered as the terminus, or point of junction of all the branches of the lower gallery.

From this shaft a main duct leads in a southeastern direction to within 45' of the eastern *peribolus* wall. Here we lost all trace of it; but it was probably continued as a built gallery, on account of the great depth of the soil over the rock, which is here 25' below the surface. The masonry of the galleries may thus have been gradually undermined, and carried away by torrents from the hills."

As appears from his observations p. 138, Newton realized that "the great stone was used to close the entrance to the sepulchral chamber in which the body of Mausolus was deposited" but desisted from going deeper into the matter. As a comparison between his plan of the Quadrangle and the plan of the re-excavated site (figs. 1.53-54) will make clear, Newton recorded at least the upper edge of the cutting for the north and east sides of the tomb chamber. He also observed the outline of the tomb-robbers' mine as far as the tomb chamber.

Apparently, however, only the angular cutting east of the tomb chamber was investigated right to the bottom, where Newton discovered "the rag-stone drain". As it appears from the pages reproduced above, he took a particular interest in the subterranean "galleries".

Appendix 3:

Commander de la Tourrette's report on the demolition of the Maussolleion AD 1522[123]

The report was published for the first time by the French polymath and doctor of jurisprudence Claude Guichard in a learned treatise on burial customs all over the world: "FUNERAILLES & diuerses manières d'enseuelir des Rommains [sic], Grecs, & autres nations, tant anciennes que modernes, descrites par Claude Guichard Docteur és droits", Lyon 1581, pp. 378-381 (reproduced in extenso on pp. 156-159, cf. translation p. 167-8):

After having referred on the preceding pages to ancient sources dealing with the burial of Maussollos and the Maussolleion, in particular the elder Pliny and Vitruvius, and to post-antique medals representing the portrait of Artemisia, Guichard takes the opportunity to narrate the events that brought about the complete demolition of the Maussolleion.

C.T. Newton reproduced and offered a translation in English of the crucial part of the narrative (HD 75-79), while the version reprinted by Anthony Luttrell in vol. 2 of the Maussolleion publication also includes the introductory passage p. 379: "Depuis l'inclination de l'Empire Rommain etc.... Salmacis, qui couloit aupres".[124]

Newton did not discuss the problematic sections and words of the text, nor have these been sufficiently dealt with in my own preliminary discussion of it,[125] while Luttrell devoted his investigations to a most important and fruitful inquiry into the contemporary background of the report, and into the circumstances under which the events narrated by Commander de la Tourrette became known to learned people and were eventually published in print, almost sixty years after they had actually taken place.[126]

In the present paper I shall discuss first the conclusions that can be drawn from historical sources concerning the identity and lives of the persons who were jointly responsible for the transmission of the story, then the report itself. It will be shown that the original report was probably garbled to some extent by the idiom of the writers quoting it, in particular that of Guichard.[127]

Evidently the version given by Guichard was not in every detail identical with the original report, for in this the participants in the operations described must have been referred to in the first person rather than in the third. However, quite possibly the change from first to third person had already taken place when Daléchamps passed on the story to Guichard.

One cannot exclude the possibility that Daléchamps quoted from memory, but considering the many facts and details that were recorded, it seems more likely that he had taken careful notes. In his edition of Pliny's Natural History that was published at Lyons in 1587,[128] six years after Guichard's book, there is not the slightest reference to the story where it might have been expected, i.e. in connection with the annotationes p. 856 concerning Pliny's description of the Maussolleion book xxxvi, 30-31, nor any reference elsewhere to Guichard and his book.

The two certainly knew each other, for Guichard is known to have consulted Daléchamps in other learned matters as well and to have held him in high esteem, as attested by the following acknowledgment in his book (p. 290):

"Ie tien d'vn docte personage de nostre temps (marginal note: Iac. Dalechampius Doct. Medic.), duquel i'admire le rare sçavoir, & honnore la douceur & humanité, qui m'a faict ceste faveur, que de m'en dire son opinion, & monstrer ce qu'il en a escrit en son livre DE FLORIBUS, que c'est le Iosmin".

ΤΕΜΙΣΑΣ ΒΑΣΙΛΙΣΣΗΣ, qui ſe liſent d'un coſté & d'autre du baſtiment, deſquelles nous pouuons remarquer, comme de ſurcroiſt, que le vray nom de ceſte Roine eſt Artemiſe, non pas Artemiſie, iaçoit que les hiſtoriens & autres auteurs, tant anciens, que modernes, l'appellent ainſi communement.

L'autre medaille que i'ay veuë de ceſte Princeſſe Carienne eſt de bronze, belle & bien mignardement moulee, laquelle ie ne voudroye pleuuir aucunement antique, encores que Monſieur de S. Irigny, entre les mains duquel elle eſt, la tienne pour telle. Le viſage que lon y void donne par trop de l'air aux viſages Rommains, ce qu'aſſez ſçauront congnoiſtre ceux, qui deſia ſe feront acquis quelque iugement en faict de medailles, pour en auoir manié & confronté pluſieurs d'une ſorte & d'autre: ioint auſſi que l'accouſtrement de teſte ſent entierement ſon accouſtrement Rommain. Quant au ſepulcre de Mauſole, qui eſt repreſenté au reuers auec ce mot ΜΑΥΣΩΛΕΙΟΝ, il ſemble auoir eſté tiré ſuyuant la deſcription de Pline, que nous auons deſchiffree cydeſſus. Au reſte elle eſt fort nette, & faicte de la main de quelque excellent ouurier, comme on pourra congnoiſtre & iuger facilement par le portraict qu'en voycy.

Autre medaille d'Artemiſe auec le Mauſolee.

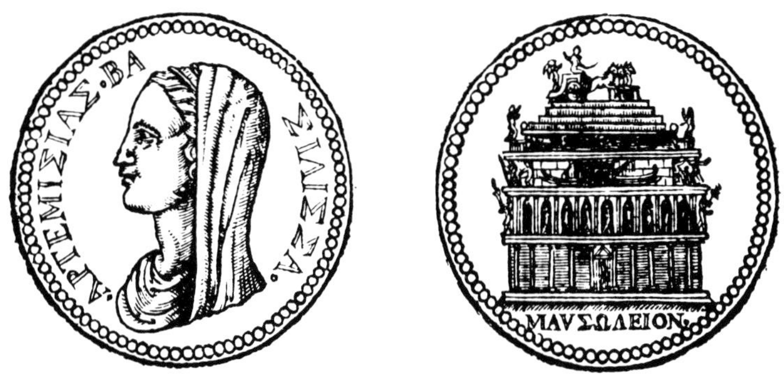

Or ne m'eſt ce pas aſſez d'auoir monſtré iuſques icy où, quand & par qui fut baſti le Mauſolee: cela ſe peut recueillir en partie des auteurs, qui en ont eſcrit par cy deuant:

uant: ie veuil, puis que l'occasion se presente si à propos, gratifier la posterité de chose, qui n'a point encor esté publiee, & deduire brieuement comment, quand & par qui cest admirable ouurage a esté desfaict & demoli. Depuis l'inclination de l'Empire Rommain, lors que par les courses des Mahometans & Persans tant de puissantes villes, riches & bien peuplees furent rauagees & destruites, l'ancienne & superbe cité d'Halycarnasse fut aussi ruïnee & reduite en vn petit village ou hameau exposé à la merci des Corsaires & escumeurs de mer, qui dure encor auiourdhuy, appellé *Mesy*. Les Cheualiers de S. Iean de Ierusalem s'estans retirés à Rhodes, & voyans ce lieu, lequel se presente le premier passant droit de l'isle en terre ferme, defensable de sa nature, & fort commode pour commander sur l'Asie, tirer viures de tous ces païs là, & empescher les courses des pyrates de Turquie & d'Egypte, ils bastirent sur la pointe droite du port, où iadis, comme nous auons remarqué cy dessus, estoit le temple de Venus & de Mercure, vn chasteau qu'on y void encor à present, lequel ils fortifierent, & appellerent la Tour S. Pierre: allechés, comme ie croy, à fortifier de ce costé, iaçoit que l'autre pointe fust de plus forte assiette, pour la commodité de la belle & cristalline fontaine Salmacis, qui couloit aupres.

L'an 1522. lors que Sultan Solyman se preparoit pour venir assaillir les Rhodiens, le Grand-maistre sçachãt l'importance de ceste place, & que le Turc ne faudroit point de l'empieter de premiere abordee, s'il pouuoit, y enuoya quelques cheualiers pour la remparer & mettre ordre à tout ce qui estoit necessaire pour soustenir l'ennemi, du nombre desquels fut le Commandeur de la Tourrette Lyonnois, lequel se treuua depuis à la prise de Rhodes, & vint en France, où il fit, de ce que ie vay dire maintenãt, le recit à monsieur d'Alechamps, personnage assez recongnu par ses doctes escrits, & que ie nomme seulement, à fin qu'on sçache de qui ie tien vne histoire si remarcable. Ces cheualiers estans arriués à Mesy, se mirent incontinent en deuoir de faire fortifier le chasteau, & pour auoir de la chaux, ne treuuans pierre aux enuirons plus propre

bb 2 pour

pour en cuire, ny qui leur vinst plus aisee, que certaines marches de marbre blanc, qui s'esleuoyent en forme de perron emmy d'un champ pres du port, là où iadis estoit la grande place d'Halycarnasse, ils firẽt abbattre & prendre pour cest effect. La pierre s'estant rencõtree bonne, fut cause, que ce peu de maçonnerie, qui paroissoit sur terre, ayant esté demoli, ils firent fouiller plus bas en esperance d'en treuuer dauantage. Ce qui leur succeda fort heureusement: car ils recongnurent en peu d'heure, que de tant plus qu'on creusoit profond, d'autant plus s'eslargissoit par le bas la fabrique, qui leur fournit par apres de pierres, non seulement à faire de la chaux, mais aussi pour bastir. Au bout de quatre ou cinq iours, apres auoir faict vne grande descouuerte, par vne apresdisnee ils virent vne ouuerture comme pour entrer dans vne caue: ils prirent de la chandelle, & deualerent dedans, où ils treuuerent vne belle grande sale carree, embellie tout au tour de colonnes de marbre, auec leurs bases, chapiteaux, architraues, frises & cornices grauees & taillees en demy-bosse: l'entredeux des colonnes estoit reuestu de lastres, listeaux ou plattes bandes de marbres de diuerses couleurs ornees de moulures & sculptures conformes au reste de l'œuure, & rapportés propremẽt sur le fonds blãc de la muraille, où ne se voyoit qu'histoires taillees, & toutes batailles à demyrelief. Ce qu'ayans admiré de prime face, & apres auoir estimé en leur fantasie la singularité de l'ouurage, en fin ils defirent, briserent & rompirent, pour s'en seruir comme ils auoyent faict du demeurant. Outre ceste sale ils treuuerent apres vne porte fort basse, qui conduisoit à vne autre, comme antichambre, ou il y auoit vn sepulcre auec son vase & son tymbre de marbre blanc, fort beau & reluisant à merueilles, lequel, pour n'auoir pas eu assez de temps, ils ne descouurirent, la retraicte estant desia sonnee. Le lendemain apres qu'ils y furent retournés, ils treuuerẽt la tombe descouuerte, & la terre semee tout autour de force petits morceaux de drap d'or, & paillettes de mesme metal: qui leur fit penser, que les corsaires, qui escumoyent alors le long de toute ceste coste, ayans eu quelque vent de ce qui auoit

auoit esté descouuert en ce lieu là, y vindrent de nuict, & osterent le couuercle du sepulcre : & tient on qu'ils y treuuerent des grandes richesses & thresors. Ainsi ce superbe sepulcre, compté pour l'un des sept miracles & ouurages merueilleux du monde, apres auoir eschappé la fureur des Barbares, & demeuré l'espace de 2247. ans debout, du moins enseueli dedans les ruïnes de la ville d'Halycarnasse, fut descouuert & aboli pour remparer le chasteau S. Pierre, par les cheualiers croisés de Rhodes, lesquels en furent incontinent apres chassés par le Turc, & de toute l'Asie quant & quant.

Ie passeray aux sepultures des nations, qui habitent à present l'Asie, & par mesme moyen mettray fin à ce chapitre, apres que i'auray dit encor ce mot à propos des Cariens, que Theuet en sa Cosmographie ° estime auoir veu le sepulcre de la Roine Artemise à l'une des portes de la ville de Rhodes, ioingnant les murailles assez pres du port. Mais aussi bien le se peut il imaginer là, comme il a faict le Mausolee, pres d'Halycarnasse, & non pas dedans, & la statue d'Artemise, qui marquoit la cité de Rhodes en signe de seruitude, sur vne petite montagne qui est aupres, au lieu qu'elle estoit posee en l'une des plus apparentes places de la ville. Ie ne veuil pareillement oublier, encor qu'il ne me souuienne point maintenant de l'auteur qui l'escrit, que les Cariens auoyent iadis accoustumé d'enseuelir les morts auec leurs armes, & signammēt auec les petits boucliers, dont ils se seruoyent à la guerre. Et voyla quant aux peuples anciens de l'Asie.

o liu -. chap. 4.

Des funerailles & sepultures des peuples qui se treuuent à present en Asie. CHAP. VI.

MAINTENANT nous passerons aux cerimonies funebres obseruees de nostre temps, & cōmencerons par celles des INDIENS ORIENTAVX, puis que c'est la nation de laquelle nous auons le plus à discourir : Et d'autant que la region de l'Inde est de grande estendue, & habitee de plusieurs sortes

bb 3 de peu

Daléchamps may have found the Commander's report of no avail; at any rate, it was of course not directly relevant to Pliny's text.

"De la Tourrette" could possibly have been the personal name of Daléchamps' informant, but his title "Commandeur" strongly suggests that he was one of those Hospitallers who held the Commandery of la Tourrette in the Priory of Auvergne.[129] Luttrell has traced the lives of six of these commanders who might have been identical with the one mentioned in the report,[130] were it not that five of them would either have been too young or too old to fit in convincingly with the basic dates deducible from the report:

(1) Fr. Ligerius was granted La Tourrette in 1505, but died already in 1507 or 1508, i.e. many years before the final demolition of the Maussolleion took place in 1522.
(2) Fr. Annet Constant became a Commander of La Tourrette in 1508 and died about 1528, i.e. at a time when Daléchamps was still in his boyhood.
(3) Fr. Lionet Regnault was granted La Tourrette in 1540 and died in about 1545, definitely before Daléchamps settled at Lyons in 1552, where Regnault is not known to have resided.
(4) Fr. Geuffroy Regnault became Commander of La Tourrette in 1545 and died in about 1573, but is not mentioned in any source before 1537, and is unlikely to have been in Bodrum in 1522.
(5) Fr. Jacques des Roches became Commander of La Tourrette in 1564 and died in 1587. In 1522 he would probably have been too young to take part in the Rhodian Hospitallers' activities in Bodrum.

The qualifications of these candidates are evidently inadequate as compared to those of no. 6 on the list, Fr. Georges de Vauzelles:

(6) De Vauzelles was granted the Commandery of La Tourrette in 1528 and lived thereafter at Lyons until his death between 1553 and 1557. Since Daléchamps settled at Lyons in 1552, the two could well have become acquainted there. De Vauzelles exchanged the Commandery of La Tourrette for that of Temple d'Ayen in 1540, but was apparently better known among the people he knew at Lyons in his former capacity. Thus in a book on Roman religion published at Lyons in 1557 (Discours de la Religion des anciens Romains), the author Guillaume du Choul refers to "Messire George de Vauzelles, Chevalier de Rhodes, Commandeur de la Torrette", to whom he was indebted for the information on the Colossus of Rhodes in a book which de Vauzelles had brought with him from Greece.

Georges and his two brothers Jean and Matthieu lived together and were known as "the three illustrious brothers". Jean was a writer and social reformer, had an excellent library and numerous literary friends and correspondents, while Matthieu was an important lawyer and politician. Both were patrons at the Hôtel-Dieu (principal hospital) at Lyons to which Daléchamps was appointed in 1552.

Since Georges was at Rhodes both in 1519 and during the siege in 1522, where he participated actively in its defence, and later lived until his death at Lyons, where he could hardly have failed to make the acquaintance of Daléchamps, the evidence is clearly in favour of the possibility that the anonymous "Commandeur de la Tourrette Lyonnois" was in actual fact identical with Fr. Georges de Vauzelles.

The report proper begins with the passage "L'an 1522. lors que Sultan Solyman etc. ..." and ends with the words "grandes richesses et thresors". Basically original are, of course, only the statements clearly deriving from eyewitness observations that cannot reasonably well be ascribed to Daléchamps or to Guichard, such as the following:

(1) It is stated that beneath "certain steps of white marble" (certaines marches de marbre blanc) the Knights found not only more material that could be used for making lime (non seulement à faire de la chaux), but also stones suitable for building (aussi pour bastir). This seems to imply that the latter stones were not of marble, but of a different geological composition, as were in

fact the foundation blocks of greenish tufa used in the Maussolleion.

(2) The detailed description of many individual features in the decoration of the walls in the larger of the subterranean rooms could hardly have been devised by people who had not been present in person at their discovery (cf. below, p. 164f).

(3) It is mentioned that the door leading from the larger compartment into the anteroom was "very low" (fort basse).

Apparently de la Tourrette found this feature strikingly disproportionate to the impressive dimensions of the compartment.

(4) Soon after the tomb had been discovered, and before the Knights had had time to inspect the place in every detail, the retreat had been sounded and they had had to withdraw to the Castle. Since they had to use candles to find their way in the darkness of the subterranean rooms, they might as well have continued their work in the night, but the surroundings of the Castle were basically in enemy hands, particularly so in the night-time.

From the very beginning of its existence, it seems to have been the principal purpose of the Castle at Bodrum to maintain a symbolic claim of sovereignty on the Asiatic continent. Rather than posing a threat of any importance, the garrison had to undergo a constant siege by the surrounding Turkish community. In 1470 it was continuously engaged with the Turks, and in 1472 a Venetian fleet had to be sent to come to its rescue.[131]

In 1520 there was peace with the Turks who twice weekly sold foodstuffs and other items to the garrison, but the worry was a small mound from which the Turks would be able to do much damage to the Castle.[132] In 1522 the tension had probably become even more critical.

(5) The zeal with which the knights destroyed the wall decoration in the larger room (defirent, briserent et rompirent) may well be interpreted in the light of the religious aversion to pagan antiquities officially maintained by the Hospitallers.

(6) The discovery that the tomb had been robbed and that the floor was "strewn all over with tiny pieces of gold cloth and appliqués of the same metal" (semee tout autour de force petits morceaux de drap d'or, & paillettes de mesme metal) must have been made by the Knights, which conclusion is corroborated by the recent finds of similar remains in the tomb chamber and in the grave-robbers' mine.[133]

In contrast to the facts of the report, the last lines "Ainsi ce superbe sepulcre etc. ... de toute l'Asie quant & quant" are retrospective in character and were evidently added by a commentator, presumably Guichard. Suspiciously excursive and literary in style is also the topographical specification "là où jadis estoit la grande place d'Halycarnasse". This is also found a few pages before (p. 373) in somewhat similar terms: "le lieu où jadis estoit situee la ville de Halycarnasse".

In the report proper there is no other explicit reference to Halikarnassos, and even more conspicuous is the absence of any reference to Maussollos and the Maussolleion. There is not the slightest indication that de la Tourrette associated the tomb that had been discovered with that of the Maussolleion, or that he was inclined to interpret the evidence to that effect. This might have been tempting, if he had known that "Mesy" was identical with ancient Halicarnassus, and that this was the place where the Maussolleion was situated. To all appearances it was not his ambition to offer an exhaustive explanation and interpretation of what he had seen, but just to state the tangible facts of the discovery as precisely as he could, which is an important argument in favour of his credibility.

His description does not even suggest the possibility that the tomb should be identified with that of Maussollos, quite the reverse, for it is said to be placed in a kind of anteroom (comme antichambre) subordinate to the spacious and richly decorated room which particularly impressed the Knights, and which obviously would have been a much more suitable resting-place for a potentate like Maussollos. E SILENTIO, therefore, one must conclude that nothing remained in the larger room to suggest the existence of a burial.

Guichard made no attempt to interpret de la Tourrette's description, but was satisfied to draw the conclusion that the demolished ruins must have been those of the Maussolleion and to leave open the issue whether or not the Knights had actually been aware at the time of their discovery that they were removing the last remains of one of the Seven Wonders of the World.

The report does not differ markedly in style from the parts of the book manifestly written by Guichard himself. It does not seem unlikely, though, that being himself a Lyonnese associating with intellectual circles at Lyons, Georges de Vauzelles would have expressed himself in much the same terms as Guichard. Some expressions used in the report are in fact more or less closely paralleled in Guichard's own stylistic repertory, as I had the opportunity to observe by reading his book in its entirety:

(1) "defirent, briserent et rompirent" cf. p. 66: "brisoit, rompoit, & ruoit"; p. 120: "abbatus, defendus, abolis".
(2) "histoires taillees, et toutes batailles à demy relief" cf. p. 493: "un cloistre ... lequel estoit tout taillé d'histoires de demy bosse representans la guerre que le Roy fit contre les Bactrianiens, qui s'estoyent rebellés (the tomb of King Osymandyas, Diod. Sic. 1.47); p. 119: "faisoyent historier leur sepulcres, et tailler en demi-bosse leur triomphes & trofees".
(3) "morceaux de drap d'or, et paillettes de mesme metal" cf. p. 145: "feuilles d'or battu, ou de paillettes de mesme metal".
(4) "colonnes de marbre, auec leurs bases, chapiteaux, architraues, frises & cornices" cf. p. 170: "colonnes, accompagnees de leurs bases, chapiteaux, architraue, & frontispice".
(5) "& deualerent dedans" cf. p. 349: "devaloyent dedans".
(6) "Outre ceste sale ils treuuerent ... vne autre, comme antichambre" cf. p. 491: "on passe ... en d'autres salles, antichambres, & galleries" (the Labyrinth in Egypt, Herodotus 2,148).
(7) "un sepulchre ... de marbre blanc, fort beau et reluisant à merueilles"
The adverbial construction "à merueilles" is unlikely to have been quoted verbatim from the original report, and was more probably due to Guichard, cf. the following passage p. 347:

"Mais, pour reuenir aux Rois de Perse, celuy oseroit bien s'abuser, qui a mis en auant, qu'une grande tour bastie de marbre blanc, laquelle il dit avoir veuë pres la ville de Souses, belle & haute à merueilles, & ayant au dedans les plus magnifiques tombes du monde, la pluspart encore entieres, seruoit anciennement de sepulture aux Rois Persans.

Car cela est rebroué par l'autorité de plusieurs segnalés historiens que nous auons allegué cy dessus (Strabo, Xenophon, Arrian). Et il n'y eut que Cyrus, qui fut enterré en Pasargades, pource qu'il le commanda: Et son sepulchre fut dressé au iardin royal etc."

In this account which was quoted from the contemporary cosmographer Theuet, "à merueilles" may well imply irony on the part of Guichard, who obviously found the whole story unbelievable.

On the other hand, in Guichard's rendering of de la Tourrette's report, the same phrase should more probably be understood to express justifiable enthusiasm on the part of the eyewitness, the reliability of whom Guichard found no reason to question. There is not the slightest indication elsewhere in the report that he did not consider the evidence of his informant perfectly trustworthy.
(8) On the use of expressions presumably quoted directly from the report, such as LASTRES and LISTEAUX, see below.

The description of the tomb – "vn sepulcre auec son vase & son tymbre de marbre blanc, fort beau et reluisant à merueilles" – is remarkably brief, and the terms primarily used to characterize it – VASE and TYMBRE – are difficult to interpret.

The information that pirates "removed the lid of the tomb" (osterent le couuercle du sepulchre) implies that it had the form of a receptacle closed at the top by a lid, cf. Guichard's description of the opening of Numa Pompilius' coffers: "de sçavoir que les couuercles estans ostés, on treuua l'un des coffres totalement vuide" (p. 29).

However, instead of making use of technical terms like those elsewhere found in his book to designate tombs of a sarcophagus-like type such as "sarcophague";[134] "sarceuil";[135] "cercueil";[136] "caisse de pierre";[137] "coffre (du corps, de marbre, de pierre, de terre cuite)";[138] "receptacle du corps en guise de coffre accompagné de son couuercle à dos d'asne";[139] "chasse", or "vaisseau"[140] – Guichard prefers the much less commonplace words VASE and TYMBRE. Nevertheless, the use of the possessive pronoun in the expressions SON VASE and SON TYMBRE must mean that rather than being in any way exceptional, VASE and TYMBRE were components characteristic of tombs in general or at least of types of tombs familiar to Guichard, and presumably to his informant as well.

In a number of cases, Guichard uses VASE as synonymous with URNE.[141] However, if this was its meaning in the case under discussion, the expression "osterent le couuercle" would be rather misleading, for it would have required no piratical violence but just a minimum of effort to remove the lid of an urn.

Besides, if one of the two components were an urn, it would be hard to imagine any complementary component equally relevant to the basic requirements of a tomb. But VASE is not known to have been used in any other sense in contexts of sepulchral relevance, and it may therefore be suspected that Guichard used it as synonymous with VAS, or that a misprint occurred.

In addition to VAS, ancient Latin and late Latin also had the form VASUM, and both continued to be in use in the Romance languages. Besides meaning "vessel", VASUM could also refer to a tomb or a sarcophagus, as in a sepulchral Christian inscription from the Narbonensis: CORPUS HOC VASO SITUM. In Romance Gaul, the meaning "sarcophagus" prevailed in Francoprovencal which was the language spoken in and around Lyons, where de Vauzelles and Guichard lived.[142]

VAS is used by Guichard in a passage referring to the habit in Antiquity of decorating tombs with flowers and herbs (p. 287):

"Au regard des herbes & des fleurs, nous apprenons d'une infinité de passages, qu'ils en couronnoyent, embouquettoyent, & sursemoyent ordinairement LES PILASTRES, VAS & LAMES DES SEPULCRES, & singulierement lors qu'ils y celebroyent quelque commemoration ou anniversaire".

In this context, VAS (plural) appears to refer to the lids on top of sarcophagi, while PILASTRES and LAMES must be understood to mean upright monuments[143] and stone slabs covering the graves,[144] respectively. Much the same choice of various categories of externally visible funerary equipment is exemplified in a passage dealing with the customs of washing, anointing, and scenting graves in Antiquity (p. 301):

"Car le pluspart des Grecs avoyent accoustumé de lauer, oindre, & parfumer ... LES LAMES, TYMBRES, & PILASTRES DES SEPULCRES"

in which TYMBRES takes the place of VAS in the first-mentioned passage and appears to be largely synonymous with this, the difference between the two being presumably that while VAS alludes primarily to the receptacle, TYMBRE applies in particular to its lid.

Judging from other contexts in which the word is used by Guichard, TYMBRE may signify any object serving the purpose of crowning a basic structure underneath. Thus the member resembling a broad-brimmed hat like the Greek PETASOS which was placed on top of the bronze disk forming the roof of the lower storey of King Porsenna's fabulous memorial at Chiusi as described by the elder Pliny (NH 36.91), is referred to as a TYMBRE (p. 436):

"Chacune desquelles (pyramides) ... estoyent tellement plantees et appointees, qu'elles portoyent à la cime une grosse boule de bronce (orbis aeneus), qui les prenait toutes (unus omnibus impositus), laquelle estoit TYMBREE d'un chappeau à l'impériale de mesme metal (et petasus) ... Sur ce TYMBRE estoyent encor", etc.[145]

In this context, the verb derived from TYMBRE: TYMBRER, must mean "to round off" or "to crown". In the same sense, TYMBRER is used to describe imperial badges and coats of arms decorating the personal belongings of Charles V, such as shield and helmet, that were carried in procession at his funeral in 1558.[146]

Judging from the above-mentioned evidence, the tomb described in de la Tourrette's report must have had the form of a sarcophagus consisting of a receptacle and its lid. It may have been a specimen of simple design, but the choice of the term TYMBRE rather than COUUERCLE leaves open the possibility that the lid was a piece of some individual attraction.

The same conclusion can be drawn from an analysis of the sentence structure. FORT BEAU & RELUISANT À MERUEILLES must refer, in the first place, to TYMBRE. This is evidently the focal point of the description, while if equal attention were to be paid to VASE, the adjectives should have read in the plural form FORT BEAUX ET RELUISAN(T)S À MERUEILLES. As there is no comma between TYMBRE and DE MARBRE BLANC, the latter word must logically apply to TYMBRE. At any rate, the context does not necessarily imply that VASE should be understood as well.

Possibly, therefore, the receptacle was made of a stone different from, and perhaps less costly than white marble, such as the bluish limestone that was used to face parts of the superstructure of the Maussolleion and the retaining walls supporting its terrace.[147]

On the issue whether the sarcophagus described by de la Tourrette was identical with the one, of which fragments have been found at the British and Danish excavations of the Quadrangle, see above, chapter 19.

In addition to the finds of gold appliqués and other pieces of jewelry already referred to, the re-excavation of the Maussolleion site has also brought to light other remains that invite a critical comparison with de la Tourrette's report: in particular the tomb chamber and its corridor, as well as the mine dug by the grave-robbers who looted the tomb.

The tomb-robbers' mine

As Anthony Luttrell has established,[148] stones from the Maussolleion were used after 1494 for the enlargement of the western ramparts of the Castle, and possibly this work had not been completely finished, when in 1522 the Grand Master decided to send a contingent of Knights from Rhodes to speed up all due preparations for the defence against the Turks.

The last phases of building operations in the Castle involving the use of material from the Maussolleion are recorded on coats of arms dating from 1517-18.[149] If utilization of its stones had stopped at that time, its ruins might well have been partially covered by earth and overgrown by weeds, when the Knights from Rhodes arrived four or five years later. At that time, according to the report, all that was visible was a kind of platform (PERRON) of steps of white marble, whose purpose it would not have been possible to establish until the burial in one of the subterranean chambers was discovered.

Presumably the shaft marking the entrance to the robbers' mine was hidden underneath shrubs and weeds, and the mine itself partly silted up with mud deposited by seasonal torrents of rainwater and therefore not accessible (cf. above, p. 118).

At any rate, the way the Knights discovered the larger compartment was from above, probably by coming across the corbelled vault with which the excavated tomb chamber must be assumed to have been covered.

The larger room and the decoration of its walls

This room (sale) is characterized as large (grande) and square (carree) i.e. giving the impression of being square, but not implicitly said to be exactly quadratic in plan – under the circumstances hardly anybody would have cared to measure its sides. This description is perfectly compatible with the dimensions of the excavated tomb chamber, which measured c. 6.25 × 6.80 m.[150]

No columns supporting the ceiling are mentioned – they were probably rendered superfluous by a corbelled vault – but the walls were decorated all around with a colonnaded structure represented in half-relief (demy-bosse), whose components are enumerated in the correct sequence counting from bottom to top: column base, capital, architrave, frieze, and cornice.[151]

Having bases, the columns must have been Ionic or Corinthian rather than Doric. The frieze may have been of the type traditionally connected with the Corinthian Order (cf. the Lysicrates Monument at Athens), though it is not inconceivable that Ionic columns might have been combined with a Doric triglyph frieze, as was the case in Maussollos' Andron at Labraunda.[152]

If it is assumed that the room had a height of about 4 m, and that the colonnade and its entablature covered the wall from bottom to top entirely, there might have been six columns on the longer sides and five on the shorter, not including the corner supports (fig. 17.1, 3-4). What particularly attracted de la Tourrette's attention, in addition to the columns and their entablature, were the richly decorated fields between the columns:

"L'entredeux des colonnes estoit reuestu de lastres, listeaux ou plattes bandes de marbres de diuerses couleurs ornees de moulures & sculptures conformes au reste de l'oeuvre, & rapportés proprement sur le fonds blanc de la muraille, où ne se voyoit qu'histoires taillees, & toutes batailles à demyrelief."

The description lists in one long sequence of words various ornamental components: LASTRES, LISTEAUX, PLATTES BANDES, MOULURES, SCULPTURES – which are characterized by means of a number of adjectives and an adjectival construction: ORNEES, CONFORMES, RAPPORTÉS, DE MARBRES DE DIUERSES COULEURS – but the context in which all these terms should be interpreted and understood to make sense, is far from clear.

Judging from the syntactical structure, ORNEES (fem. plur.) must refer not only to LASTRES and PLATTES BANDES (both fem. plur.), but also to LISTEAUX (masc. plur.), and should therefore read ORNÉS (masc. plur.). Besides, unless ORNEES and RAPPORTÉS are understood as coordinate sentence members, the passage is grammatically incoherent. If it is assumed that the original reading was ORNÉS and that a copyist or the typographer changed the gender to make it fit the preceding feminine noun COULEURS, this correction will make the meaning much clearer:

"The space between the columns was faced with slabs, bands, or borders of marbles of different colours decorated with mouldings and sculptures in conformity with the rest of the composition [i.e. the architectural framework of the colonnade] and properly attached to the white ground of the wall, on which nothing was to be seen except engraved stories, all battle-scenes sculptured in half relief."

LASTRE and LISTEL are both loan words adopted from Italian (LASTRA, LISTELLO), and it is remarkable that LASTRE does not occur anywhere else in Guichard's text and is not at all exemplified in 16th century French literature! Presumably, therefore, these terms were not chosen by Guichard but were quoted from the original report. Of multinational composition, the Hospitallers must have been familiar with the colloquial use of many words from other languages than their native tongue.

The last part of the description may be understood to imply that one and the same frieze was depicted as if running behind the columns and below the ceiling of an imaginary portico. Presumably the subject-matter represented was an Amazonomachia or a Centauromachia, themes that were also shown on the friezes decorating the outside of the Maussolleion.

A wall decoration of the kind suggested would in principle have resembled that of the external PTERON of the Maussolleion and even more representations in low relief such as the Sarcophagus of the Mourning Women from Sidon and the facade of the early Hellenistic altar in the sanctuary of Athena at Priene.[153] Possibly the structure including slabs, bands and borders (lastres, listeaux, plattes bandes) had the function of representing a podium, on top of which were seen statues (sculptures) placed between the columns.

Apparently, however, it did not occur to de la Tourrette that the decoration should be understood to represent a three-dimensional structure; and contrary to what he believed, the wall facing could hardly have consisted of pieces of marble. More probably it was made of the medium traditionally used for wall decoration in classical Antiquity: moulded stucco painted in imitation of variously coloured marbles. This technique reached a high level of perfection that may have impressed de la Tourrette to such an extent as to convince him of the costliness and authenticity of the material.

As demonstrated above (p. 94), the evidence suggests that the walls were constructed of foundation slabs of greenish tufa. For one thing, traces on the vertical surface of the bedrock behind the walls indicate that they were composed of courses of the same height as that of the foundation slabs, c. 30 cm. Besides, to judge from the slabs from the lowest course surviving in situ (fig. 17.2), the masonry facing the tomb chamber was bonded with that of the anteroom and the corridor. Five courses of the masonry adjoining the plug-block on its south side survived in Newton's day and can be seen on his photos figs. 10.5-6, where the top level of the sequence is exactly flush with the platform around the tomb chamber at level 678 (L8). The following courses were therefore bonded with the masonry forming the core of the building on all sides of corridor, anteroom, and tomb chamber.

White marble might have been used to throw into relief the walls of the tomb chamber as compared to those of greenish tufa in the corridor. If so, however, the finer stone would immediately have made it clear to tomb-robbers approaching through the mine that they had found what they were looking for. It would in that case have been unnecessary for them to trace the wall to its full extent, and pointless to push the mine even further before trying to break through to see what was behind the wall, in which endeavour they could not have failed to succeed.

It is perhaps conceivable that some of the fragments of the c. 30 cm high header courses of white marble that can be reasonably attributed to the exterior facing of the building came from the tomb chamber; but, on the other hand, unlikely that a room of such prominence would have been left with a wholly blank facade and no architectural articulation whatsoever. Evidently there was no orthostat course (this must have equalled at least three foundation courses in height), the Chariot frieze would have been too long to fit the dimensions of the tomb chamber,[154] and the excavations have not brought to light any other architectural members which are clearly from the Maussolleion, but not attributable to any part of its exterior. While the green stone might well have served as an adhesive ground for the application of stucco, a revetment of marble would have had to have the form of thin slabs attached to the background by means of metal hooks, a complicated technique for which no evidence was found in the tomb chamber or elsewhere in the Quadrangle, and which is not known to have been applied anywhere in Classical Greece.

At the time of the Roman Empire the method was widely used as a cheap way of facing shapeless concrete masonry with an attractive surface. But in this combination there was a clear distinction between the function of the core, which was purely structural, and that of the revetment, whose only purpose was to cover and conceal the core of concrete. Even where it was technically possible, it had become unreasonably expensive to use monolithic marble in basic structures of buildings as luxurious and colossal as those of ancient Rome.

The foundation slabs of tufa that formed the core of the superstructure in the Maussolleion were revetted with marble, but in the form of c. 30 cm high and 60 cm deep headers and c. 40 cm thick and 60 cm high stretchers which were all solidly bonded with the masonry of the core and were as much as the tufa slabs an integral part of the structure. Of monolithic marble were also the c. 30 cm high and c. 90 cm deep steps of which the roof pyramid was composed. Even though the inside of the building was of tufa (using marble throughout would have been wasteful extravagance), no conspicuous attempt was made to economize on the use of marble on the outside. Consequently, if it had been decided to build the walls of the tomb chamber of marble, such an intention would undoubtedly have been effectuated regardless of the expenditure involved.

Consisting of the purest lime itself, stucco

would have been no less useful than marble as a basis for burning lime. Most of the stucco would probably have stuck to the tufa slabs to which it had been applied, but since none of these stones appear to have remained on the site, they were presumably all brought to the Castle and incorporated in its masonry.

As suggested in the reconstruction drawing fig. 17.1, the core of the architectural framework represented on the walls of the tomb chamber, in particular the column shafts, was probably hewn out from the wall itself, and if reused in the Castle the blocks might have been placed with their outside facing inwards. Possibly the extraordinary thickness of the east wall should not be explained as a measure intended to reinforce structural stability on this particular side, as has been suggested above (p. 55). Perhaps more likely, it may have been its principal purpose to permit the elaboration of an architectural framework represented not merely in low relief, as on the other sides, but in high relief with the columns and figures between them projecting in full from the wall plane, thereby setting off to advantage the background in front of which Maussollos' ossuary was to be seen.

No remains were observed during the excavation of the tomb chamber in 1972 which could be identified as fragments of stucco or of marble slabs that might have come from the wall decoration of the tomb chamber. The crumbling pieces of stucco that would have fallen from the walls when their ashlars were taken down, and would have accumulated on the marble pavement, must have been cleared away before the pavement slabs and the course of foundation slabs underneath them could be broken up.

Anteroom and tomb

In addition to the larger room, the Knights found "a very low door" (une porte fort basse) leading into what "looked like an anteroom" (comme antichambre), in which there was a tomb (sepulcre). As argued above (chapter 17) the existence of a separate anteroom placed between the corridor and the tomb chamber is corroborated by the archaeological evidence.

The purpose of the anteroom was probably to provide more space than the corridor afforded for a sham doorway moulded in stucco of monumental dimensions fitting the size of the tomb chamber, but giving access only through a passage in one of its lower panels.

Translation

In consequence of the textual analysis and interpretation carried out above, the report in its entirety should read in translation as follows:

"In the year 1522, when Sultan Solyman made preparations for the attack on the Rhodians, the Grand Master, being aware of the importance of this place and realizing that the Turks would seize it at the first assault, sent some knights thither to repair it and to make all due preparations to resist the enemy. Among the number of these was the Commander de la Tourrette from Lyon, who afterwards was present at the taking of Rhodes and came to France, where he related, what I am now about to narrate, to Monsieur d'Alechamps, a person sufficiently known by his learned writings, and whose name I mention here only for the purpose of making my source for so singular a story known:

When the Knights had arrived at Mesy, they commenced immediately fortifying the castle, and as they did not find any stone in the neighbourhood, wherewith to make lime, more suitable or more easily got at than certain steps of white marble, which rose like a platform of stone in the middle of a field near the harbour where formerly was the grand place of Halicarnassus, they ordered them to be pulled down and appropriated for the abovementioned purpose.

When the stone was found to be good, and the little masonry remaining above ground had been demolished, they let the digging go deeper in the hope of finding more, and in this they were highly successful, for in a short time they perceived that the deeper they went, the more the structure widened downwards, supplying them with more stones, not only for making lime, but also for building.

After four or five days, when they had laid bare a great space, they saw one afternoon an opening as into a cellar. Taking a candle, they descended into it, where they found a beautiful, large, square room, adorned all around with columns of marble, with their bases, capitals, architraves, friezes and cornices engraved and carved in half-relief. The space between the columns was lined with slabs, bands, or borders of marbles of different colours ornamented with mouldings and sculptures in accordance with the rest of the composition, and properly attached to the white background of the wall, where representations of historical events were engraved, all representing battle-scenes in half-relief. Having at first admired the work, and formed in their imagination an idea of its singularity, they finally demolished it, broke it up, and pulled it to pieces, applying it to the same purpose as they had done with the rest.

In addition to this room they found afterwards a very low door which led into another room, like an anteroom, where there was a tomb with its receptacle and its lid of white marble, very beautiful and of marvellous lustre, which, for want of time, they did not open, the retreat having already sounded. The day after, when they had returned, they found the tomb opened, and the earth all round strewn with tiny pieces of cloth of gold and appliqués of the same metal. This made them suppose that the pirates who hovered at that time along the neighbouring coast, having some inkling of what had been discovered, had come there at night and had removed the lid of the tomb: and it is believed that they discovered in it immense treasures.

It was thus that this magnificent tomb, which ranked among the seven miracles and wonderful works of the world, after having escaped the brutality of the barbarians, and having for the space of 2247 years[155] remained standing, or at least buried within the ruins of the town of Halikarnassos,[156] was discovered and, for the purpose of repairing the Castle of St. Peter, done away with entirely by the Knights of Rhodes, who immediately afterwards were driven out of the castle by the Turks, and at the same time of the whole of Asia".

Appendix 4

Comparanda relatable to the fragments of a double-door and of a sarcophagus lid found in the Maussolleion foundations

A: DOUBLE-DOORS

Double-doors of marble strikingly similar to the one reconstructed from fragments found inside the Quadrangle of the Maussolleion have been discovered in chamber tombs in a number of other places on the Halikarnassos peninsula and in adjoining parts of Caria:

1. Double-door from the chamber tomb discovered in 1976 in the Yokuşbaşi district in the eastern outskirts of Halikarnassos and reconstructed in the moat of the Castle at Bodrum (fig.28.1).[157]

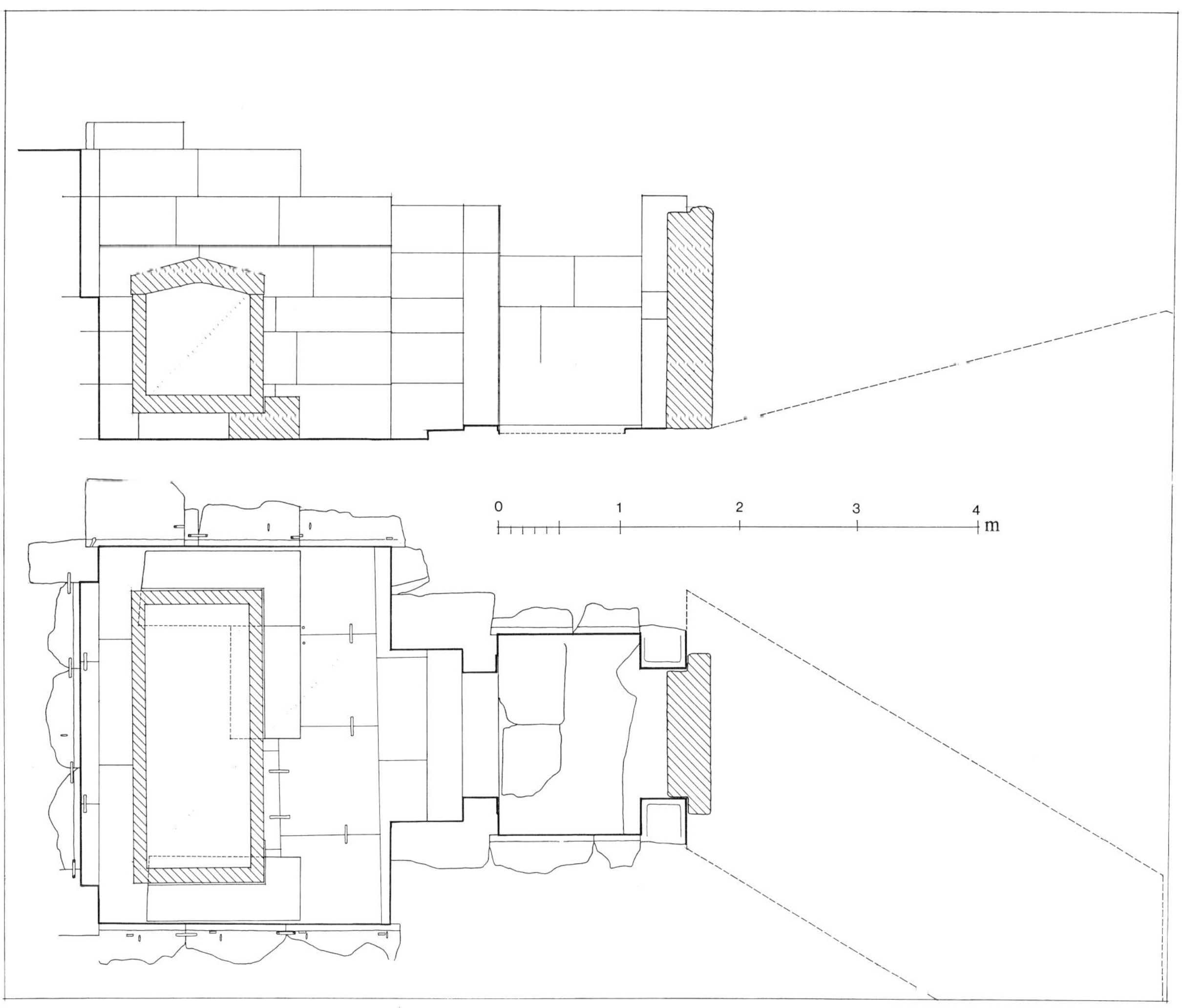

Fig. 28.1. Chamber tomb from the Yokuşbaşi district in the outskirts of Halikarnasssos, plan and longitudinal section.

Fig. 28.2. Yokuşbaşi tomb. Close-up of tomb chamber and sarcophagus.

The tomb chamber was entered through a double-door of white marble (figs. 28.3-8). Substantial fragments survive of both door-leaves. On the front, each door-leaf has two recessed panels between three cross-ties. Each cross-tie is decorated with three horizontal rows of knobs, the middle one consisting of four, those above and below it each of three knobs.

The knobs, semicircular or slightly parabolic in section, have not been turned on a lathe and separately added, but are carved in the door-leaves. Those on the cross ties are of the same size as the ones decorating the vertical fillets bordering the panels.

The door-leaves measure 98-100 mm in maximum thickness (not including the knobs). The panels on the front are 12 mm deep, while those on the back reach a depth gradually amounting to c. 34 mm near the

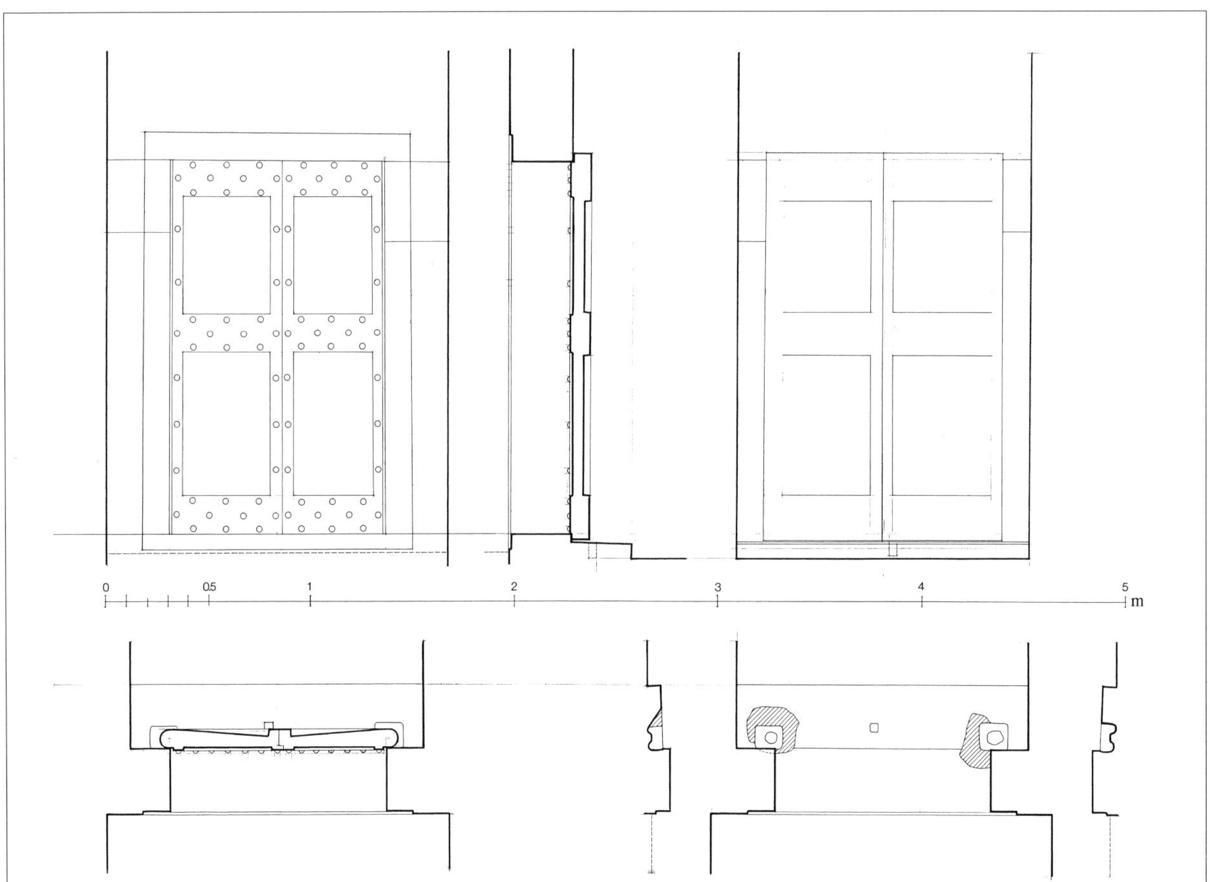

Fig. 28.3. Yokuşbaşi tomb, reconstructed double-door of white marble, section, plans, and elevations.

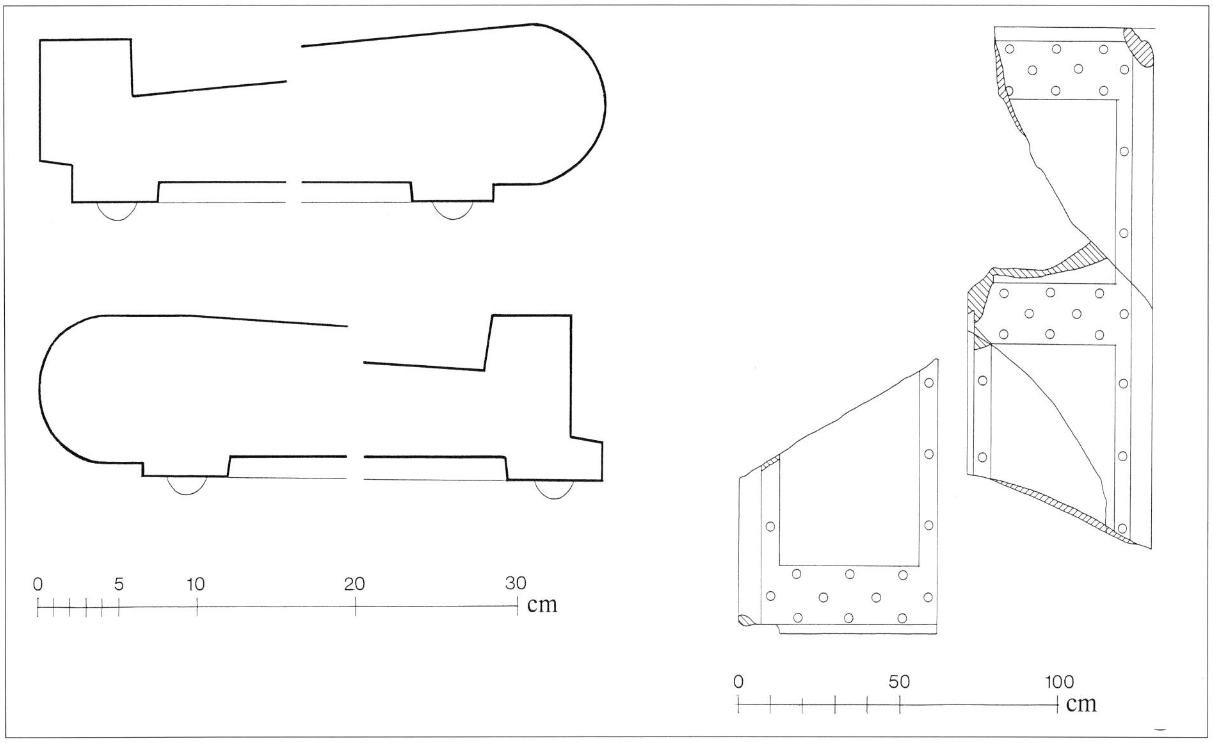

Fig. 28.4. Yokuşbaşi tomb. Surviving fragments of the door-leaves and cross-sections recording details of both leaves.

middle of the doorway, i.e. at the point where the overhang of each door-leaf reached a maximum, undoubtedly with a view to reducing its weight and rendering the use of wheels to support it during rotation unnecessary.

The complete width, inclusive of both door-leaves, was c. 119 cm, and the width of the door opening must have been at least 105 cm. Depending on the number of spacings between the knobs on the vertical fillets along the lower panels, the complete height of the door was either c. 182 or c. 203 cm (fig. 28.3).

The pivots that once projected from the ends of each door-leaf are broken off and lost. However, deep rectangular cuttings on top of the threshold indicate where bronze sockets designed to hold the lower pivots were fastened with molten lead. Almost midway between them is a cutting, c. 4 × 4 cm square, for the vertical metal bar with which the door could be locked. For information on the architectural details of the tomb see below, SARCOPHAGI 1.

2. Double-door from the so-called "School Yard Tomb" at Milas (fig. 28.9).[158]

   The knobs on the cross-ties are distributed exactly as on the door-leaves of the Yokuşbaşi tomb and are all of the same size, though smaller. Pivotal projections of cylindrical form survive at both ends of each door-leaf.

3. Double-door from chamber tomb at Beçin south of Milas.[159]

   The knobs on the cross-ties are distributed exactly as on the door-leaves from the abovementioned tombs at Yokuşbaşi and Milas.

In the garden of the archaeological Museum at Milas are door-leaves from two double doors having the same distribution of knobs on the cross-ties, figs. 28.10-11.[160]

B: SARCOPHAGI

1. Sarcophagus from the Yokuşbaşi tomb[161]
   The tomb chamber is occupied by a sarcophagus of bluish limestone consisting of a simple monolithic receptacle of rectangular form, 95 cm high, 108 cm wide and 230 cm long, and a lid of gable-shaped form.

   Inside, the receptacle is 80 cm deep, 87 cm

Fig. 28.5-8. Yokuşbaşi tomb. Photos of the surviving fragments of door- leaves.

wide, and 210 cm long. Part of its edge, and the adjoining part of the lid, was broken when the tomb was looted. The front of the receptacle is tooth-chiselled but for a narrow margin along the edges. The other sides and the back are dressed along their vertical edges and the edge along the top with a 6 cm broad tooth-chiselled margin inside which the surface has been pecked with a fine point in much the same way as the ashlars of the eastern retaining wall of the Maussolleion Terrace.[162]

The lid, which has a lifting boss at the middle of either end, has been tooled with the pointed chisel and additionally flattened with the toothed chisel, most carefully on the front, while on the other sides the toothed chisel has been used only to accentuate the edges.

The sarcophagus rests in a rebate cut in a low podium of white marble supporting the receptacle along the front and the sides. Inside the receptacle and where it is covered by the rebate, it has been roughly tooled with the pointed chisel.

There is no evidence for the date of the tomb except its architectural features which may be described briefly in the following terms:

The tomb is encased on all sides in modern masonry laid in cement mortar. Its walls are therefore visible only on the inside. They may have been composed originally of two rows of ashlars of which the outermost one is lost. Those of the remaining row are smoothed with the claw chisel on the front, but left with a quarry-face on their backs.[163]

The masonry consists mainly of courses of stretchers, two or three per each course of headers. The material is bluish limestone, occasionally supplemented with blocks of white marble. The ashlars were connected with one another by means of metal clamps.

The tomb chamber measures c. 3 m in width and 2.30 m in depth. In its rear wall (the one opposite to the entrance) is a shallow, 15 cm deep and 242 cm wide recess. It begins 114 cm above the pavement and can be followed to a height of 118 cm (232 cm above the pavement), but must originally have been higher.[164]

If the lintel rested on top of the doorpost on the right (as seen from the entrance), i.e. at a level of 175 cm above the threshold, this would just have sufficed to hold a doorway of the lower size (c. 182 cm, cf. above), taking into account the projecting parts overlapping lintel and threshold. Behind the doorway is a 60 cm deep and 137 cm wide recess permitting the door-leaves to be opened without encroaching on the passage into the tomb chamber.

The tomb chamber is paved with large rectangular flags of the same limestone as the one used for the walls and held together by means of metal clamps. The surface is tooled with the pointed chisel, but a 10-15 cm wide tooth-chiselled band with a corroded outline parallel to the entrance wall and c. 62 cms from it suggests the possibility that the sarcophagus was placed c. 14 cm closer to the entrance wall than in the reconstruction.

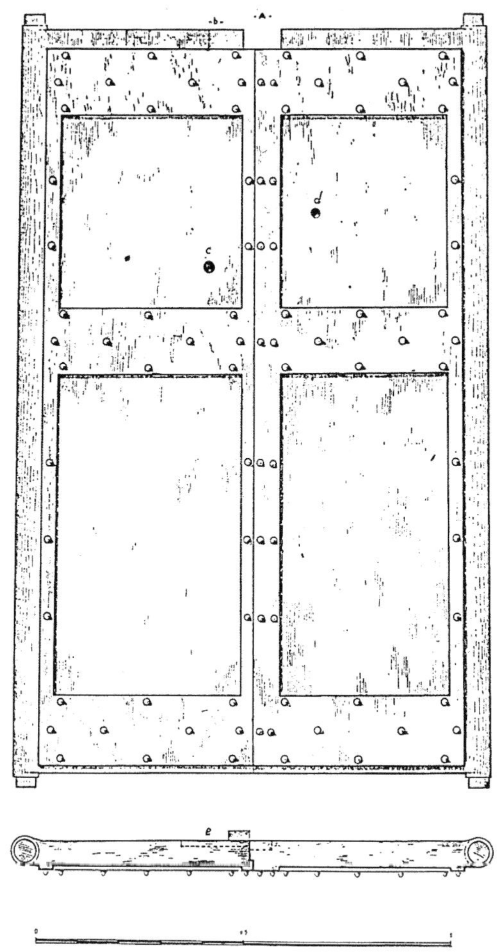

Fig. 28.9. Double-door from so-called "School Yard Tomb", Milas (A. Akarca, A Hellenistic Tomb in Mylasa, Belleten 16, 1952, 367-405, Lev. lxxvii).

The tomb is entered from a long ramp sloping downwards at an oblique angle in relation to the axis of the entrance. In the reconstruction, the 103 cm wide opening is closed by a plug-block of greenish tufa, but the doorposts are higher than the plug-block which does not seem to fit.

As the tomb was not measured before its

Fig. 28.10-11. Two leaves from different double-doors of marble, in the garden of the archaeological museum at Milas.

removal, and photos illustrating the state of preservation in which it was found are not available, it is not possible to check the correctness of the reconstruction in all dimensions and details.

2. Plain sarcophagi of the same type as the one in the Yokuşbaşi tomb, some more coarsely tooled, several of greenish tufa.

As attested by the tomb of the "Carian Princess", which is datable in the last quarter of the fourth century BC,[165] such sarcophagi could be used for burials even of prosperous and socially high-ranking individuals. A number of similar sarcophagi deprived of their context, but probably found in the outskirts of Bodrum, are exhibited in the lower garden of the Bodrum Museum.[166] The only point of similarity between the lids of the above-mentioned sarcophagi and the lid reconstructed from fragments found in the Maussolleion Quadrangle is their gable-like shape. So far, the only fragment of a lid perfectly similar to the latter has been found at Kos (chapter 20, fragment e).

Notes

1 In particular: K. Jeppesen, TOT OPERUM OPUS, Ergebnisse der dänischen Forschungen zum Maussolleion von Halikarnass seit 1966, JdI 107 (1992) 59-102; Das Maussolleion von Halikarnass, Forschungsbericht 1997, Proceedings of the Danish Institute at Athens II (1998) 161-231.

2 Pl. E2,44-47 (opposite the interval 44-47 on the scale).

3 Pl. E1,19-24, A,B and C, cf. Newton HD 101f., below, Appendix 2.
The drums, which may well have been intended for one and the same column, measure c. 85 cm (A), c. 135 cm (B), and c. 81 cm (C) in height; c. 96 cm (A), c. 95 cm (B), and c. 97 cm (C) in diameter. They have been roughly dressed with the pointed chisel.
A recessed margin at each end indicates the thickness of the layer (apergon) which was to protect the drums during their transport and final placement.

4 Pedersen (1991) 1, 12f.

5 Cf. the preliminary observations Jeppesen (1998) 197f.

6 Pedersen (1991) 2, 7-18, trenches R11, R10, and R1.

7 It remains to solve this problem, once a convenient opportunity be afforded. Achmet's well may prove considerably deeper than Suliman's and therefore less easily accessible.

8 Jeppesen (1992) 81, Tf. 22.3.

9 Below the level previously attained, Maussolleion fragments continued to turn up, among these a fragment from the top of the Quadriga base. At a depth of 4.10 m below the surface (i.e. at level c. 268) groundwater intruded, thus necessitating the continuous use of pumps, until the bottom of the well was eventually reached at a depth c. 6.60 m below the surface (i.e. just 18 cm above sea level).Right to the bottom the fill was mixed with marble fragments from the Maussolleion and fragments of greenish tufa.

10 Carstens (1999) I, 6, figs. 2-3.

11 Two slabs of that size found inside the Quadrangle, but not in situ, have the following dimensions: 96 × 134 × 33 cm and 87 × 134 × 28 cm., respectively. Since they differ considerably in thickness, the chances are that they came from different courses, and none of them seems to fit in with the slabs of C9 in situ which are c. 30 cm high.

12 Zahle/Jeppesen (1975) 71f.

13 This is Newton's interpretation of the evidence (HD 143), but cf. below chapter 17, p. 88.

14 On the geological composition of the bedrock, see Appendix 1.

15 Cf. Højlund (1981) 43.

16 Højlund (1981), 49f.

17 Since it cannot have been the function of these structures to buttress the foundations of the Maussolleion, the designation used by Newton, "pier", is somewhat misleading, and "pillar" seems more appropriate.

18 Newton HD, 101 f.

19 Pedersen (1991) I, 12 f.

20 For the interpretation of Pliny's description of the Maussolleion, cf. Jeppesen (1998) 164, 210. In the current text editions, the passage recording the horizontal dimensions of the building runs as follows:

PATET AB AUSTRO ET SEPTENTRIONE SEXAGENOS TERNOS PEDES, BREUIUS A FRONTIBUS, TOTO CIRCUMITU PEDES CCCCXXXX etc.

It is rightly and universally agreed that the measurement specified for each of the longer sides of the building, 63 ft., must be basically wrong if the figure given for the circumference, 440 ft., is correct, and vice versa.
Judging from the archeological evidence (see the main text below) the reading 440 ft. may well be perfectly correct (for the alternative readings: CCCCXI, CCCC UNDECIM or CCCC UNDE CUM, cf. Jeppesen (1986) 53), but if so, the longer side of the building must have been more than 110 ft. long, i.e. at least about twice as long as indicated in the surviving version. Besides, the figure 63 is overly specific as compared to the other maximum dimensions given by Pliny which are round numbers (circumference 440, total height 140 ft.).
Even if the suspect figure is emended to read, for example, cxiii instead of lxiii (Mayhoff), this correction will not eliminate the fundamental oddity in the construction of the sentence, its roundabout way of stating simple numerical facts.
Instead of specifying the length both of the longer and the shorter sides and leaving it to the reader to calculate the circumference, or

of specifying the circumference and drawing attention to the oblong plan of the building without defining any of its side lengths, the MS text combines the two possibilities. What makes this version unlikely to be the original one, is the complexity of its construction, which is incompatible with the brevity in Pliny's description of the main features of the building. To be in keeping with this, the passage must have read differently, possibly in the following terms:

PATET AB AUSTRO ET SEPTENTRIONE LATIUS, PAULO BREVIUS A FRONTIBUS, TOTO CIRCUMITU PEDES CCCCXXXX etc.

"It is widest on the south and north sides, a little shorter on the fronts, in full circumference 440 ft".
This would imply that at some stage of the manuscript tradition PAULO was abbreviated to read P. which was subsequently interpreted to mean PEDES, thus requiring that LATIUS should be understood to represent a numeral. Possibly "latius" was read as "lx tius" and transcribed to read "sexagenus ternus" which form is found in the MSS nos. 3, 5, and 8 of Group A, no. 8 being the earliest MS surviving (8/9 century), while all the later MSS including the Bamberg codex (no.1) have the form "sexagenos ternos" (Jeppesen (1986) 14, 19, 47).

21 Jeppesen (1992) 76f.
22 As maintained by W. Hoepfner, cf. Jeppesen (1998) 207.
23 Jeppesen (1976) 97.
24 Jeppesen (1998) 161f.
25 The existence of a curvature is suggested by the slightly convex top surface of an euthynteria block and a crepidoma block in the British Museum (1857.12- 20.316/317).
A number of similar blocks incorporated in the walls of the Castle at Bodrum are not directly accessible. Besides, measuring-instruments of great precision would be required to record the evidence exactly.
26 IG VIII 3073, 134 f.: kanona makron me elatton podon eikosi, pachos hex daktylon, hypsos hemipodiou.
27 Bundgaard (1957) 137 assumes that the pavement was planned to become "slightly convex, like the floor in the side corridors of the Parthenon", but this is not explicitly indicated in the inscription.
28 Jeppesen (1998) 187f.
29 Though a tempting possibility, the spacing of 144" = 9' previously suggested (Jeppesen (1992) 88; (1998) 161) would imply the use of a foot unit of only 31.67 cm.
30 This is true, for example, of the corner blocks of bluish limestone Jeppesen (1998) 182, Abb.12.
31 Cf. the cross-sections of the building, Jeppesen (1992) pl. 29,1-2. For an alternative explanation of the extraordinary thickness of the east wall, see below p. 167.
32 Pedersen (1991) I, pl. VII, fig. 252, at d.
33 Newton HD, pl. IV; Pedersen (1991) I, 83f., fig. 89.
34 Pedersen (1991) I, 123f., cf. Biliotti's plan of his excavations reproduced ibid.
35 Only corner slabs might be larger, as exemplified by the corner slab of course C9 in situ at the SW corner which measures 142 × 145 cm, cf. above fig. 1.59.
36 Jeppesen (1992) 63.
37 This viewpoint is rightly emphasized by Poul Pedersen (1991) I, 85: "Indirectly the poor occurrence of antique building stone in the western part of the terrace suggests that this sector was of a different nature" [i.e., from that of the area south and east of the monument].
In his opinion, therefore, "a park or ALSOS would harmonize well with the picture the investigations have given".
38 Jeppesen (1994) 79f.
39 Jeppesen (1998) 196f.
40 Højlund (1981), cf. Jeppesen (1994) 81 f.
41 Hell. iv.1.15: therai ... en perieirgmenois paradeisois.
42 Anabasis 1.2.7: paradeisos megas agrion therion pleres.
43 Anabasis 2.4.14: paradeisos dasys ... pantoion dendron.
44 Jeppesen (1992) 80f., pls. 27.2 and 28.1.
45 Pedersen (1991) I, 34f.
46 Pedersen (1991) I, 85f.; II, 67f., fig. 267 (trench N/O2).
47 Newton HD 143, cf. our Appendix 2.
48 Cf. Inclosure in No. 11, List of Cases shipped in Her Majesty's ship "Gorgon", Waywell (1978) Appendix 1:
128 Idem [cf. 127 which reads "Cask, various fragments].
129 Fragment of Lion; fragment of Lioness; Architectural fragments; fragment of figure from Frieze.
136 Fragment of colossal Female figure, from

waist to hips, from near the well, Omer's field, Mausoleum.

138 Cask, various fragments, chiefly architecture.

The invoices attached to the casks in which Newton's finds were shipped to England are, as in the above-mentioned cases, anything but complete lists, specifying only spectacular pieces and referring to other finds in terms too cursory to permit individual identification of the marbles actually referred to.

49 Waywell (1978) cat.nos. 655 and 656 pl. 43. There is no reference to the identification suggested by Newton.

50 Fragment B: Walker/ Matthews (1997) 53, Table 1, no. 22 (erroneously labelled as "chariot shaft").

51 Walker/Matthews (1997) 51.

52 Cf. the tomb at Langaza, JdI 26 (1911) 207, fig. 19 (Th. Macridy).

53 Cf. the ribs on the bronze collars which held the dowels by means of which the plug-block was fastened (figs. 11.1-2).

54 The tomb chamber in "Philip's Tomb" measured 4.46 × 4.46 m, Andronikos (1984) 97.

55 Højlund (1981) 41f.

56 As attested by the door opening leading into the tomb chamber of the Mausoleum at Belevi, a height of 1.42 m might well be considered perfectly sufficient in a sepulchral context (EPHESOS VI, Das Mausoleum von Belevi (1979), 60, Abb. 46,48).

57 Roos (1972) pl.49, tombs B1, B6, B8, and C50; cf. pls. 23, 27, 29, 38.

58 Diodoros xvi.45.7.

59 Supplemental to John Gifford's observations in 1974 (Appendix 1) may be mentioned that during the excavation in 1996 of the Turkish well at the NE corner of the tomb chamber (square 10/10, cf. above p. 9f.), its bottom was found at a depth of 6.6 m below its top level (678), i.e. at level 018, 4.6 m below the bottom of the tomb chamber (level 478).

On 28th September of the same year the surface of the water reached a height about 2.5 m above the bottom of the well, i.e. c. 2 m below the tomb chamber.

60 Oldfield (1895) 349, pls. xxiii-xxiv.

61 Cf. The Princeton Encyclopedia of Classical Sites (1976) 672, s.v. Pantikapaion (Kertch).

62 I.e. the pyramid of Meidum and the bent pyramid at Dahshur (4th Dynasty, c. 2575-2465 BC): Mark Lehner, The Complete Pyramids (Thames and Hudson 1997) 97 f., ill. pp. 97, 98, 102, 104.

63 The Gebe Kilise tomb, Radt (1970) Abb.19; Carstens (1999) 51, figs. 25-31.

64 For SOROS meaning "sarcophagus of stone", cf. Theophrastos, de Igne, 46.

65 In a previous report (Jeppesen (1992) 69) the find-spot of this piece was erroneously specified as "immediately before the entrance to the tomb chamber" i.e. in square 5/9, but the figures written on it are not 5/9, but 9/5, a position not in front of the tomb chamber, but south of it near the southern staircase.

66 In the report, the figures for fragments b, c, d are specified to three decimal places: 4.383, 4.366, 4.462 and -3.257, -2.867, -2.970.

67 Letter of 27 August 1999.

68 Letter of 9 March 2000.

69 Cf. the Sarcophagus of the Mourning Women, Koenigs/Philipp (1996) 135, Abb.4.

70 The pediments on the Sarcophagus of the Mourning Women are decorated with sculptural groups carved in relief, but these pediments are rather more spacious than those of the sarcophagus from the Maussolleion, c. 115 cm in length, and 17 cm in height, Koenigs/Philipp (1996) 135 Abb.4.

71 Koenigs/Philipp (1996) Abb. 3-7.

72 Jeppesen (1955) pl. vi.

According to the dedicatory inscription on the architrave (ibid. 26f., pl. xxi), the South Propylaea were dedicated by Idrieus, who reigned between 351 and 344 BC. However, as a comparison with sima mouldings from other late Classical buildings in Ionic style at Labraunda makes clear (cf. Hellström/Thieme (1982) fig. 16), the sima of the South Propylaea should hardly be seen as typical of its time, but only as one of the varieties exemplified in the surviving repertory.

73 Jeppesen (1955) pl. xi,4-9.

74 IDRIEYS EKATOM(N.., barely legible on Jeppesen (1955) pl. x,7.

75 Cf. the selection given in an appendix by Jonas Crampa, Westholm (1963) 121f, 1-3.

76 Özet (1994) 88.

77 For further references cf. Appendix 4.

78 cf. Jeppesen (1986) chapter 3.

Aulus Gellius reports (Noctes Atticae 10.18) that Maussollos was buried at a splendid funeral (funere magnifico sepultus est), and probably the use of the verb SEPELIO implies that his body was cremated.

This is also what must be inferred from Aulus Gellius' story about Artemisia's exceptional behaviour at the funeral where she "mingled

Maussollos' bones and ashes with spices, ground them into the form of a powder, put them in water and drank them" (ossa cineremque ejus mixta odoribus contusaque in faciem pulveris aquae indidit ebibitque). Whatever was the truth of the matter, to make sense at all the story must imply that Maussollos' body was known to or assumed to have been cremated on a pyre.

In the gold larnax deposited in the tomb chamber at Vergina Manolis Andronikos observed "carefully placed burnt bones." "There is no doubt" he added "that the bones had been collected up after the cremation with the utmost care. They had then been washed – in wine, of course – wrapped in an all-purple cloth and placed in the larnax." (Andronikos (1984) 170) As emphasized by Andronikos, these finds agree strikingly with the epic description of Achilles' and Hector's burials (Odyssey 24.40 f.; Iliad 24.788 f.). There is every reason to believe, therefore, that the traditional epic model for princely burials – cremation on a pyre, and pious collection of the burnt bones – was copied deliberately in historical times and also maintained at Maussollos' funeral.

79 Hornblower (1982) 40f. Idrieus died in 344/43 BC, Pixodaros probably about 336, and Idrieus' sister and wife Ada even later, after having adopted Alexander the Great as her son after his arrival in Caria in 334 BC.

80 Strabo 656: ATEKNOS.

81 Multaque alia violenti amoris indicia fecisse dicitur. Molita quoque est ingenti impetu operis conservandae mariti memoriae sepulcrum illud memoratissimum etc.

82 Harpokration (s.v. Artemisia) quoting Theopompos: phthinadi nosoi lephtheisan dia ten lypen ten epi tou andros kai adelphou Mausolou apothanein; Cicero, Tusc. Disp. 3.31: luctu … confecta contabuit.

83 On the pre-Maussollan cemetery, cf. chapter 24.

84 I am obliged to Jan Stubbe Østergaard, Ny Carlsberg Glyptotek, for the following reference: Guntram Koch, Sarkophage der Römischen Kaiserzeit (Darmstadt 1993) 41, notes 165-166. Koch lists a substantial variety of examples, not a few of which are from a period when marble had become scarce.

However, in the Museo Nazionale Romano is a sarcophagus with a composite lid presumably dating from the mid-second century AD. It was made for a boy referred to in the dedication as "clarissimus puer" (his parents were probably high-ranking people) and measures therefore only c. 40 × 50 × 160 cm.

According to the laconic description of the lid given by Luisa Musso (A. Giuliano, Museo Nazionale Romano, Le Sculture I.2, 84, no. 3), "il coperchio è spaccato [sic]", while Koch o.c. observes: "Der Deckel ist aus drei Teilen sehr sorgfältig zusammengesetzt; eines hat dunklere Färbung und besteht vielleicht aus anderem Marmor".

However, to judge from the photo p. 85 in the catalogue showing the front of the sarcophagus and its lid, the lid consists of two halves, the left one of which has a darker hue than the one on the right. Unless "zwei" should be read instead of "drei" in Koch's description, the point needs clarification.

85 Cf. Hornblower (1982) 40.

86 Cf. above p. 101.

87 Jeppesen (1998) Abb. 10.3 (Appendix: Gf).

88 Newton HD 107.

89 The maximum depth given by Bodil Bundgaard Rasmussen (1998), 66 as 112 cm, is probably due to an error in printing.

90 Cf. Zahle/Jeppesen (1975) 72.

91 Cf. the preliminary report Rasmussen (1998).

92 This summary is largely quoted from Bodil Bundgaard Rasmussen's paper at the conference on Greek Gold at the British Museum in 1998: Gold Ornaments from the Mausoleum at Halikarnassos, The Art of the Greek Goldsmith pp. 66-71.

However, the catalogue that was given in the paper comprised only objects of gold, and those from the cavity were listed indiscriminately with those from the robbers' mine without indication of their individual find-spots. A full description and discussion of the archaeological setting of the finds superseding Mrs. Bundgaard Rasmussen's provisional presentation will be found in chapters 21 and 22 of the present volume.

93 M.A. Özet, The tomb of a noble woman from the Hekatomnid period, HalStud I (1994) 94, group I, fig. 19.

94 Vergina (1984) 79, fig. 42; CR 1878/79, 135.

95 S. Drougou, Der Stoff von Vergina: Ein vorläufiger Bericht, AMITOS (1987).

96 Jaro (1995).

97 CR 1878/79 135-136, pl. V 4.

98 Gold der Steppe (1991), Kat. Nr. 153, G.T. Kovpanenko, Die sarmatische "Prinzessin" aus der Sokolova Mogila, 221-226, Abb.6.

99 Miller (1997) 80, fig. 27.
100 Miller (1997) 81, suggests that it was made in an Attic oikos or a specialized workshop staffed with foreign slaves.
101 Mesará (1924) 111,9, pl. LVII, no. 497.
102 Vergina (1984), figs. 99-100.
103 Williams (1998) 72.
104 Williams (1998) 111-121 (P. Craddock et al., The Refining of Gold in the Classical World).
105 Vergina (1984) fig. 42.
106 Cf. above, note 78.
107 Part 2, comprising (1) sherds of late classical Attic pottery, (2) fragments of alabaster jars, (3) sherds of ribbed glass vessels, and (4) fragments of ivory or bone, will be published in connection with similar objects from other parts of the Quadrangle in a forthcoming volume.
108 The Royal City of Susa (1992-93) no. 177, fig. 54, cf. MDP 8, pp. 29-58, fig. 93, pl. 6:4-6.
109 Pasargadai (1978) 168 f., pl. 156d.
110 BM 1857.12-20.178; Williams (1998) 72.
111 Now in the British Museum, Meiggs and Lewis, Selection of Greek Historical Inscriptions (Oxford 1969) No. 32.
112 Compare the transfer of bones and funerary furnishings from graves on Delos to the neighbouring island of Rheneia under Peisistratos and once again in 426 BC (Herodotos 1.64 et al.).
113 Newton HD 147; cf. Newton's description of similar fillings between the pillars 1-4 on the north side of the Quadrangle, and above the western staircase, HD 101.
114 Jeppesen (1992) 62.
115 Carstens claims note 438, that "these finds were never published", but does not mention that a specimen of the stamped ware referred to is illustrated pl. 15 fig. 5 in the same article.
116 The observations on which the present study is based were made in 1974, when John Gifford worked at the INA, but very kindly also took an interest in the work of the Danish expedition on the Maussolleion site. Since we have no reason for suspecting that any of the view-points and conclusions expressed in his report may no longer be as tenable as before, or require modification or supplementation, it is reproduced in full. His study was made at a time when the site had just been opened and offered the best opportunities for a thorough examination of its geological configurations that could be hoped for, while such conditions no longer prevail after the surface of the bedrock within the Quadrangle has had to be covered almost entirely by protective dry walls in 1996.
117 Footnote: See Herod. ii.121.
118 Footnote: These slabs extended as far as the lower gallery, to be described hereafter, of which they formed the roof.
119 Footnote: In the Plan this drain is marked "Marble Drain". It is also shown in the upper View, Plate VIII.
120 Footnote: In the pyramid of the tomb near Constantine, called the Madrazen, was a staircase leading into the interior, the entrance to which was closed by a slab which is thus described: "Elle était glissée comme un tiroir vertical, dans une rainure en pierre de taille, et l'on devait la soulever au moyen d'une machine." – Annuaire de la Société Archéol. de la Province de Constantine, 1856-7. Paris 1858, p. 62.
121 Footnote: On the distinction between *thyein* and *enagizein*, see Liddell and Scott, Lexicon, *s.v. enagizo.* Bulls were sacrificed to heroes, such as Mausolus must have been accounted after his death,- see Boeckh, C.I.No.1051. Hence, probably, the bones which were discovered with the *alabastra.*
122 Footnote: This rubble wall, having been considered by Lieut. Smith as of comparatively recent origin, is not laid down in Plate III.
123 Cf. Jeppesen (1992) 67-71.
124 Luttrell (1986), Appendices, select texts, p. 186f.
125 Jeppesen (1992) 67-71.
126 Cf. Luttrell (1986) 170-174.
127 I am indebted to Anthony Luttrell, Bath, and Povl Skårup, Institute of Roman Philology at Århus University, Denmark, for revising my manuscript and giving their expert advice on historical and linguistic issues.
128 C. Plinii Historiae Mundi Libri xxxvi.
129 Luttrell (1986) 170.
130 Luttrell (1986) 170-172.
131 Luttrell (1986) 164.
132 Luttrell (1986) 165.
133 Cf. chapter 21.
134 P. 107: "dont nous retenons encor le mot de Sarcueil".
135 Pp. 107, 162, 340, 412, 456, 468, 471, 472, 484, 485, 505, 528, 539, 540, 541.
136 Pp. 537, 456: sercueil.
137 P. 26.
138 Pp. 29, 331, 487, 479, 274.
139 P. 118.
140 P. 345.
141 Pp. 81-83, 89f., 261. In the literature of the 15th and 16th centuries, the use of the term "tym-

bre" is exemplified in a variety of different meanings more or less synonymous with "vase", so "auge, fontaine, bassin" (manger, fountain, basin, from the period 1530-1622), and "vase, cruche" (1564, Rab.; 1584).

142 Walter v. Wartburg, Französisches Etymologisches Wörterbuch, 14 (1961) 189f., s.v. VAS.

143 Guichard's distinction between PILASTRE, PERRON and STELE: "& permit tant seulement d'eriger sur la fosse un PILASTRE ou PERRON haut de trois coudees"; "ces PERRONS ou PILASTRES qu'ils appelloyent STELAS" (both quotations on p. 274) is based on the terms used by Cicero in his description of the luxury restrictions imposed at Athens by Demetrios of Phaleron at the end of the fourth century BC (de legibus 2.26.66):
"nam super terrae tumulum noluit quidquam statui, nisi COLUMELLAM tribus cubitis nec altiorem aut MENSAM aut LABELLUM etc."

144 Cf. "ou de faire un coffre de pierre pour mettre le corps, ou bien poser une LAME dessus de la longueur du mort" (p. 274); "les uns se contentoyent de mettre une LAME platte couchee sur la tombe" (p. 118); W.v.Wartburg, Französisches Etymologisches Wörterbuch 5 (1950) 140 s.v. LAMINA I,1,a. Fr. lame f. "pierre sépulchrale, qui couvre le tombeau" (12 Jh.- 1656).

145 For the interpretation of Pliny's passage, cf. Jeppesen (1986) 55-57.

146 "Estoyent portés apres quatre escussons couronnés, l'armet Imperial TYMBRÉ du diademe, l'escu TYMBRÉ aussi ayant l'ordre à l'entour, etc." (p. 536); "Le premier escuyer ... porte l'armet TYMBRÉ à la royale" (p. 543). For exemplifications elsewhere of the meaning of TYMBRE/TYMBRER cf. W.v.Wartburg, Französisches Etymologisches Wörterbuch XXXIII,2 (1967) s.v. TYMPANUM 1,c.

147 Pedersen (1991) 1, 12f.; Jeppesen (1998) 183f.

148 Luttrell (1986) 167.

149 Luttrell (1986) 203, [30], shield xl from 1517; ibid.204, shield cvi a from 1518.

150 Cf. above p. 92.

151 Enumerated in much the same way as in Guichard's description of colonnaded fronts on Roman coins, pp. 170, 188.

152 Hellström/Thieme (1981) fig.18.

153 Jeppesen (1998) 202.

154 Jeppesen (1998) 210. In all probability, the frieze was placed below the ceiling of the colonnade, ibid. 176f.

155 Between Maussollos' death in 353/2 BC and the departure of the Knights in 1522 AD 1874 years had passed, i.e. 373 years less than the number estimated in the report. According to the latter, the Maussolleion must have been built in 725 BC.

156 This modification of the statement is omitted in Newton's translation.

157 Carstens (1999) 67f., figs. 61-64.

158 Carstens (1999) 72f., figs. 68-70.

159 Carstens (1999) 74f., fig. 73.

160 Provenance not indicated, but probably from the Milas region.

161 Carstens (1999) 1, 67f, figs. 61-62.

162 Pedersen (1991) I, 59f., figs. 67-70.

163 Cf. the construction of the north peribolos wall of the Maussolleion Terrace, Pedersen (1991) I, 24f.

164 Though being much shallower, this recess bears some resemblance to the niches in the rear walls of the Andrones at Labraunda, cf. Hellström (1997) 109f., fig. 209, but there is no indication suggesting its purpose.

165 The date is based on the find of a fluted oinochoe in the tomb, Özet (1994) 89, fig. 3; cf. Carstens (1999) 90f., figs. 112-114.

166 Carstens (1999) 94f., figs. 116-123.

Bibliography

ABC (1854)
S. Reinach, Antiquités du Bosphore Cimmérien (1854)

Amandry (1958)
P. Amandry, Orfèvrerie Achéménide, AntK 1958, 9-23

AMITOS (1987)
S. Drougou and C. Saatsoglu-Paliadele (eds.) AMHTOC, Timetikos tomos gia ton kathegiti Manoli Androniko (1987)

Artamonov (1969)
M.I.Artamonov, Treasures from Scythian Tombs in the Hermitage Museum (Leningrad 1969)

BMCJ (1911)
F.H.Marshall, Catalogue of the Jewellery, Greek, Etruscan and Roman, in the Departments of Antiquities, British Museum (1911)

Breglia (1966)
L. Breglia, Le Antiche Rotte del Mediterraneo Documentate da Monete e Pesi (Roma 1966)

Breitenstein (1941)
N. Breitenstein, Catalogue of the Terracottas in the Danish National Museum (1941)

Brooklyn (1984)
P.F.Davidson and A. Oliver, Ancient Greek and Roman Jewelry in the Brooklyn Museum (1984)

Bundgaard, J.A. (1957)
Mnesicles, A Greek Architect at Work (Copenhagen/Oslo).

Carapanos (1878)
C. Carapanos, Dodone et ses ruines (1878)

Carstens, A.M. (1999)
Death Matters, Funerary Architecture on the Halikarnassos Peninsula, Ph.D. Diss., Dept. of Archaeology and Ethnology, University of Copenhagen, vols. 1-2 (Copenhagen).

CR
Compte-rendus de la Commission Impériale Archéologique (1859-88)

From the Land of the Scythians (1973/74)
BMetrMus, special issue xxxii, no. 5 (1973/74)

Gold der Steppe (1991)
R. Rolle et al. (eds.), Gold der Steppe; Archäologie der Ukraine (Schleswig 1991)

Greek Gold (1994)
D. Williams and J. Ogden, Greek Gold: Jewellery of the Classical World (1994)

Greifenhagen I/II
A. Greifenhagen, Schmuckarbeiten in Edelmetall, I Fundgruppen, II Einzelstücke (Berlin 1970 and 1975)

HalSt
Halicarnassian Studies
1 (1994) Hekatomnid Caria and the Ionian Renaissance (Acts of the International Symposium at the Department of Greek and Roman Studies, Odense University, 28-29 November, 1991).

Hellström, P./ Thieme, T. (1981)
The Androns at Labraunda, a Preliminary Account of their Architecture, Bulletin 16, 1981, The Museum of Mediterranean and Near Eastern Antiquities, Stockholm, 59-74.

Hellström, P./ Thieme, T. (1982)
Labraunda, vol.1, part 3: The Temple of Zeus (Stockholm).

Hellström, P. (1997)
Sculpture from Labraunda, SSCD 109-113.

Hill (1904)
G.F.Hill, Catalogue of Greek Coins of Cyprus (British Museum 1904)

History of Beads (1987)
Lois Sherr Dubin, The History of Beads from 30,000 B.C. to the Present, with over 5.000 beads reproduced in colour (Thames and Hudson 1987).

Hogarth (1908)
D. Hogarth, Excavations at Ephesus (1908)

Hornblower, S. (1982)
Mausolus (Oxford).

Højlund, F. (1981)
The Deposit of Sacrificed Animals at the Entrance to the Tomb Chamber, REPORTS 1, 21-90.

Jaro (1995)
M. Jaro, Manufacturing technique of gold threads and their imitations on museum textiles. Chronology of the preparation of metal threads. Results of the scientific investigations. Yearbook of the Textile Museum, Budapest, 8 (1995, special issue)

Jeppesen, K. (1955)
Labraunda, vol. 1, part 1: The Propylaea (Lund).

Jeppesen, K. (1976)
Neue Ergebnisse zur Wiederherstellung des Maussolleions von Halikarnassos, IstMitt 26, 47-99.

Jeppesen, K. (1981)
Preface and Introduction, REPORTS 1, 7-20.

Jeppesen, K. (1986)
The Ancient Greek and Latin Writers, REPORTS 2, 5-113.

Jeppesen, K. (1992)
Tot Operum Opus, Ergebnisse der dänischen Forschungen zum Maussolleion von Halikarnass seit 1966, JdI 107, 59-102.

Jeppesen, K. (1994)
Founder Cult and Maussolleion, HalSt 1, 73-84.

Jeppesen, K. (1998)
Das Maussolleion von Halikarnass, Forschungsbericht 1997, Proceedings of the Danish Institute at Athens, II, 161-231.

Koenigs, W./ Philipp, H. (1996)
Proportion und Grösse, SÄULE UND GEBÄLK (Mainz) 133-147.

Louvre (1924)
A. de Ridder, Catalogue sommaire des bijoux antiques du Musée National du Louvre (1924)

Luttrell, A. (1986)
The Later History of the Maussolleion and its Utilization in the Hospitaller Castle at Bodrum, REPORTS 2, 114-214.

Mesará (1924)
S. Xanthoudides, The Vaulted Tombs of Mesará (Liverpool 1924)

Miller, M.C. (1997)
Athens and Persia in the Fifth Century BC. A study in cultural receptivity. Cambridge U.P., 1997.

Newton HD (1862-63)
C.T.Newton, A History of Discoveries etc., vols. 1-2, 1862-63 (London).

Oldfield, E. (1895)
The Mausoleum at Halicarnassus. A new Restoration, ARCHAEOLOGIA liv 1895, 273-362.

Pasargadai (1978)
D. Stronach, Pasargadai (1978).

Pedersen, P. (1991)
The Maussolleion Terrace and Accessory Structures, REPORTS 3, 1: Text and Appendices, 7-208; 2: Catalogue, 7-134.

Pedersen, P. (1994)
The Ionian Renaissance and some aspects of its origin within the field of architecture and planning, HalSt 1, 11-35.

Providence (1976)
Bulletin of Rhode Island School of Design (Providence, Rhode Island), Museum Notes (June 1976)

Radt, W. (1970)
Siedlungen und Bauten auf der Halbinsel von Halikarnassos unter besonderer Berücksichtigung der archaischen Epoche, IstMitt Beih. 3, 1970.

Rasmussen, B.B. (1998)
Gold Ornaments from the Mausoleum at Halikarnassos, in Dyfri Williams, "The Art of the Greek Goldsmith" (1998) 66 f.

REPORTS
The Maussolleion at Halikarnassos, Reports of the Danish Archeological Expedition to Bodrum, Jutland Archeological Society Publications XV:1-4 (1981-2000).

XV:1 (1981), The Sacrificial Deposit.

XV:2 (1986), The Written Sources and their Archaeological Background, parts 1-2.

XV:3 (1991), The Maussolleion Terrace and Accessory Structures, Text and Appendices (vol. 1), Catalogue (vol. 2).

XV:4 (2000), The Quadrangle, The Foundations of the Maussolleion and its Sepulchral Compartments.

Roos, P. (1972)
The Rock-Tombs of Caunus. 1. The Architecture (Gothenburg).

Rudolph (1995)
W. Rudolph, A Golden Legacy: Jewelry from the Burton Y. Berry Collection (1995)

SINDOS (1985)
J. Vokotopoulou et al. (eds.), Sindos (1985)

SSCD
Sculptors and Sculpture of Caria and the Dodecanese, British Museum Press, 1997.

Sørensen, K. Aaris (1981)
A Zoological Analysis of the Osteological Material from the Sacrificial Layer at the Maussolleion at Halikarnassos, REPORTS 1, 92-110.

Taranto (1984)
M. de Juliis, Gli ori di Taranto in età ellenistica (Milano 1984)

The Royal City of Susa (1992-93)
The Royal City of Susa, ancient near eastern treasures in the Louvre, publ. in connection with the exhibition held at the Metropolitan Museum of Art, Nov. 1992-March 1993, ed. P.O. Harper et al.

Thrakische Kunst (1973)
I. Venedikov u. T. Gerasimov, Thrakische Kunst (Wien-München 1973)

Vergina (1984)
M. Andronikos, Vergina: The Royal Tombs and the Ancient City (1984)

Walker, S./ Matthews, K.J. (1997)
The marbles of the Mausoleum, SSCD 49-59.

Captions for E1-15

"Within area x/y" indicates the interval between the integers × and y on the metre scale opposite which the object referred to is situated on the drawing (e.g. 14.46 – 19.78 = 14/20).

Horizontal striation delimits approximately the extent of softer layers of bedrock (claystone) in distinction to the harder ones (sandstone). For levels and sections, cf. figs. 1.54-55.

E1
Section from west towards east, looking north:

Within area 11/24:
Vertical surfaces of bedrock with traces of quarrying activities, and pillars P1 and P18.

On the bottom there are three discarded column drums of bedrock roughly tooled with the pointed chisel (also observed by Newton, see p. 9, note 3), and possibly from one and the same column shaft.

Within area 23/37:
Behind the pillars P2, P3, and P4 the foundations of ashlars of bedrock and the euthynteria course for the northern peribolos wall of white marble (now lost) are seen. Still lying on top of the euthynteria course (but not in situ), two toichobate blocks of bluish limestone were found.

Within area 36/43:
Vertical faces of bedrock cut for the foundations of the Maussolleion. Pillar P5 rests on top of the edge of the foundation cutting.

Area 42/53:
The bedrock rises abruptly from level L8 to level L14 (courses C8-13). Beneath the part of pillar P6 projecting from the edge of the foundation cutting is a compact mass of chippings of green lava, presumably from the cutting of foundation slabs.

Adjoining the left side of the pillar is a row of rock-cut blocks, possibly part of a wall incorporating the pillar.

The section crosses a shallow depression in the bedrock cut to accommodate 2 × 4 foundation slabs of course C14 whose height it would otherwise have been necessary to curtail (within area 47-51).

At the right side of pillar P7 the foundation cutting rises some 80 cm, thus revealing its roughly cut vertical side flattened with a pointed tool.

Within area 52/58:
From the NW corner of course C14 eight slabs remain in situ representing 4 × 5 rows, one of them forming the eastern border of the foundations, while remains of the two northernmost rows are missing, apart from pry-cuttings indicating their positions.